THE STONE WOMAN

By the same author

NON-FICTION

The Clash of Fundamentalisms (2002)
Bush in Babylon: The Recolonisation of Iraq (2003)
The Nehrus and the Gandhis: An Indian Dynasty (4th edition 2005)
Speaking of Empire and Resistance: Conversations with Tariq Ali (2005)
Rough Music: Blair, Bombs, Baghdad, London, Terror (2005)
Street Fighting Years: An Autobiography of the Sixties (New edition 2005)
Pirates of the Caribbean (2006)
Conversation with Edward Said (2006)
The Leopard and the Fox: A Pakistani Tragedy (2007)
A Banker for All Seasons: Crooks and Cheats Inc. (2007)
The Duel: Pakistan on the Flight Path of American Power (2008)
The Assassination: Who Killed Indira Gandhi? (2008)
Protocols of the Elders of Sodom (2009)
The Obama Syndrome: Surrender at Home, War Abroad (2010)
On History: Tariq Ali and Oliver Stone in Conversation (2011)
The Extreme Centre: A Warning (2015)

FICTION

OTHER TITLES IN THE ISLAM QUINTET

Shadows of the Pomegranate Tree (1991)
The Book of Saladin (1998)
A Sultan in Palermo (2005)
Night of the Golden Butterfly (2010)

THE FALL OF COMMUNISM TRILOGY

Redemption (1991)
Fear of Mirrors (1998)

Tariq Ali

THE STONE WOMAN

VERSO
London • New York

This paperback edition published by Verso 2015
First published by Verso 2000

1 3 5 7 9 10 8 6 4 2

Verso
UK: 6 Meard Street, London W1F 0EG
US: 20 Jay Street, Suite 1010, Brooklyn, NY 11201
www.versobooks.com

Verso is the imprint of New Left Books

ISBN-13: 978-1-78168-004-9

British Library Cataloguing in Publication Data
A catalogue record for this book is available from the British Library

Library of Congress Cataloging-in-Publication Data
A catalog record for this book is available from the Library of Congress

Typeset in Fournier by M Rules
Printed in the US by Maple Press

For

Susan Watkins

whose love and comradeship has

sustained me through good times and bad

for the last twenty years.

Contents

ONE

The summer of 1899; Nilofer returns home after an enforced absence; Yusuf Pasha's exile; Iskander Pasha suffers a stroke

Myths always overpower truth in family histories. Ten days ago, I asked my father why, almost two hundred years ago, our great forebear, Yusuf Pasha, had been disgraced and sent into exile by the Sultan in Istanbul. My son, Orhan, on whose behalf I made this request, was sitting next to me shyly, stealing an occasional look at his grandfather, whom he had never seen before.

When one first arrives here after a long absence, through the winding roads and the green hills, the mixture of scents becomes overpowering and it becomes difficult not to think of Yusuf Pasha. This was the palace of his exile and its fragile, undying beauty never fails to overwhelm me. As children we often travelled from Istanbul in the dust-stifling heat of the summer sun, but long before we actually felt the cooling breeze on our skins, the sight of the sea had already lifted our spirits. We knew the journey would soon be over.

It was Yusuf Pasha who instructed the architect to find a remote space, but not too distant from Istanbul. He wanted the house built on the edge of solitude, but within reach of his friends. The location of the building had to mirror the punishment inflicted on him. It was both very close and far removed from the site of his triumphs in the old city. That was the only concession he made to the conditions imposed on him by the Sultan.

The structure of the house is palatial. Some compromises had been made, but the house was essentially an act of defiance. It was Yusuf Pasha's message to the Sultan: I may have been banished from the capital of the Empire, but the style in which I live will never change. And when his friends arrived to stay here, the noise and laughter were heard in the palace at Istanbul.

An army of apricot, walnut and almond trees was planted to guard his exile and shield the house from the storms that mark the advent of winter. Every summer, for as long as I can remember, we had played in their shade; played and laughed and cursed and made each other cry as children often do when they are alone. The garden at the back of the house was a haven, its tranquillity emphasised whenever the sea in the background became stormy. We would come here to unwind and inhale the intoxicating early morning breeze after our first night in the house. The unendurable tedium of the Istanbul summer was replaced by the magic of Yusuf Pasha's palace. The first time I came here I was not yet three, and yet I remember that day very clearly. It was raining and I became very upset because the rain was wetting the sea.

And there were other memories. Passionate memories. Anguished memories. The torment and pleasure of stolen moments during late-night trysts. The scents of the grass in the orange grove at night, which relaxed the heart. It was here that I first kissed Orhan's father, "that ugly, skinny Dmitri, Greek school inspector from Konya" as my mother had called him, with a stern and inflexible expression that hardened her eyes. That he was a Greek was bad enough, but his job as an inspector of rural schools made it all so much worse. It was the combination that really upset her. She would not have minded at all if Dmitri had belonged to one of the Phanariot families of old

Constantinople. How could her only daughter bring such disgrace to the house of Iskander Pasha?

This attitude was uncharacteristic of her. She was never bothered by family trees. It was simply that she had another suitor in mind. She had wanted me to marry her uncle Sifrah's oldest son. I had been promised to my cousin soon after my birth. And this most gentle and even-tempered of women had exploded with rage and frustration at the news that I wanted to marry a nobody.

It was my married half-sister, Zeynep, who told her that the cousin for whom she had intended me was not interested in women at all, not even as engines for procreation. Zeynep began to embroider tales. Her language became infected by the wantonness she was describing and my mother felt her elaborate descriptions were unsuitable for my unmarried ears. She painted my poor cousin in such dark and lecherous colours that I was asked to leave the room.

Later that day my mother lamented bitterly as she kissed and embraced me. Zeynep had convinced her that our poor cousin was a merciless monster and my mother was weeping in self-reproach at the thought that she might have forced her only daughter to marry such a depraved beast and thus have become the direct cause of my lifelong unhappiness. Naturally, I forgave her and we talked and laughed about what might have been. I'm not sure whether she ever discovered that Zeynep had invented everything. When my much-maligned cousin became ill during a wave of typhoid and died soon afterwards, Zeynep thought it better if the truth was concealed from my mother. This had one unfortunate result. At her nephew's funeral in Smyrna and to the great consternation of my uncle Sifrah, my mother found it difficult to display any signs of grief and when I forced myself to squeeze out a few tears she looked at me in shocked surprise.

All that lay in the past. The most important truth for me was that after nine years of exile I was back again. My father had forgiven me for running away.

He wanted to see my son. I wanted to see the Stone Woman. Throughout my childhood my sister and I had found hiding places among the caves near an ancient rock which must once have been a statue of a pagan goddess. It overlooked the almond orchards behind our house and, when we saw it from a distance, it looked most like a woman. It dominated the tiny hillock on which it stood, surrounded by ruins and rocks. It was not Aphrodite or Athena. Them we recognised. This one bore traces of a mysterious veil, which became visible only when the sun set. Her face was hidden. Perhaps, Zeynep said, it was a local goddess, long since forgotten. Perhaps the sculptor had been in a hurry. Perhaps the Christians had been on the march and circumstances had compelled him to change his mind. Perhaps she was not a goddess at all, but the first carved image of Mariam, the mother of Jesus. We could never agree on her identity and so she became the Stone Woman. As children we used to confide in her, ask her intimate questions, imagine her replies.

One day we discovered that our mothers and aunts and women servants did the same. We used to hide behind the rocks and listen to their tales of woe. It was the only way we knew what was really taking place inside the big house. And in this way, the Stone Woman became the repository of all our hidden pain. Secrets are terrible things. Even when they are necessary they begin to corrode our souls. It is always better to be open, and the Stone Woman enabled all the women in this house to disgorge their secrets and thus live a healthy inner life themselves.

"Mother," whispered Orhan as he clutched my arm tight, "will Grandfather ever tell me why this palace was built?"

There were many versions of the Yusuf Pasha story in our family, some of them quite hostile to our ancestor, but these were usually the preserve of those great-uncles and great-aunts whose side of the family had been disinherited by mine. We all knew that Yusuf Pasha wrote erotic poetry, that except for the few verses passed down orally from one generation to the next, it had all been burnt. Why had the poetry been destroyed? By whom?

I used to ask my father this question, at least once a year, before my exile. He would smile and ignore my question completely. I thought that perhaps my father was embarrassed to discuss this aspect with his children, especially a daughter. Not this time. Perhaps it was the presence of Orhan. This was the first time that he had seen Orhan. Perhaps my father wanted to pass the story to a male of the younger generation. Or perhaps he was simply feeling relaxed. It was not till later that I realised he must have had a premonition of the disaster that was about to strike him.

It was late in the afternoon and still warm. The sun was on its way to the west. Its rays had turned a crimson gold, bathing every aspect of the garden in magic. Nothing had changed in the summer routines of this old house. The old magnolia trees with their large leaves were glistening in the dying rays of the sun. My father had just woken up after a refreshing nap. His face was relaxed. As he grew older, sleep worked on him like an elixir. The lines that marked his forehead seemed to evaporate. Looking at him, I realised how much I had missed him these last nine years. I kissed his hand and repeated my question. He smiled, but did not reply immediately.

He waited.

I, too, waited, recalling the afternoon routines of the summer months. Without speaking a word, my father took Orhan's hand and drew the boy close to him. He began to stroke the boy's head. Orhan knew his grandfather from a fading photograph that I had taken with me and kept near my bed. As he grew I had told him stories of my childhood and the old house that looked down on the sea.

And then old Petrossian, the major-domo of our house, who had been with our family since he was born, appeared. A young boy, not much older than Orhan, followed him carrying a tray. Old Petrossian served my father a coffee in exactly the same way as he had done for the last thirty years or more and, probably, just as his father had served my grandfather all those years ago. His habits were unchanged. He ignored me completely in my father's presence, as was his custom. When I was a young girl this used to annoy me greatly. I would stick out a tongue at him or make a rude gesture, but nothing I did could alter the pattern of his behaviour. As I grew older I had learnt to disregard his presence. He became invisible to me. Was it my imagination or had he smiled today? He had, but in acknowledgement of Orhan's presence. A new male had entered the household and Petrossian was pleased. After inquiring with a respectful tilt of his head whether my father needed anything else and receiving a reply in the negative, Petrossian and the grandson he was training to take his place in our household left us alone. For a while none of us spoke. I had forgotten how calm this space could be and how rapidly it soothed my senses.

"You ask why Yusuf Pasha was sent here two hundred years ago?"

I nodded eagerly, unable to conceal my excitement. Now that I was a mother of two, I was considered mature enough to be told the official version.

My father began to speak in a tone that was both intimate and authoritative, as if the events which he was describing had taken place last week in his presence here, instead of two hundred years ago, in a palace, on the banks of the Bosporus, in Istanbul. But as he spoke he avoided my gaze altogether. His eyes were firmly fixed on the face of little Orhan, observing the child's reaction. Perhaps my father recalled his own childhood and how he had first heard the story. As for Orhan, he was bewitched by his grandfather. His eyes sparkled with amusement and anticipation as my father assumed the broad and exaggerated tones of a village story-teller.

‘ As was his wont, the Sultan sent for Yusuf Pasha in the evening. Our great forebear arrived and made his bows. He had grown up with the Sultan. They knew each other well. A serving woman placed a goblet of wine in front of him. The Sultan asked his friend to recite a new poem. Yusuf Pasha was in a strange mood that day. Nobody knows why. He was such an accomplished courtier that, usually, any request from his sovereign was treated as a command from heaven. He was so quick-witted that he could invent and recite a quatrain on the spot. But not that evening. Nobody knows why. Perhaps he had been aroused from a lover's bed and was angry. Perhaps he was simply fed up with being a courtier. Perhaps he was suffering from severe indigestion. Nobody knows why.

When the Sultan observed that his friend remained silent, he became genuinely concerned. He inquired after his health. He offered to summon his own physician. Yusuf Pasha thanked him, but declined the offer. He looked around him and saw nothing but slave-girls and eunuchs. This was not new, but on that particular day it annoyed our ancestor. Nobody knows why. After a long silence, he asked the Sultan for permission to speak and it was granted.

"O great ruler and fount of all wisdom, Sultan of the civilised world and Caliph of our faith, this servant craves your forgiveness. The fickle muse has deserted me and no verse enters this empty head today. With your permission I will become a story-teller tonight, but I urge your sublime majesty to listen carefully, for that of which I am about to speak is true."

The Sultan was by now genuinely curious and the entire Court swayed as it leant forward to hear Yusuf Pasha's words.

"Five hundred and thirty-eight years before the birth of the Christian saint, Jesus, there was a powerful Empire in Persia. On its throne there sat a great king by the name of Cyrus. In that auspicious year Cyrus was proclaimed King of Kings in Babylon, a region now ruled by our own great and wise Sultan. That year the Great Persian Empire appeared invincible. It dominated the world. It was admired for its toleration. The Persians accepted all worshippers, respected all customs and, in their new territories, they adapted themselves to the different schemes of governing. All appeared to be well. The Empire flourished, dealing with its enemies like an individual swatting a flea.

"Two hundred years later the heirs of Cyrus had become the pawns of eunuchs and women. The satraps of the Empire had become disloyal. Its officials, corrupt, callous and inefficient. The enormous riches of Mesopotamia saved the Empire from collapse, but the longer it was delayed, the more overwhelming it was when it finally happened. And thus it was that the Greeks gained influence. Their language spread. And thus it was that long before the birth of Alexander the route of his conquest had already been built.

"Then one year, without any warning, ten thousand Greek soldiers slew their Persian patron, made their officers prisoners and marched from the city we now call Baghdad to Anatolia. Nothing stood in their way. And soon people began to realise that if only ten thousand soldiers could do this, then rulers and leaders were unnecessary . . ."

Yusuf Pasha had not yet finished his story, but the sight of the Sultan's face interrupted his flow. He fell silent and dared not look his ruler in the eye. The Sultan developed a rage, rose to his feet and stormed out of the room. Yusuf Pasha feared the worst. All he had intended was to warn the friend of his youth against sloth and sensuality and the suffocating influence of eunuchs. He had wished to apprise his ruler of the eternal law, which teaches that nothing is eternal. Instead the Sultan had taken the story as an ill-omened reference to the Ottoman dynasty. To himself. Anyone else would have been executed, but it was probably shared childhood memories that favoured the quality of mercy. Yusuf Pasha was punished very lightly. He was exiled from Istanbul. For ever. The Sultan did not wish to be in the same city as him. And that is how he came here with his family to this isolated wilderness surrounded by ancient rocks and decided that it was here that he would build his palace in exile. He yearned for the old city, but he never saw the Bosporus again.

They say that the Sultan, too, missed his company and often yearned for his presence, but the courtiers, who had always been jealous of Yusuf Pasha's influence, made sure that the two friends never saw each other again. That's all. Does that satisfy you, my little pigeon? And you, Orhan, will you remember what I have said and repeat it to your children one day, when I am dead and gone? ’

Orhan smiled and nodded. I maintained an expressionless face. I knew my father had spoken half-truths. I had heard other stories about Yusuf Pasha from aunts and uncles belonging to another branch of our family, children of a great-uncle whom my father loathed and whose children were never encouraged to visit us here or in Istanbul.

They had told tales that were far more exciting, much more real and infinitely more convincing. They spoke of how Yusuf Pasha had fallen in love with the Sultan's favourite white slave, and of how they had been caught while copulating. The slave had been executed on the spot and his genitals fed to the dogs outside the royal kitchen. Yusuf Pasha, according to this version, had been whipped in public and sent away to live out the rest of his life in disgrace. Perhaps my father's version was also true. Perhaps no single narrative could explain our ancestor's fall from grace. Or perhaps nobody knew the real reason and all the existing versions were false.

Perhaps.

I had no desire to offend my father after such a long estrangement and so I refrained from questioning him further. I had upset him a great deal all those years ago by falling in love with a visiting school inspector, running away with him, becoming his wife, carrying his children and appreciating his poetry, which I now realise was very bad, but which at the time had sounded beautiful. Poetry, alas, had always been Dmitri's true profession, but he had to earn a living. That is why he had started teaching. In this way he could earn some money and look after his mother. His father had died in Bosnia, fighting for our Empire. It was the soft voice in which he recited his poems that had first touched my heart.

All this had happened in Konya, where I had been staying with the family of my best friend. She had shown me the delights of Konya. We had seen the tombs of the old Seljuk kings and peeped inside the Sufi houses. It was here that I had first met Dmitri. I was seventeen years old at the time and he was almost thirty.

I wanted to escape from the stifling atmosphere of my house. Dmitri and his poetry appeared as the road to happiness. For a while I was happy, but it had never been enough to obscure the pain I felt at being banished from my family home. I missed my mother and soon I began to ache for the comfort of our home. More than everything else, I missed the summers here, in this house overlooking the sea.

I had wanted to leave home, but on my own terms. My father's edict declaring me an outlaw had come as a real blow. I hated him then. I hated his narrow-mindedness. I hated the way he treated my brothers and especially Halil, who, like the spirited stallion he was, refused to be disciplined. My father would whip him sometimes in front of the whole family. That was when I hated my father the most. But Halil's spirit remained unbroken. My father regarded Halil as a lazy, disrespectful anarchist and was, as a result, astounded when Halil enlisted in the army and because of his family history was rapidly promoted and assigned to duties in the palace.

Iskander Pasha doubted his younger son's motives and in this he was not so far wrong. Father could be ever so refined and elegant in the Parisian salons where he served as ambassador from the Sublime Porte to the French Republic for many years. That is what we were told by my older brother,

Salman, who had been permitted to accompany him and had received his higher education at the Academy in Paris, which made him a lover of all things French, except its men.

Whenever Father returned to Istanbul with new pieces of furniture and fabrics and paintings of naked women for the western portion of the house, and perfumes for his wives, our spirits would lift. Halil would whisper, "Perhaps, this time, he has become a modern." We would all giggle in great anticipation. Perhaps there would be a New Year's Eve Ball in our house. We would wear dresses and dance and drink champagne, just like our father and Salman did in Paris and Berlin. Idle dreams. Life never changed. In the familiar environment of his city and his country, Father reverted to the behaviour and mannerisms of a Turkish aristocrat.

This was the first time since my runaway marriage that I had been invited to return to our old summer house, but only with Orhan. Dmitri and my adorable little Emineh stayed at home. Perhaps next year, my mother promised. Perhaps never, I had shouted angrily. My mother visited me three times, but always in secret, bringing clothes for the children and money for me. She acted as an intermediary and, slowly, relations with my father had been restored. We began to communicate with each other. After two years of exchanging polite and unbearably formal letters, he asked me to bring Orhan to the summer house. I'm glad I did as he had asked. I had been close to refusing his request. I wanted to insist that I would not see him unless I could bring my daughter as well, but Dmitri, my husband, convinced me that I was being foolish and headstrong. Now, I'm glad I did not let pride stand in the way. If I had apologised for my defiance and pleaded my case at his feet, I would have been forgiven a long time ago. Contrary to the impression I may have created, Iskander Pasha was neither a cruel nor a vindictive man. He was a creature of his time, strict and orthodox in his approach to us.

That first night, when Orhan was asleep, I left the house and walked through the orchards, the familiar smell of thyme and the pepper tree reviving many old memories. The Stone Woman was still there and I found myself whispering to her.

"I've come back, Stone Woman. I've come back with a little boy. I missed you, Stone Woman. There were many things I could not tell my husband. Nine years is a long time to go without speaking of one's longings."

Three days after my father told Orhan the story of Yusuf Pasha, he suffered a stroke. The door of his bedroom was half open. The windows leading to the balcony were wide open and a gentle breeze had brought with it the sweet smell of lemons. My mother always went into his room early in the morning to open the windows so that he could smell the sea. That morning she had entered the room and found him breathing strangely, lying on his side. She turned his body round. His face was mute and pale. His eyes were staring into the distance and she knew, instinctively, that they were searching for something outside this life. He had felt death's chill and he did not wish to prolong his life.

He was paralysed, unable to move his legs, incapable of speech and, if his eyes were an indication, praying to Allah every conscious minute to bring his presence in this world to an end. Allah ignored his pleas and slowly, very slowly, Iskander Pasha began to recover. Life returned to his legs. With the help of Petrossian he began to walk again, but his powers of speech were gone for ever. We would never hear his voice again. His demands and commands were henceforth written on small pieces of paper and brought to us on a little silver tray.

And so it came about that every day, after the evening meal, a group of us would gather in the old room with the balcony overlooking the sea. Once everyone was comfortably seated, Father would sip some tea from the corner of his mouth – his face had been cruelly affected by the stroke – and while Petrossian's grandson, Akim, gently massaged his feet, he would lie back and insist that we tell him stories.

It had never been easy to relax in my father's presence. He had always been a demanding man. Ever intolerant of even the mildest form of criticism directed against his own conduct, past or present, he was always finding fault in others.

My brothers and sister, who had been summoned to his bedside from different parts of the Empire, were convinced that his affliction would make him more tolerant. I was sure they were wrong.

TWO

The family begins to assemble; the Baron makes an impressive entrance; Salman's melancholy

I was lying in bed in a darkened room, a cold compress covering my face and forehead. I was resting to soothe a dull headache that refused to go away. That was the day Salman and Halil arrived to see our speechless father. I was not on the terrace with the rest of the family and all the servants to see them disembark from our old coach, which, flanked on each side by six cavalrymen, had transported them from Istanbul. I was later told by my mother how the sight of my father sitting motionless on a large chair had shaken both men. They had fallen to their knees on either side of him and kissed his hands. It was Halil, in his general's uniform, who was the first to realise that silences can easily become oppressive.

"I'm pleased you're still alive, Ata. Heaven alone could have helped me if Allah had decided to make us orphans. This brute of a brother of mine would have ordered Petrossian to strangle me with a silken cord."

The thought was so ridiculous that a smile appeared on the face of the old man, a signal for the loud laughter from the entire assembly that woke me so rudely. But the headache had disappeared and I jumped out of bed, wet my face with water and ran downstairs to greet them. I arrived in time to see Halil take Orhan in his arms. He tickled the boy's neck with his moustache and then threw him up into the air, hugging him warmly as he came down again. Then he introduced Orhan to the uncle he had never seen. Orhan looked at the new uncle with a shy smile and Salman awkwardly patted the boy on the head.

I had not seen Salman for nearly fifteen years. He had left home when I was thirteen. I remembered him as tall and slim with thick black hair and a deep, melodious voice. I was startled when I first glimpsed his silhouette on the terrace. For a moment I thought it was Father. Salman had aged. He was not yet fifty, but his hair was grey and thin. He seemed shorter than when I last saw him. His body had grown larger, his face was over-fleshed, he walked with a slight stoop and his eyes were sad. Cruel Egypt. Why had it aged him thus? We embraced and kissed. His voice was distant.

"And now you're a mother, Nilofer."

Those were the only words he spoke to me that day. His tone had expressed surprise, as if bringing children into the world had somehow become a novelty. For some reason Salman's tone and his remark irritated me. I'm not sure why this was so, but I remember feeling slightly angry. Perhaps because it suggested a refusal to see or treat me as a grown woman. I was still a child in his eyes. Before I could think of a suitably cutting reply, Petrossian had taken him away for a private audience with our father.

Then it was Halil's turn. He had never lost contact with us and made a point of communicating regularly with Orhan's father. He had been of great help to us during bad times, making sure we were properly fed and clothed after Dmitri and most of the Greeks in Konya had been deprived of their livelihood as a punishment. I had last seen Halil when he arrived without warning on a beautiful spring afternoon in Konya. Orhan was three years old at the time, but he never forgot his uncle, or rather the moustache, which always irritated him. I looked at Halil. He was as handsome as ever and the uniform suited him. I often wondered how it had happened that the most mischievous member of my family had accepted the disciplines and routines of the army. As he embraced me, he whispered.

"I'm glad you came. Did he tell Orhan a story?"

I nodded.

"Yusuf Pasha?"

"Who else?"

"Which version?"

We laughed.

As we were about to follow the rest of the family into the house, Halil noticed the rising dust on the distant track that led to our house. It had to be another carriage, but whom did it contain? Iskander Pasha was known throughout his family for his antisocial habits and his bad temper. As a consequence, very few people arrived at our Istanbul house uninvited and I can't remember anyone ever coming here. Traditional hospitality was alien to my father as far as his own extended family was concerned. He was particularly hostile to his first cousins and their progeny, but could also be distant from his brothers. Because of all this, unexpected visitors had always been a pleasant surprise for us when we were children, especially Uncle Kemal, who never arrived without a coach full of presents.

"Is someone else expected today?"

"No."

Halil and I stayed on the terrace waiting for the coach to arrive. We looked at each other and giggled. Who dared arrive at our father's house in such a fashion? When we were very small, the house had belonged to Grandfather and at that time it was always full of guests. Three bedrooms were always kept in a state of readiness for Grandfather's closest friends, who walked in and out at their own pleasure. The entire staff was aware that they could arrive any day and at any hour, accompanied by their own manservants. That was a long time ago. Soon after my father had been given this house, he had made it clear that Grandfather's old friends were not welcome. This created a scandal in the family. Grandmother had objected and in unusually strong language for her, but my father remained adamant. His style was different and he had never liked the lechers who hung around the house during his father's time, making life miserable for the more attractive maidservants.

The carriage drew up, and we recognised the coachman and the manservant perched next to him. Halil chuckled as we walked down the stairs to greet our father's older brother, Memed Pasha, and his friend, Baron Jakob von Hassberg. Both men, now in their early seventies, appeared in good health. Their complexions, usually very pale, had been touched by the sun. They were dressed in cream-coloured summer suits and straw hats, but the cut was not identical. Each believed firmly in the superiority of his own tailor. My father could never conceal his irritation when these two men discussed their clothes. Halil saluted the Prussian fondly and respectfully kissed his uncle's hand.

"Welcome to your house, Uncle and you, too, Baron. An unexpected pleasure. We had no idea you were in the country."

"Nor did we till we arrived," replied Memed Pasha. "The train from Berlin was late as usual."

"Only after it had crossed the Ottoman frontier, Memed," interjected the Baron. "You must be fair. It arrived in perfect time at the border. We are very proud of our trains."

Memed Pasha ignored the remark and turned to Halil. "Is it true that death's arrow pierced my brother, but he refused to fall? Well?"

"I'm not sure I understand your question, Uncle."

He looked at me.

"Our father has lost the power to speak, Uncle," I muttered. "Otherwise he is well again, though he will always need help to walk."

"I don't regard that as a complete tragedy. He always talked too much. Do you know what your mother has ordered for supper? Is there any champagne in the house? I thought not! We've brought a few cases from the Baron's estate. I spent too many melancholy evenings in this wretched house when I was your age. Never again. Is there any ice in the pit?"

I nodded.

"Good. Have them cool a few bottles for this evening, child, and tell Petrossian to prepare our rooms. I'm sure they haven't been aired for thirty years. And you, young man, take me to see my brother."

Father did not much care for Memed Pasha, but he was never impolite to him, and for a very good reason. When my grandfather died, Memed Pasha, being the oldest son, inherited the family residence in Istanbul as well as this house, which he had always disliked. We had never understood his antipathy. How could any person be unhappy in these surroundings? We never discussed the matter in too much detail because Uncle Memed's prejudice had benefited us greatly. Our curiosity was overtaken by joy. We loved this house. We loved our Stone Woman. I remember the excitement when our father told us that Uncle Memed had given us this house as a present. Halil, Zeynep and I had clapped our hands and hugged each other. Salman had remained grave and asked an awkward question. "Will it revert to his children after you're dead?"

Father had glared at him in silence as if to say, you imbecile, we've just been given this house and you are already thinking of my death. My mother had attempted to suppress a smile. None of us would have known the reason for her merriment had Zeynep, aware of my mother's routine, not hidden behind a rock after sunset that day and heard Mother talking to the Stone Woman.

‘ What should one tell the children these days, Stone Woman? How far can we go?

Poor Salman. All he wanted to know was whether he would ever inherit this house. My husband looked at him as if he had attempted a murder. Even though I'm not his mother, I feel fond of the boy. I wish his father would talk to him. Tell him how much he really loves him. It's not Salman's fault his mother died giving birth to him. He feels his father's indifference. Most of the time Iskander Pasha sees his first wife in the boy's face and loves him, but there are moments when he looks at Salman with hatred as if he had consciously killed his mother. Once I asked Iskander Pasha about his first wife. He became very angry with me and insisted that I must never question him on this matter again. I had asked so that I could console him, but he was very strange. It did make me wonder whether he had anything to hide. What is it with the boys in this family, Stone Woman? Once they have reached puberty they seem to become aloof, look on their mothers and sisters as inferior beings. I hope Halil never becomes like that. Even though I'm not his real mother, I will do my best to stop him.

As for Memed Pasha, what can I say? Nobody would have objected if he had also married and produced children, but he refused and his father punished him severely for his disobedience. He was kept under permanent watch and special tutors were hired to educate him. Who could have known that this young Baron who came here over fifty years ago to teach Memed and his brothers the German language would become so attached to Memed? Not even the servants suspected. Petrossian's father was questioned in some detail when the whole business was discovered, but he swore in the name of his Allah that he had not known.

If only you could speak, Stone Woman. You could tell Salman that his uncle Memed will never have children and that Salman will one day inherit this house. '

Zeynep told me. I told Halil. Halil broke the news to Salman and Salman began to laugh. He would stop, look at us with a serious expression, but could not maintain his composure for more than a few seconds. He would collapse. His laughter became uncontrollable. The room had filled up, with Petrossian and even the maids – normally very quiet, but now infected by the strange mirth which swept through the house like a summer storm. Everyone wanted to share the joke, but Salman could not bring himself to speak.

Halil, Zeynep and I became quiet and even a bit frightened, especially when Iskander Pasha came down the stairs. At first he smiled, but Salman, on seeing his father, laughed even more. The atmosphere became tense. Petrossian, alert to his master's moods, shepherded the maids out of the room. It was only after they had left that Iskander Pasha asked in a deceptively soft voice, "Why are you laughing, Salman?"

Salman suddenly stopped laughing. He wiped the tears off his face and looked straight into our father's eyes.

"I'm laughing, Ata, at my own blindness and stupidity. How could I have been so foolish as to ask you about Uncle Memed's heirs? I mean barons, even of the Prussian variety, have not yet been known to bear children."

My mother took a deep breath. Iskander Pasha could not contain his rage. All I remember is his predatory profile as he clenched his fist and hit Salman on the face. My brother staggered backwards, horrified.

"If ever again you refer disrespectfully to your uncle in my presence or that of your mother, I will disinherit you. Is that understood?"

Salman, his eyes filled with tears of anger and hurt and bitterness, nodded silently. Iskander Pasha left the room. I was not yet nine years old, but I really hated my father at that moment. This was the first time I had ever seen him strike anyone.

I took Salman's hand in mine, while Zeynep fetched him some water before stroking the cheek that had sustained the blow. Halil's face had become pale. Like me, he was greatly dismayed, but for him it went much deeper. I don't think he ever respected our father again. I was very young, but I never forgot that afternoon.

It was not simply the act of violence against Salman that had upset us so much, but the explosion of a frustrated bitterness that had lain concealed below the surface. The mask had been torn aside to reveal a twisted face with heavy and coarse features. Salman was twenty-six that year. All four of us, all Iskander Pasha's children, had left the house together as if in a delirium. We walked to a flat rock, not far below where the Stone Woman stood, hidden from us by a grove of pine trees.

Each of us had our own favourite place on this rock, but this was the first time we had all come here together. The surface of the rock was dented, but completely level. Nature had played little part in this process. Petrossian insisted that it was here that Yusuf Pasha sat to compose his more lyrical verses with the sea stretching out before him. Several stonemasons had worked hard to flatten the rock and smooth its surface.

We sat down in silence and stared at the sea, till the sight had soothed the turbulent waves tormenting our hearts. We remained there for a long time, waiting for the sun to set. Halil had been the first to speak. He had repeated those selfsame words concerning Uncle Memed that had caused the offence. Then Zeynep repeated them, but when it was my turn, Salman put his hand on my mouth to stop me.

"Little princess, you should never speak of what you still do not understand."

And we had all begun to laugh again, to exorcise the memory of what had happened that day. Salman, touched by our response, had confessed that he wanted to leave home for ever. He would never visit this house again or return to Istanbul. He would travel to Aleppo or Cairo or perhaps even further away, to lands where there were no Ottomans. Only then would he feel really free.

We were heartbroken. At least get married first, Zeynep had pleaded.

Why not join the army, Halil had suggested. They talked of their hopes for themselves and their children, who were yet to be born. They became engrossed in their own lives. All this was new to me. I was still too young to join in or even understand much of what they were saying, but the emotional intensity was such that the day remains vivid in my memory. I had never seen them like this before. Their faces wore animated expressions and they sounded happy and I remember how that had made me happy. It was almost as if the tragedy of that afternoon had become a turning point in their lives and filled them with hope for the future. Even Zeynep, whose placid temperament was a joke in our family, was angry and excited that day. None of us wanted to re-enter the house that evening. We were in full revolt against Iskander Pasha and his whole world. When Petrossian, who always knew where we were, arrived and informed us it was time for the evening meal, we ignored him completely. Then he sat down next to us and with honeyed words of conciliation, he gently cajoled us to return. Salman provided the lead and the rest of us reluctantly followed him back.

I'm not sure exactly when Salman left our home. I think it could not have been too long after being struck by Iskander Pasha. All I remember is the panic that gripped the whole family when Salman announced at breakfast one day that he had decided to leave his job and see the world for the next few years. Since he worked in Uncle Kemal's shipping company there would be no real problem in returning whenever he wished.

Zeynep and Halil's mother had looked after Salman soon after he was born, since his own mother had died during childbirth. She was a distant cousin and had always showered me with affection. Her marriage to Iskander Pasha had been arranged in a hurry. He was desolate at the time, but had bowed to family pressure and married her to provide Salman with a mother. She looked after him, tended to all his needs and did become his mother. She loved him as if he were her own son and always defended him fiercely, even after the birth of her own children, Halil and Zeynep.

She rarely stayed in the summer house and had not been present to witness Salman's humiliation, but the news had been relayed to her in Istanbul and my mother was sure that Iskander Pasha would have felt the whiplash of her tongue. Perhaps she tried to persuade Salman not to go. If so, she failed. He had arrived at a decision and nothing would dissuade him. He told us he would travel for some time and let us know when he decided to settle in a particular town.

A penitent father offered him money for his travels, but Salman refused. He had saved enough from his salary over the last four years. He embraced us all and left. We did not hear from him for many months. Then letters began to arrive, but irregularly. A year after he left a message was received from Uncle Kemal, who had just returned from Alexandria. He informed us that he had stayed with Salman, who was successfully trading in diamonds and married to a local woman. He had sent a letter for Zeynep's mother. Its contents were never divulged to any of us. Zeynep searched every hiding place in her mother's room but failed to uncover the letter. One day, in a state of total despair, we asked Petrossian if he knew what had been said in the letter. He shook his head sadly.

"If too many stones are thrown at a person, he stops being frightened of them."

To this day I am not sure what Petrossian meant by that remark. Zeynep and I had nodded our heads sagely and burst out laughing when he left the room.

It was strange that they had all arrived here on the same day. What memories would float through Iskander Pasha, when he saw Salman, Uncle Memed and the Baron walking into his room together? Halil later reported to me that Father had wept on seeing Salman, embraced him gently and kissed his cheeks. Salman was touched, but his eyes remained dry. The gesture had come too late. The pride exhibited by grown men is something I have noticed for a long time, but never really understood. It is something that was not completely absent in but firmly suppressed by my husband Dmitri.

As the days passed I had occasion to observe Salman. My brother who, in his youth, had been the most lively and ambitious of us all, was now afflicted by a melancholy that made him bitter. I think it was his inability to accomplish more in his life that caused him great anxiety. It was almost as if his success as a diamond merchant lay at the root of his unhappiness. He was never satisfied. He had married an Egyptian woman in Alexandria, "a beautiful Copt" in Uncle Kemal's words, but had kept her from meeting his family. Even now as his father lay disabled by a stroke, Salman had not brought his sons to see their grandfather at least once. Halil alone had been invited to Egypt and accorded the privilege of meeting Salman's wife and children. On one occasion when I persisted in questioning Halil about Salman's indifference I received a sharp and surprising reply.

"Salman is very depressed by the fact that the Empire has been irreparably decadent for three hundred years. I'm aware of this fact as well, but Salman takes it personally."

My instincts rejected such reasoning. I recognised Salman's impatience with the rituals of Istanbul life. He was deeply frustrated and wanted change, but, at best, this could only be a partial reason. I could not believe that my brother, once so mischievous and full of fun, had become so deeply affected by a sense of hopelessness in relation to history. Our family had always made history. How could we now let it crush us? There had to be another reason for Salman's sadness and I was determined to discover its roots.

THREE

The Baron reads an extract from the Qabus Nama *on "Romantic Passion"; the unfinished story of Enver the Albanian; Sabiha and the Circassian maid who thought the only way of escape was to fly*

"Your Ottoman Empire is like a drunken prostitute, lying with her legs wide open, neither knowing nor caring who will take her next. Do I exaggerate, Memed?"

The Baron and Uncle Memed were on their second bottle of champagne.

"As usual Baron, you express lofty thoughts with great clarity," replied Memed, "but I do wonder sometimes whether the great master Hegel might have been a bit disappointed in you. According to your contemporaries, you showed great promise as a student in Berlin . . ."

The Baron's interruption took the form of laughter, which resembled the staccato burst of gun-fire: ha-ha-ha-ha, ha-ha-ha-ha, ha-ha-ha and a final ha. This was not the sort of laughter which starts as a smile and develops at a slow rhythm. His laughter was part of his verbal armoury, deployed to humiliate, crush, interrupt or divert any opposition.

"Whenever I visit this family, I'm lost to the real world, Memed. The real world, as I've often told you, is the world of ants. The only way human beings can survive in this world is to become like ants. It is our future. It beckons us, but you resist. You pretend that your home is the real world and in this fashion you keep the monsters at bay, but for how long, Memed? For how long? Your Empire is so bankrupt that you can no longer even afford to buy time as you have done for nearly three hundred years."

My uncle remained silent for a while. He replied in a soft voice. "What your philosophers call progress, my dear Baron, has created an inner drought in human beings. They show a callow disregard for each other. Look at France, a country we both love, not to mention England. There is no solidarity between human beings. No belief in common except to survive and get rich, no matter what the cost. Perhaps this is the way of the world. This is where we will all end up one day. Not you and me, of course. We will have died long before that day, and who can say we will not have died happy? Why shouldn't we seek pleasure in each other's company. Why shouldn't I enjoy my life, this house, my family . . ."

The Baron roared with laughter, but this time it was real.

"Why do you laugh?"

"I just recalled the *Qabus Nama*. When I was translating it into German I found it incredibly dull and commonplace, not worthy of even the slightest attention. I remember thinking: if this is the moral code for the Sultan and his princes, it is hardly surprising that they degenerated so rapidly. Even feeble heads filled with imperial vapours could safely ignore this nonsense. There was, however, one arresting passage. It was headed 'Romantic Passion' and I recited it so often to my wayward uncles and cousins that I never forgot the words. I was reminded of it when you spoke of those who are interested only in getting rich. Listen now, old Memed, to the wisdom of the *Qabus Nama*: 'For your part resist falling in love and guard against becoming a lover, for a lover's life is beset with unhappiness, particularly when he is without means. The penniless lover can never achieve his aim, more particularly when he is elderly; the goal cannot be reached except with the aid of money, and a lover not possessed of it will succeed only in tormenting his soul.'"

It was Memed's turn to smile. "To be elderly and penniless is bad enough without being tormented by irrational emotions. There is a lot of truth in that, I suppose. It is true we are getting old, my dear Baron, but I don't think that the passage you have memorised so ably could affect us in any way. I think even if we were penniless, we would find pleasure in each other's company. Perhaps we should open another bottle to mark the uselessness of the *Qabus Nama*."

Father's sitting-room, organised and decorated on the model of a French salon, was full today. Prior to his illness, Ottoman women had been barred from entering this sanctuary. French females, we had noticed, were permitted entry, but only if accompanied by their husbands or fathers. As a rule, this, the most beautiful and spacious room in the house, was reserved exclusively for male friends and visitors.

Once when Father was in Paris, Zeynep and I and our two mothers had come into this room, ordered mint tea and rose-water and then had settled down to play cards. I loved watching the changing moods of the sea from the three large balcony windows that lit the room during the day. We had used the space every single day, to the great amusement of the maids. They, too, had enjoyed being here in the absence of Petrossian.

Everything was different now. This is where we met after dinner every evening to exchange information and listen to a story, before retiring for the evening. Father had frowned at the exchange between Uncle Memed and the Baron. The reference to prostitutes in the presence of his wife and daughters must have irritated him. Orhan was fast asleep on a chaise-longue near a window and had not heard the remark.

Iskander Pasha lifted the stick that never left his side and banged it hard on the floor. This was the signal to end all the whispered conversations in different corners of the room and for the story-teller to begin. Uncle Memed cleared his throat. Salman smiled. Halil played nervously with his moustache. My mother, Sara, tightened the shawl around her. Zeynep and I looked at each other, trying hard to restrain our mirth. If Uncle Memed was going to speak, anything was possible.

Father, looking slightly nervous, summoned Petrossian and pointed in the direction of Orhan. The gesture was understood. My sleeping Orhan was lifted gently and taken away. I now wished I had brought my little daughter Emineh here as well. I wanted her to be part of our family. Uncle Memed assumed a look of fake humility and began to speak.

‘ I will now tell you the story of our great Albanian ancestor Enver, as it was transcribed on the dictation of his son. The document itself used to be read once every five years on the occasion of our Prophet's birthday, when the whole family assembled to celebrate the feast. The ritual was considered necessary so that we never forgot our humble origins. Unfortunately, it was lost about fifty or sixty years ago. Some say that our grandfather Mahmut Pasha destroyed the slim bound volume because he was in the process of reinventing the history of our family and the truth, even though it was four centuries old, disconcerted him. Mahmut Pasha did manage to produce an alternative book which still sits in the library unread and unloved, though the calligraphy is exquisite.

Those of us who have attempted to read it have given up after the second set of lies, according to which the founder of our family was of pure Arab blood and descended from the tribe of the Prophet rather than an Albanian whose first job was to clear the mounds of horse-dung that had accumulated on the edges of an Ottoman military encampment in that region. He cleared the dung with such efficiency that his prowess was noted and appreciated. He was brought back to Istanbul by the Aga in command of the encampment and later became responsible for cleanliness and hygiene inside the palace.

Mahmut Pasha manufactured untruths because he intended to marry a niece of the Sultan and thought it prudent to improve his pedigree. I think the falsehood was unnecessary. The Sultan probably knew the truth in any case and was unconcerned. Though I wish he had objected to the suit on other grounds and spared our family an unnecessary tragedy.

The Ertogruls have always preferred their ministers and courtiers to acknowledge their modest backgrounds. The Sultan creates and destroys Viziers. It is easier to maintain this style in the absence of a nobility. The knowledge that they are the only true hereditary ruling family gives our Sultans a feeling of stability and self-confidence, based on a belief that the Ertogruls are the only genuine hereditary ruling family in the history of our great Empire. Alas, this is true. And, incidentally, it is one reason why this Empire is rotting before our eyes. The colourful description of the Baron is close to the truth. Sultan Abdul Hamid II knows this. When I accompanied him to Berlin last year, he asked me: "Do you think I will be the last Caliph of Islam?" I smiled, without replying.

My grandfather Mahmut was a vain and conceited peacock, but he was not a complete imbecile. He must have been aware of Ertogrul sensitivities. The Sultan traces his descent from Osman, who founded the dynasty. Why did our idiot grandfather claim descent from the Prophet? Why did he feel the need to embellish the truth? Why create an imaginary world from which our family supposedly emerged? Grandfather made a complete fool of himself. His book was foolish and vainglorious, divided evenly between fantasy and fact.

Our family, of course, knew the truth, but though they laughed at Mahmut and found his conduct to be an embarrassment, none of them had the courage to confront him. If a delegation of stern-visaged family elders had called on him and insisted he stop lying, it might have had a temporary effect. Who knows? Perhaps it didn't really matter. After all, despite Mahmut Pasha's well-known habit of embroidering the truth, he was permitted to marry a niece of the Sultan and she, in due course, gave birth to our father and his three sisters. Not that this stopped the Sultan and his courtiers from laughing at Mahmut.

My aunt once told me that whenever Mahmut Pasha visited the court to pay his respects, the Sultan would question him about his book, forcing him to repeat some of his more absurd inventions before the assembled courtiers. The Sultan, of course, maintained his poise during the reading, while encouraging the sycophants to release their mirth at regular intervals, and so it came about that Mahmut Pasha's recitations were always punctuated by the noise of suppressed laughter.

What did he think while all this was going on? How could his greatly vaunted pride survive this ritual humiliation? When he came home from the palace, he would tell his wife how her uncle had honoured him once again and how the Vizier had congratulated him on the composition of a very important and top secret *aide-mémoire* which he, Mahmut, had drafted on the Russian Question and which had been despatched, without a single alteration, to the Chancellery in Berlin.

Did our beautiful grandmother, Sabiha, whose portrait welcomes visitors as they enter the house in Istanbul, believe any of this nonsense? I think not. She had married him not because he was good-looking or wealthy or a habitual liar, but simply because her father had decided that Mahmut Pasha would make a kind and good husband. I note that the mother of Orhan is smiling. She is asking herself, could our great-grandmother have been that stupid? And the answer, my lovely Nilofer, is a simple yes.

Your great-grandmother Sabiha was undoubtedly very pretty. The drawing is accurate enough in this regard but Bragadini, who painted her, was not, alas, a very gifted artist. He painted only what he saw. He lacked both intelligence and a real interest which might have pushed him to peer underneath and locate her real character. He failed abysmally to uncover her interior. She had a fair skin, luscious lips, a broad forehead, dark flowing tresses, blue eyes and it was claimed by him who knew that underneath her robes she possessed a body that was an "embarrassment of riches". For myself I hate this phrase, but Grandfather Mahmut used it often when in his cups, as a boast and an explanation to old friends who wondered aloud how he could possibly tolerate her mindless obsession with all things trivial.

Mahmut himself was not a very profound person. He had chosen not to burden himself with too much knowledge but, Allah be praised, how he enjoyed the three pastimes common to believers since the days of the Prophet. My grandfather loved wine, hunting and fornication and in that order. He could not hunt without a drink and he could not mount my grandmother without having killed some unfortunate beast. Even a rabbit helped him perform well in this respect.

Unfortunately for him, Sabiha regarded all three practices with the utmost repugnance. She had grown up in the palace. Even as an eight-year-old she had observed men in their cups and spoke often of how the sight had filled her with nausea, without ever being more specific. Who knows what she saw or experienced as a child in the palace where the Caliphs of our faith held sway, or how deeply it affected her? It was said that her father's decision to marry a Japanese courtesan had upset her greatly. In the conflicts that followed her father always backed his new wife against his children. Sabiha felt abandoned and it coloured her attitude to men and the power they possessed, but this is not what she told her friends.

They were informed casually that Mahmut Pasha was not a real man, that she derived no pleasure through coupling with him. That he was less effective than a dog and that after his children were born he had, Allah be praised, become impotent. However hard she tried, his little radish refused to stir. In fact she did not try at all. She never permitted him in her bed again.

Mahmut Pasha, self-loving and pleasure-seeking as ever, was enraged by these slurs on his manhood. He responded characteristically by lifting a Circassian serving wench from the kitchen and transporting her to a chamber near his bedroom. She became his mistress. Petrossian's grandfather was the Sultan of our kitchen at the time. He, too, had a soft spot for the woman, but bowed before the superior will of his master.

The Circassian – to this day I have never heard her real name mentioned – was illiterate. As a young girl, she had been bought for the household from a passing trader in Istanbul and trained as a kitchen maid. They say she possessed a natural intelligence. They say she made Mahmut Pasha laugh a great deal and, most important of all, she rejuvenated him between his legs. It was not long before news of her existence began to spread outside the family.

She began to accompany Mahmut Pasha on his hunting trips. Her presence compelled him to reverse the order of his pleasures. Now he could not hunt until he had been pleasured by the Circassian and only after the sport was over did they both share a cup of wine. He should have married her, but Mahmut Pasha was a coward. He was cowed by three fears. He feared the Sultan's displeasure. He feared a decline in his own social status. He feared the wrath of his father.

None the less he frustrated all Sabiha's attempts to have her

Circassian rival removed from the scene. Why did Sabiha care so much about this particular concubine? The practice was as common then as it is now. I think it was the public humiliation that upset her. If my grandfather had remained discreet she would not have felt insulted, but Mahmut Shah was angry with Sabiha for impugning his virility. And so he refused to hide his wench from the public gaze. He liked her to dress in the fashion of a lady so that he could show her to his friends. Halil's mother once found a carefully preserved, beautiful, though faded, Parisian gown in a small box in this house. It had belonged to the Circassian.

One day, she disappeared from our house in Istanbul. At first Sabiha was delighted, but a month passed and she noticed that her rival's absence, far from affecting Mahmut Pasha adversely, appeared to have improved his humour. Sabiha realised that something was being hidden from her. She sent for Petrossian's grandfather, but he denied all knowledge of anything related to his master's passion.

I think it must have been one of the maids who, jealous of the social ascent achieved by her Circassian peer, told her mistress the truth. The Circassian was carrying Mahmut Pasha's child and had been sent here for the period of her confinement. Who knows but that the child was intended to be born in this very room and in this very bed where Iskander Pasha now lies, unable to speak, but frowning at me because he disapproves of this story? Forgive me, dear brother. But every beginning needs an end. You disagree? ❜

My father was writing a note on his pad that I took to my uncle, who smiled.

"Iskander says there was no ending. That everything else is supposition. That evil tongues in the servants' quarters manufactured tales that were untrue. He is tired and wants to sleep and suggests we continue tomorrow. We must respect his wishes, but the end will not take long.

"There was an ending, and it was of a tragic nature. Mahmut Pasha's Circassian disappeared with the unborn child. She was never seen again. When I was little the servants used to frighten me with stories of a baby ghost whose screams were often heard outside this balcony. Ask Petrossian and he will tell you that Sabiha had her murdered. He claims he heard the story from his father. So there was an ending, even though Mahmut Pasha, like his descendant Iskander, preferred to believe that she had run away. He offered a big reward to anyone who brought him news of her, but it was never claimed."

With these words the Baron and Uncle Memed rose, bowed graciously in the direction of my father, who had shut his eyes in disapproval, and left the room. We followed in silence.

FOUR

The Circassian tells her truth to the Stone Woman and bemoans her fate; how the rich cancel the love of the poor

'Will you listen to my tale of woe, Stone Woman, or do your ears welcome only the voice of the Pasha and his family? I've been in this house for over three months. I'm well looked after and fed by the caretaker and his wife and I'm happy to be away from Istanbul, but in my solitude, I miss Hikmet more than ever before. I wake up every day long before the birds. It is still not light and the stars have yet to fade. I can't sleep. Hikmet's face and his voice fill my dreams and make me miserable. Look at me. I am eight months pregnant with Mahmut Pasha's child but my heart is still heavier than my stomach.

In my dreams I see Hikmet in his soldier's uniform. He is looking at me with bitterness in his grey eyes. They speak to me: "We trusted you, but you would not wait. You betrayed our love for a rich man's comfort." I plead forgiveness. I beg for mercy, but inside myself I know that his eyes are speaking the truth. I was pledged to him. I was even preparing to ask the mistress for permission to marry him, when the cursed day arrived and our lord, Mahmut Pasha, catching sight of me, began to twirl his moustache. It was the fatal sign of which I had first been warned when I was a girl of ten, and now, eight years later, it had happened. My heart sank straight to my feet.

The house maids still warn any new addition to the household that there is a longstanding tradition in this family. When the master looks at any one of them and begins to play with his moustache, it is a sign that the call to his bed will come for that night. And it always did, Stone Woman. It always did. And not just for the maids. There were a few young coachmen who received the summons. One of them ran away and was never seen again. The maids spoke often of Mahmut Pasha's habits, but their crudeness offended my ears. I preferred to forget their stories.

I was, after all, only a kitchen maid, not even permitted near the other rooms of the house. My task was to help the cooks and make sure they had all the ingredients they needed for their dishes. When I was much younger, I never thought of myself as a person whom the master even noticed and so I was never worried like some of the other maids, those who carried their breasts like over-ripe melons.

He saw me from the window one day as I was sitting on a bench near the vegetable garden and washing cucumbers. I averted my glance from his, but he rushed down and passed in front of me. I stood up and covered my head. He smiled and fondled his moustache. O cruel fate, Stone Woman. I knew I was doomed. I wanted to run away before the night came. As luck would have it, my clean-shaven Hikmet with his dark red hair, who stood daily on guard duty outside the house, had gone back to his village to attend his mother's funeral. I was alone. I swear in Allah's name that if Hikmet had been there that day I would have run away with him, but it was not to be. The call came in the shape of the oldest maidservant in the house. She, who boasted of how she had warmed the bed of Mahmut Pasha as well as his father and grandfather, was now approaching her fiftieth year. In the past she had used her privileged position to lord it over the other servants. They had despised and feared her, but that was some time ago. Now she had been reduced to the status of the Pasha's procuress, but this had made her warm-hearted. I think, deep in herself, she understood the humiliation. To try and make it easier for us she would say: "I have known three generations of this family," she used to tell us, "and this young master is the kindest of them all. He will not be violent with you. He will not hurt you in any way as his grandfather did when his lust was aroused."

Her reassuring words had little effect on me. I lay in my narrow little bed and wept without restraint. Later, when the old woman took me to the Pasha's chamber, I fell on my knees and kissed Mahmut Pasha's feet. I beseeched him to spare my honour. I whispered that I was promised to another. I confessed my love for Hikmet. I told of my desire to be a mother and to give my children the love that had been denied me. In my foolishness I thought my honesty might impress him, but it had a completely different effect. He took my pleas for resistance and this inflamed him further. He made me undress and then he pushed me back on his bed and took his pleasure. For my part, and this, I swear to you, Stone Woman, is the truth, I felt only anger and sadness and helplessness. No enjoyment did I feel, not even momentarily. The blood I saw on my legs frightened me. All the while his ungainly body, with its mounds of flesh, was heaving over me. I became inwardly angry with my parents for dying when I was only three and I cursed my grandfather for selling me like a piece of cloth to a passing merchant.

He noticed my indifference. This angered him. "Return tomorrow night," he said as he dismissed me in the voice a master uses when reprimanding an ungrateful slave.

I returned the next night and the one after and every night after that one. My indifference only seemed to arouse him and he became ever more determined to break my will. He wanted me to say that I enjoyed him. He would look at me and ask whether I could ever love him. I never replied to these questions, but I also ceased to resist. He bought me clothes, gave me expensive jewellery and, on one occasion, dressed me in the clothes of a European lady and took me to the reception at the German Embassy, where he introduced me as his European wife, who had lost the power of speech after the tragic death of her father. He moved me to a special room in the house and I was given my own maid. One day he was entertaining some guests in his own rooms. I was seated next to him, watching the men getting more and more drunk. A few of them looked at me with desire in their eyes. Suddenly his wife, the princess Sabiha, walked into the room. She was intoxicated with anger. She stood there for a moment, ignoring his frown. She screamed abuse at him, informing his friends that he was worse than a eunuch. As he stood to escort her out of the room, she undid her trousers and lifted her tunic to reveal her most private parts. As the men averted their eyes, she shouted at her husband: "Wasn't this good enough for you? Answer me, you sweeper of horse-shit!" The Pasha's face had frozen in horror. Her performance had a magical effect. I have never seen men in their cups sober themselves so quickly. Then, satisfied with what she had done, Sabiha swept out of the room. Previously I had never liked her and this was long before I was chosen by the Pasha. She was rude to us and her chambermaids loathed her. After this display I began to admire her. I wanted to speak with her and explain my own despair, but I never found the courage to face her anger. I pray that Allah will forgive my cowardice.

But I could not stop thinking of Hikmet. The only time I forced

Hikmet out of my head was when the master was taking his pleasure of me. I never enjoyed those moments. They told me that the mistress had sent a message to Hikmet and told him what had happened. He was never seen again. I wanted him to come to me, Stone Woman. I would have cleaned his feet with my tears, begged him to forgive me and take me with him, far away from here, but he never returned to the house. Perhaps he did not love me enough. Perhaps he was scared off by the Pasha or perhaps a pregnant purse, heavy with coins, bought his disappearance.

And now I carry the child of a man I despise. I'm sure it's a boy and that makes me even more angry. I will not have his child. I will not bring this poor creature into the world. I will jump into the sky and I will fly away, Stone Woman. When I get tired of flying I will fall into the sea and when they find me, I will be floating on the water, like a bloated, dead fish, but with my eyes shut. I will be in a sleep as deep as the sea. Do you understand why I'm doing this, Stone Woman? To punish him. These cursed Beys and Pashas think they are gods. They believe all they have to say to a poor girl is, "I love you, have my child", and she will be so grateful for their affection, their food, their clothes, their money that she will ask for nothing more from this world. I dreaded his touch. My worst fear was that one day the Pasha would put his poisonous seed in me and it would sprout. And yet when it happened I was no longer frightened. I became very calm. I knew what had to be done. There was no more anguish in my life.

The day I lost my Hikmet, with his soft skin and smiling eyes, the sun stopped shining for me. In Istanbul, the Pasha tried to avoid leaving me on my own. He thought his company kept me cheerful. I felt more alone when he was with me than at any other time and especially when he was filled with lust and groaned like a donkey on heat. Not a day passed when I didn't ask myself what I should do with my life.

What shall I do, Stone Woman? You listen, but you never reply. If only you could speak. Just once. Can you see the sky tonight? There is a crescent moon, which always travels fast as if in search of a lover, but it will soon become full-blown, like my belly, and when it does I know what I will do. I will go to the cliffs and fly to join the moon. I will laugh as I leap. The distance will disappear and on that day I will know that no other man will ever enter my life again. I will laugh at the thought of the Pasha's fat face, white with anger, when they tell him that his slave-girl has freed herself. He will know why I did this and that will hurt him even more. He will know I left this world because I could no longer bear his touch or that of his child. He will never be able to admit this truth to anyone, but I hope the secret devours his insides. I want his death to be pure agony. My only regret is that I will not live to see that day. ’

FIVE

Petrossian tells of the glory days of the Ottoman Empire; Salman insists that the borders between fiction and history have become blurred; Nilofer writes a farewell letter to her Greek husband; Orhan's belated circumcision at the hands of young Selim

I first saw the strange gestures he was making from a distance. They made me smile. I knew precisely what the old Armenian was doing. Like everything else in this house, it revived memories of my own childhood. Scenes from my past were being repeated, but this time for the benefit of my son. I was pleased. Petrossian was engaged in a weekly household ritual, which he would never entrust to anyone else. He was polishing my father's old silver shaving bowl. It was an item that had been brought back from Paris many years ago. He treasured it greatly and, for that reason, Petrossian had taken it upon himself to ensure that the bowl never lost its lustre. Normally such tasks were assigned to less important servants, but Petrossian, who always accompanied Iskander Pasha to Paris, must have known the value attached by his master to this particular object.

Orhan and the children from the servants' quarters were watching him, trance-like, just as we used to when we were young. I walked slowly in their direction, but I knew which story was being retold even before I heard the words being spoken. I was pleased and irritated at the same time. I wanted

Orhan to be part of this world, to be accepted by my father, but I wanted things to change. Here it seemed that, like the Stone Woman, everything stood still.

"And do you think, my young master Orhan, that Memed the Conqueror listened to the whimpers and the moans of his frightened old woman of a Vizier? No. He raised his hand to say 'Enough'. The Sultan had heard enough of such talk. Now he wanted to take the city they called Constantinople. He wanted to stand erect on the old walls of Byzantium and look at Europe. Memed knew that if we were going to be a power in Europe we had to take that city. Without it our Empire would always be one-eyed. We needed Constantinople to look at what lay beyond the Bosporus.

"They say that it was a beautiful spring day when the Sultan Memed gave the orders to prepare for battle and lay siege to the city. We will build a fortress on the other side of the water to control all access to their city. It will fall. Memed the Great was sure of this and his strong will and determination infected every soldier. Mothers told their sons to go and fight for the honour of their faith. Imagine the excitement that must have swept through the army. The Sultan has ordered that we will take the city. His Exalted Majesty has ordered the soldiers be properly fed. That night hundreds of lambs were covered with fresh herbs and roasted on spits for the soldiers. The exquisite scent of grilled meat pervaded the entire encampment. I'm sure it must have reached the defenders of Constantinople . . ."

Why does nothing in this house ever change? When I was told this same story by this same story-teller, I'm sure it was goats and not lambs that were being prepared, and perhaps ten years from now it will be peacocks. I have stopped caring. It makes no difference and yet I could not help being touched as I watched Orhan's face alight with excitement. His eyes were fixed on Petrossian. My little boy had entered the world of Sultans and holy wars. How different all this was from the bedtime stories Dmitri and I told him at home. I had brought him up on stories of our family, of my uncles and aunts and all our cousins in different parts of our Empire. It was a way of instructing him in the geography of our world and its cities. These were tales of happiness and adventures, designed to make him feel at ease with the world inhabited by his family.

Orhan's father never spoke of our great Empire. In this way he avoided both denigration and praise. The vices and glories of the Ottomans were not a subject very close to Dmitri's heart. His own people had fought to free themselves from our rule only a few dozen years ago. Dmitri, not surprisingly, was on their side, though as a school teacher he had to keep his opinions to himself. Even at home we rarely discussed these matters. In fact, if I'm honest with myself, I would have to admit that ever since our marriage we rarely spoke of anything important. There were occasions when I deliberately provoked him. He would lose his temper with me, curse the day he had fallen in love with an Ottoman. Remarks of this nature only made me laugh, which was unfortunate since it only served to prolong his irritation. He found it difficult to believe that both my brothers were more critical than he of the Sultans and their Court, but then, as Dmitri never failed to point out, they had nothing to fear.

Dmitri is a good man. Of this I'm sure. And yet there are times when goodness becomes a bit wearisome. After my daughter was born I began to wonder whether I had made a mistake. Had I really loved him, or was it my father's opposition that had closed my mind to any other alternative? The value of defying Iskander Pasha had long since depreciated, leaving me alone to confront my daily existence. I was tired of Dmitri. Tired of his jokes. Tired of his bad poetry. Tired of his resentments. Tired of seeing him wear the same style of clothes every single day and, what made all this doubly bad, I had tired of his body. It no longer gave me pleasure. There was nothing left. My life became a burden. I felt stifled.

He felt my growing indifference. It was difficult to hide my feelings all the time. His pride was hurt. Inside his head he must have begun to hate me. Sometimes I caught a look on his face that gave him away, but he restrained his anger. He was fearful that one day I might take the children and return to my father's house. That must be why he suffered my alienation in complete silence and this made everything worse. He never allowed it to affect outward appearances and this only succeeded in enraging me further. I would have thought more of him if he had lost his reserve and hurled abuse at my face or shouted at me, but he remained silent. Most important of all, he never neglected his children. This was the big difference with our household. Here and in Istanbul the men in our family had nothing to do with children or their needs. It was the women, aided as always by an army of servants. We had only one serving-maid in Konya. Yes, just one!

Dmitri used to put Orhan to bed with stories of the ancient Greek gods and goddesses. And Orhan always wanted to be Hermes. Never Zeus or Neptune or Apollo or Mars or Cupid, but Hermes. He liked the thought of a god who was a messenger and he sometimes flew from his father to me with imagined messages. What Orhan and I really appreciated when Dmitri spoke of the old gods was that they were like human beings. They fought over each other. They had favourites on earth. They competed for the affections of Zeus. It was all very real.

Old Petrossian's tales of Ottoman heroes could have been like that, but the old man had learnt his craft in the school of slaves. I have no idea how long Petrossian's forefathers had worked in our household, but he and we knew that the relationship was very old. There had been Petrossians in our family for nearly a hundred and fifty years. And so Memed the Conqueror was above criticism, even of the mildest variety.

When we were young, my brother Salman used to invent stories, which cast Memed in a very ugly light. He would stop Petrossian in the middle of a story and ask with an innocent expression, "But Petrossian, is this not the same Memed who had his own mother's brother boiled alive in oil and then fed his entrails to the dogs simply because the unfortunate man had been unable to control his wind in the Sultan's presence?"

Remarks of this sort were designed partially to make us laugh, which we did, and partially to challenge and irritate the story-teller. Petrossian remained impassive in the face of every provocation, neither irritated nor amused, his expression unmarked by the tiniest smile or the trace of a frown. What annoyed him was losing our attention and, at those moments, he began to resemble a shepherd whose crook has been stolen and whose sheep are straying all over the hills. Instead of ignoring Salman's jokes, Petrossian ended up taking them very seriously and he defended every imagined atrocity dreamed up by my brother to blacken the name of the Sultans.

Only once did Petrossian lose his control and laugh. Salman had interrupted him in full flow and asked for his views on an important matter.

"This concerns Sultan Selim the Sot. Do you think the stories they tell of him are true, Petrossian? They say that he drank so much that he became incapable of performing his main function as a man. This angered him greatly, because the more alcohol he consumed the more it inflamed his desire. He became desperate for the little thing between his legs to rise and commence its work, but, alas, Allah had willed otherwise. They say that when he summoned a wife to his chamber, he used to be hoisted upwards by silken cords and while he was held thus by the eunuchs, young boys with delicate hands would fondle him between the legs so that he felt some sensation while a healthy, blindfolded janissary was brought in naked. The loyal soldier would proceed to impregnate the delighted princess with tightly shut eyes; she who lay below the floating Sultan, expecting the worst, was delighted by the vigour of the surprise. And all this time, Allah's representative on earth, in a drunken stupor, would see the happiness on the face of his wife and hear her delighted squeals. So, or so they say, everyone was satisfied. Could this possibly be true? If it is so then the line of descent that our Sultans claim from Osman himself would have been decisively broken. Answer me, Petrossian!"

Petrossian had not been able to keep a straight face during this story. He had cast away his caution and laughed a great deal, much to the delight of Salman, who had never before tasted such a sweet victory. After this we became very attached to Petrossian, realising that his reserve was largely a mask.

"The devil himself must communicate these stories to you, Salman Pasha. I have no knowledge of them."

Looking at him now, I could tell from the old man's gestures and facial expressions that Constantinople had been taken. Sultan Memed had restricted the looting and was receiving the heads of the Christian churches. The adventure was over. Little Orhan was beginning to fidget. It was time to rescue him.

"Was that all true?" he asked as we walked away.

I nodded.

"Would my father say it was true?"

"I don't know, Orhan. I don't know. Are you missing him?"

He shrugged his shoulders and turned away so I could not see his face. He knew that Dmitri and I were no longer close. A child can sense these things much more than parents ever realise. My son knew we were no longer happy. And yet, in this house, far away from our cramped quarters in Konya, my anger had been pushed aside. I was in a more generous mood. I did not feel the need to punish Dmitri any longer. I did not even wish him dead. I just never wanted to be with him again. The thought of being in his arms again was so nauseous that it cramped the lower half of my stomach.

Orhan had walked away on his own. Slowly he was beginning to discover the house and the mysteries of its surroundings. Often I would see him walking towards the rocks, talking to himself. What was he thinking? What did he make of my family? Sometimes I would see him staring at my brothers, then turning his face away quickly to stop himself smiling lest I notice his pleasure. He was happy here. I could see that in his face, but I also knew that he missed his father and his sister. My mother suggested that I send a message to Dmitri, inviting him to bring Emineh here and to spend a few days with us so that his son could see him. I did not argue with her. I did as she asked.

"Dear Dmitri", I forced myself to write. "My father has suffered a stroke. Orhan's presence is a great relief for him. I plan to stay here for the rest of the summer. Then I will return to Istanbul with my family and make plans for our son's education and future. Orhan misses you and Emineh a great deal. My mother suggests that both of you come and visit us here. I think it is a good idea, provided, of course, that you expect nothing from me. Nilofer."

Our gardener's son was despatched to Konya with this letter. My mother had raised another question with me that day. It was something I had been dreading, but had banished from my mind in the hope it would go away.

"Nilofer," she said in a deceptively friendly voice, "I have something to ask you."

I nodded.

"Is Orhan circumcised?'

"Yes, of course."

"You lie, child. The maids who bathe him swear the opposite. The servants talk of nothing else."

I became silent and angry. When Orhan was born I had wanted him circumcised, but Dmitri had resisted. "It is a barbaric custom," he had argued, "and I do not wish this punishment to be inflicted on my son." I was so full of love in those early days that I could not deny him anything and I had acquiesced, though even then I had been uneasy. The memory of my weakness angered me now as I looked into my mother's beautiful eyes.

"It must be done, Nilofer. Your father's faith and mine are agreed on the importance of this ritual. The sooner it happens the better. I have summoned Hasan from Istanbul."

I screamed. "No! He's nearly ninety years old. What if his hand slips! He's going to die soon, but why should he deprive my Orhan of his manhood? The boy is too old now, Mother. Can't we spare him this torture?"

To my amazement, Mother burst out laughing. "Do you think I would let that old goat near Orhan with a razor? It's his grandson, Selim, who does the work now. Hasan has to come because he has been in the family all his life. His father used to shave Iskander's grandfather and Hasan circumcised your father, uncles and brothers. He accompanied your father to Paris as the household barber. He would be very insulted and upset if we did not invite him to the ceremony. And remember something, Nilofer: a man is never too old for circumcision. When I was little my mother would tell me many stories of our forefathers who were not circumcised in Spain for fear the Catholics would find out they were Jews, but the moment they arrived in Istanbul, a barber was found to perform the ceremony. It was a matter of pride in those days."

I was relieved but unhappy. Tears poured down my cheeks. My mother's slender, long fingers, the nails painted with henna, stroked my face gently. How I wished Mother had been a Christian, not a Jew! Then she might have supported me. We could have bribed the barber to pretend that Orhan had been circumcised. He was old enough to bathe himself now and I did not like the thought of young maids inspecting his body in the bath every day. It was not to be.

The next day Hasan and his grandson arrived from Istanbul. Hasan had lost all his hair. He walked with a stoop and a thick stick, the bottom end of which was held together by a rusty iron rim. I received him in my mother's reception room.

"Look at you," he croaked. "You produce a boy and fail to circumcise him! Did the Greek stop you?"

"Of course not, Hasan Baba," I replied in a voice so false that I barely recognised myself. "How could I have Orhan circumcised in your absence? It would breach an old family tradition."

"I would have come to Konya," he laughed, revealing a mouth devoid of teeth, "and circumcised the father as well."

My mother tried to conceal a smile. I decided to change the subject.

"I had no idea my father took you to Paris all those years ago. That must have given you a rest from performing circumcisions."

"It gave me a rest from performing anything," he muttered. "I was taken there just for show. It suited your father. He thought the French would be impressed if his special barber accompanied him. In Paris, your father's hair was cut by an old French sodomite. For myself, I have seen better types in Istanbul. My task was reduced to trimming his beard and cutting his nails once a week. One day your father decided to humiliate me. The French barber wanted to observe an Ottoman barber at work. I was preparing my scissors to trim Iskander Pasha's hair, when he suggested that, as a special treat, I cut the Frenchman's hair instead. At first I was angry, but then I saw in this offer an opportunity to avenge the insult. I pretended to be cheerful and friendly. I seated the Frenchman in a chair. I massaged his head with oil so that he relaxed completely. He shut his eyes to enjoy the sensation. I gave him a soldier's haircut. He screamed with rage as his grey locks fell on the floor, but it was too late. He cursed me, but I had won. Your father had to buy him a very expensive wig and give him a weighty purse. After that incident the Frenchman could not bring himself to look me in the eye. He would turn his powdered face away every time he saw me, but I would go close to him and whisper: 'Istanbul couture. Très bien, eh, monsieur?'" Hasan cackled like a hen at the memory.

I couldn't resist teasing him. "How did you occupy yourself otherwise, Hasan Baba? I have heard that you began to dress like a Parisian and visited night clubs. Some say you even kept a Frenchwoman."

"May Allah pluck out the tongue that spread such poison," he replied. "I spent most of my time in Paris studying the Koran."

The lie was so brazen that all three of us burst out laughing. Then he asked for permission to introduce us to his grandson, Selim.

"He's opened a barber's shop in Istanbul, with three apprentices, one of whom is very talented. The Westerners are his main customers. He was reluctant to follow me, but I told him it was a privilege to circumcise the grandson of Iskander Pasha. Selim! Selim!"

A young man who could not have been more than twenty-five years of age entered the room and bowed stiffly in our direction. My mother motioned that he should sit down and he took a seat without any trace of awkwardness. My first impression was favourable. He had an intelligent face. He was clean-shaven and dressed in Western clothes and did not look at the ground in fake humility when I spoke to him. Unlike Hasan, he spoke with a soft, reassuring voice.

"Orhan Bey is nearly ten years old and I realise you must be worried about the ceremony, *hanim effendi*, but it will be safe and painless. The thought of it frightens him and that is what will make him scream, not the actual circumcision. Have you determined the day?"

"In three days' time. Are you sure you can be away from Istanbul that long?"

He smiled. "I told them I would be away for a week, *hanim effendi*."

My mother indicated with a slight nod that the two men could leave. As he was walking away, Hasan remembered that he had not yet offered his condolences on my father's affliction.

"I am off now to pay my respects to Iskander Pasha. It will be the first time that I will do the talking and he will have to listen. Perhaps the shock will be such that Allah will return his tongue to him."

After they had left I asked my mother how we should break the news to Orhan. To my astonishment, she informed me that she had already done so and that the boy had been greatly relieved.

"He tells me that he was teased at school for being different. He says he will bear the pain like a man."

"How else could he bear it, Mother?"

And so it happened that Orhan was dressed in a beautifully embroidered silk robe and as the maidservants sang next door, Selim the barber snipped off the offending skin. Orhan did not scream or cry. He smiled. My father, who had insisted on being present, applauded and presented Orhan with a purse, pregnant with gold coins. It had been given to him on the day of his circumcision. The Baron and Uncle Memed entered the room and kissed Orhan. My mother had gone to the kitchen herself and supervised the making of *ure*. Orhan had not yet tasted this sweet.

"What is it made of?" he asked my mother after he had tasted the first morsel she presented to him in a silver ladle.

"They say that this was first made when Noah realised there was not enough food left in the Ark. He instructed the women to put everything in a pot for one last big meal. In the big pot went wheat and raisins and apricots and dates and figs and dried beans and the mixture was boiled for many hours, until it looked like this. Now will you stand up, Orhan, and come with me so that we can distribute the *ure* to the servants."

"Before I do that, can I offer some to Selim?"

"Of course," I shouted with relief. "He must be the first."

SIX

Iskander Pasha asks his visitors to explain the decline of the Empire; the Baron points to a flaw in the Circle of Equity; Salman's deep-rooted cynicism

Father's health was improving daily. He could now walk on his own and, as my mother confided to me, he was an active lover once again, all the more passionate for having lived through a period of denial. His face, too, was much improved. The paleness had evaporated and the sun had restored his colour. He was reading a great deal, mainly French novels. He loved Balzac and Stendhal, but hated Zola. He would write in his notebook that Zola was a scoundrel and an anarchist, but his written words never became an adequate substitute for speech. If he could speak he would have cursed Zola in language he was too embarrassed to put down on paper. He knew that his powers of speech had deserted him for ever and this was something he found difficult to accept.

But he became more and more assertive, more and more as he used to be when we gathered in his room for our stories. He was now determined to prevent a discussion of family history. He wanted to encourage more elevated talk. One evening he inscribed a question in bold capitals on his book and Petrossian held it up before us in turn. It read: CAN ANY OF YOU EXPLAIN WHY WE

DECLINE SO RAPIDLY? IF RUSSIAN TSAR AND AUSTRIAN EMPEROR ARE STILL SO POWERFUL, WHY NOT OUR SULTAN?

Everyone was present. Memed and the Baron looked at each other wearily. Salman gave a sly smile. Zeynep kissed Iskander Pasha's hands and took her leave. Halil, alone, showed any sign of interest.

"We failed to renew ourselves, Ata. And this is the price we have to pay. We allowed the clergy too much power in determining the future of this state. Istanbul could have been the capital of invention and modernity like Cordoba and Baghdad in the old days, but these wretched beards that established the laws of our state were frightened of losing their monopoly of power and knowledge. I forget the name of the fool who told the Sultan that if the palace relaxed its control, our religion would be finished. At the beginning of the sixteenth century, every major city in the West had its own printing press, while Sultan Selim threatened any person who showed even the slightest interest in it with death."

Iskander Pasha was waving his hands to interrupt his son. Halil paused while I read my father's note.

"The fear wasn't totally unjustified, Halil. The Sultan's ministers kept a very close watch on Europe. The Grand Vizier was aware that in three crucial years, from 1517 till 1520, the printing press destroyed the monopoly of the Catholic Church: three hundred thousand copies of Martin Luther's work were printed and distributed in this time."

"With great respect, Ata, I was aware of that fact, but the price we paid for our retreat into the past was a heavy one. We sealed off the Empire from a crucially important technological advance. The *ulema*, may they roast in hell, opposed modernisation on principle. Most of the Sultans and the eunuchs and janissaries who surrounded them accepted this view. It is an outrage that we kept the printing press at a distance to prevent the spread of knowledge. And even if you disagree on the printing press, though I really can't see how you can, surely you must accept that the ban on public clocks was simply senseless. Here, too, the damned beards insisted that time was not linear. It was sacred and circular and could only be determined by the muezzin's call to prayer. I think our decline is well deserved. This Empire is melting away before our eyes and the clergy and the Sultan watch in silence. It's too late now. There's nothing they can do. The Prussians and the British want to keep us alive for their own reasons. If this had not been the case, the Russian Tsar would have eaten us alive by now. We live on borrowed time and borrowed money. Some of us in the army are already discussing the future. The Empire is gone, Ata. The only interesting question is what will take its place."

Halil's speech had made everyone thoughtful. It was Uncle Memed who was the first to speak after him.

"There is much wisdom in what you say, boy, but I don't think our troubles are the result of simply ignoring the printing press. I think the decline started a long time ago, even before Yusuf Pasha's exile. Our rulers were so delighted with our military successes that they failed to observe their limitations. There was a missing link in the Circle of Equity. Am I not correct, Baron?"

The Baron nodded his agreement. "The Circle was useful, but like the *Qabus Nama* it was first formulated by a Persian and as we are aware, the Persians make good poets, but bad politicians and even worse priests."

My father signalled for attention. I read aloud what he had written.

"My son Halil surprises me by his astuteness. I think the failure to modernise ourselves at the beginning of this century is a result of our refusal to accept the printing press and other inventions from Britain and France. Could the Baron explain why he holds the Circle of Equity in such contempt? We were taught its uses when we were being educated in the art of governance. I see nothing wrong in the political theory that has governed our Empire for centuries. It is much better than all this democracy tolerated by Bismarck."

The Baron, who had been busy munching grilled almonds and pistachios, cleared his throat in a hurry, almost choking in the process. He washed the remnants of the nuts down with some water and then moved his chair close to where my father sat cross-legged on his bed.

"We shall discuss Bismarck another time, Iskander Pasha, but it would be foolish of you to underestimate his genius. He has created a new Germany. In doing so, he has dynamited the scaffolding that protected the Austrian Empire. Berlin matters now, not Vienna. But I will save Bismarck for another day.

"This Circle of Equity which you Ottomans love so much was built on flimsy foundations, Iskander Pasha. It sounds very impressive. It was designed not to solve problems, but to make an impact. Listen now how it rolls off the tongue like Memed the Conqueror's artillery outside Constantinople. No sovereign authority without an army. No army without wealth. No wealth without loyal subjects. No loyal subjects without justice. No justice without harmony on earth. No harmony without a state. No state without law. No enforcement of law without sovereign authority. No sovereign authority without a Sultan or Caliph."

The Baron had recited the Circle with such authority that everyone present burst into applause.

"I told you it sounds good, but it always had a fatal flaw. It was based on the *devshirme*. You took babies from all over the Empire and created a caste of soldiers and administrators through long years of training and education. The state owned them, but they began to believe that they owned the state and sometimes that they were the state. It was an ambitious plan which your rulers refined, but as your great and incomparable historian Ibn Khaldun warned many centuries ago, it is dangerous to expect a group without common ties of kinship or solidarity or class to remain loyal to the sovereign authority. A common training is fine for the production of French chefs, but not for creating a strong state.

"These soldiers and bureaucrats own no property. They are not permitted any hereditary rights. It is utopian to expect them to remain selfless and pure and unaffected by wealth and privileges. Naturally, they try and acquire wealth and close ties to wealthy families. They observe the clergy. They ask themselves how it is that the Durrizade family has made the *ulema* a religious nobility from the seventh century to this day. They know it is unfair and they attempt to remedy the discrepancy. But their rise has been too sudden. They are painfully aware that what they have done is illegal. It could be used against them by their rivals or when the Sultan wishes to have any of them executed. This reduces them to a state of permanent insecurity. It creates the basis for constant intrigue. It is, therefore, impossible for these men to become pillars of stability on which the state can rest with confidence. And so, my dear Iskander Pasha, your Circle of Equity becomes a descent to chaos, a circle of self-delusion, an inferno. Without solidarity and stable institutions, old Empires crumble. New ones take their place. You have lost both the war and the battle for survival. Memed the Conqueror wanted to make Istanbul the new Rome. He succeeded too well. The Ottomans have mimicked its decline and fall in a remarkable fashion."

The Baron paused for breath and refilled his glass.

"Have you quite finished, Baron?" inquired Uncle Memed with mischief.

The Baron gave him a withering look as he sipped his champagne. "This is no time for levity, Memed. We are discussing the future of your Empire."

"But I thought we had none. Our history, according to you, has come to an end. The future clearly belongs to the Prussians, which is why I'm pleased we are such close friends. If Istanbul is renamed and handed to the Greeks by the Western powers, I shall move to Berlin."

Nobody smiled. Everyone present had been struck by the Baron's words. For a few minutes there was complete silence. Only the roar of the waves outside disrupted the reflective mood. Then my brother Halil, usually very reserved, began to speak again.

"I doubt whether the Western powers will ever agree on the future of

Istanbul. Mr Disraeli knows that we have protected the Jews for many centuries. He will not wish the city to be returned to the Greek Church. Bismarck will resist change for fear that the Greeks will be too weak and that either Great Britain or Russia will become the real master of Istanbul. The Pope in Rome will do everything to prevent the re-emergence of a rival. The result of all this will help us rebuild and prosper. Do not imagine that we have all been overcome by inertia. Let me inform the Baron that though I agree with much that he has said, including the fact that this Empire is finished, there are many officers in the Ottoman army, men like myself who are forward-thinking in their approach. We will not let everything crash to the ground. We will carve out a new state from the ruins of the old. And if the Western powers try and prevent us, we shall fight them with all our might. In this regard we shall not mimic the Roman Empire. Italy has only just emerged as a unified state, many, many centuries after the fall of Rome. We will not make the same mistake."

The Baron replied, but this time he said nothing new. They talked of ancient Rome and Istanbul. I began to lose the thread of their argument as they became more and more repetitive. Throughout this conversation, Salman had given me the impression of a person completely detached from his surroundings. His heavy eyelids and languorous movements reminded me of a *dervish* who had smoked too much opium. At one point I thought he was fast asleep. Perhaps Halil had awakened him.

"What does this mean, Halil? Should I warn my friends to evacuate their families and their trade from Alexandria? Should they move to Damascus or are we going to lose everything?"

"I'm not sure. Egypt is already out of our control, but I am nervous on behalf of your friends. I think the Bedouin will go with whoever promises them the most money. We are too weak to control that world. The fact that we are all of the same faith matters the least when power and money are at stake. The Arabs have never been sentimental in this regard. He who will pay, will have his say. Come back to Istanbul, Salman. Everything is about to change."

Salman smiled at his brother. "If someone like you has become infected with the new ideologies that are sprouting all over Europe, then perhaps there is still reason to hope. Perhaps change will come like a hurricane or an earthquake. When the wind has died down and the tremors have ceased, then I shall return to Istanbul. Not a day before. And I expect you to receive me with all the respect that I deserve. Now, if you will excuse me, I will retire. All this talk of the rise and fall of Empires has given me indigestion."

Halil laughed as he stood up to embrace Salman.

"Even I would not be so crude as to blame the short-sightedness of our Sultans for your interminable flatulence. You move too little and you eat too much. The East has not been good for you. When you return I really would not recommend Istanbul as a residence. There you will only get bigger and slower, like a female elephant about to give birth. The indigestion, as you so delicately put it, will get much worse. The city I would suggest for you is Ankara. The air is clean and vices are few."

Salman stroked his brother's cheeks affectionately. "You can bury me in Ankara, if you please, Halil, but not till I'm dead. It will cost you to shift this carcass from Istanbul, but you have my permission. The Baron is our witness."

Salman's departure brought the evening to a close. Iskander Pasha was very pleased with himself for having manipulated the discussion so successfully. There had been no personal reminiscences of the family, no discussion of our past, and this pleased him. His speech had been paralysed, but his memory had not weakened and there were recollections with which he wanted no contact at all. I felt close to him again. He had once told us that whenever he returned to Istanbul after a stay in Paris or Berlin, he found the odour of stupidity at home extremely reassuring, but was terrified that it might suffocate him if, for whatever reason, he was never able to travel again. I would ask him about that before the summer was over, but not tonight, when he looked so happy. I kissed his head and took my leave.

Silently, I followed the Baron and Uncle Memed to the moon-drenched terrace. We sat down at a table beautifully laid with silver bowls filled with almonds of three different varieties, walnuts and fruits. Petrossian uncorked another bottle and served the two men. Memed told him they would help themselves and instructed him to retire for the night.

I looked at the stars in the sky and wondered whether I would ever find true happiness and be content with my life. I often felt that my mother had sacrificed too much for the sake of a comfortable existence. She had allowed her own personality to be dwarfed by the family of Iskander Pasha. If she had married someone else her biography would have taken a different course. She had spoken once to me, in a slightly embarrassed way, of another man. She had liked him a great deal, but he was poor and when her father had rejected the suit he had emigrated to New York, where he became a very successful painter. She often wished she knew what it was that he painted. I mused over whether her true and intimate feeling for my father was one of disgust, but my thoughts were interrupted.

The two men resumed their conversation. Strange, I thought, that my presence never seems to bother them. They trust me. Perhaps they imagine that like them I, too, am unconventional. Whatever their reasons, I am flattered by their confidence.

"I sometimes get the impression, Memed, that despite our knowledge of each other, you doubt my intelligence."

"Intimacy can breed doubt and contempt in equal portions, Baron."

"So, in other words, you had no doubts regarding my intellectual superiority when I was your tutor in Istanbul."

"None whatsoever, but surely you could not have forgotten that it was also the period of our courtship, which was very intense. You taught me a great deal. Your language, German poetry and philosophy and a love of books. I can still remember the words of the first poem by Heine that you recited and your pleasure when I told you I had understood every word. We talked often of god and religion and the elasticity of so many dogmas. You showed me Berlin and Paris. You compared the growth of learned societies in German towns with the lack of any intellectual movement in provincial France. It was only after I had fully penetrated that world that I could permit you to penetrate me."

Both men burst out laughing.

SEVEN

Nilofer tells the Stone Woman that Selim has stroked her breasts in the moonlight and she is falling in love with him; she is shocked to discover that her mother has been eavesdropping

'I don't know where to begin, Stone Woman. It happened suddenly, without warning, and now I may be in worse trouble than ever before. It happened yesterday in the light of the moon. I wanted to go and count the stars on the beach and I wanted to be completely alone. So I took the tiny path that leads from the cliffs to the entrance of the cave overlooking the sea. When we were children we used to believe that it was our little secret and we were convinced that no adult knew of the path. Even if they did they would find it difficult to follow us because the track was truly little.

As I heard the gentle noise of the water caressing the sand I felt at peace with myself. When I look at the sea glistening in the moonlight and then gaze upwards to catch the stars it somehow puts everything in a different perspective. My own problems shrink into nothingness. Compared to nature, we are but tiny specks in the sand. I was in deep meditation when a familiar voice came from the dark.

"Forgive me, *hanim effendi*, but I thought I should make my presence known just in case you were overcome by a burning desire to bathe in the silken waters of this sea."

It was Selim, the grandson of Hasan Baba. I had spoken to him on a number of occasions since the circumcision. He had come to inspect Orhan's wound and make sure it was healing properly. Orhan had grown to like this young man and I, too, had to admit I found his company pleasing. I liked the fact that he never averted his eyes when I addressed him. His eyes were melancholy for so young a person, but when he laughed they shone like diamonds. I was pleased by his presence.

I know what you're thinking, Stone Woman. You have seen so much over the centuries and you think I had willed him to be present, but I swear by everything I hold dear that I had not thought of him at all. The social chasm between us was so vast that he never entered my mind except as a kind barber from Istanbul who had travelled a whole day to circumcise my son. He was, undoubtedly, an intelligent man and I must confess I was surprised when he declared his passion for the operas of Donizetti Pasha. The music was alien to me, but the way he talked about it made me yearn for the opera. Of course, none of this can explain what happened yesterday, Stone Woman.

"What are you doing here, Selim?"

"I came to watch the sky."

"And think?"

"Yes, *hanim effendi*, and think. In my world solitude is a precious commodity. I live in a house with six other people. I can't even hear myself think. This place is like paradise. You must have missed it very much when you were in Konya."

"I did, and please stop calling me *hanim effendi*. When we are alone you may call me Nilofer."

"You are beautiful, Nilofer."

"I did not give you permission to talk in this fashion. Control your tongue, you insolent boy."

He fell silent.

"I heard you making Orhan laugh yesterday. Tell me a story, Selim. Make me laugh."

He stood up and began to throw pebbles in the sea. Then he came and sat in front of me.

"I will obey you, princess. Listen, then, to my story. Once long ago in the reign of a Sultan, whose name I cannot recall, there lived a young and beautiful princess. She was a younger sister of the Sultan and he was very fond of her, largely because she kept a storehouse full of jokes. She had been blessed with prodigious powers of recollection. Her memory was the envy of the Court. She never forgot a face, its name or a conversation. She made the Sultan laugh and he rewarded her by never compelling her to get married. She would veil herself and, accompanied by six armed eunuchs, she would visit taverns and places of ill-repute and all this to collect the latest lewd jokes.

"She had refused many offers of marriage, from some of the richest families in Istanbul. She told her friends that she could never be satisfied with one man. She could not commit herself to live the life of a housebound wife. The choice was celibacy or freedom to choose her men. If she saw a man she wanted, she would summon him and lift her veil. Since she was extremely attractive, most men succumbed to her charms. They were conducted by the eunuchs to her private chamber in the palace. Here she lay on a divan awaiting them, only the most flimsy of shawls covering her naked body.

"The lover she had chosen for that particular night was dazzled by the sight of her. When she removed the shawl all was laid bare and as the fortunate man fell on his knees before her she would speak the same words that she had to many of his predecessors: 'You may gorge yourself on this feast till you are sated. Enjoy it well, for you will never see or taste another. From paradise you will proceed straight to hell.'

"The excited lover was by this time too agitated and overcome by desire to reflect on her warning. It was only after she had been pleasured that he began to show signs of nervousness, but by then it was too late. The eunuchs entered the chamber and escorted the unfortunate lover to a boat moored nearby. One of the eunuchs sang a lament for lost lovers, while the others gently circled the condemned man's neck with a cord and strangled him to death. The delicate morsel of last night's banquet was thrown into the Bosporus so that the fish could feed on him. The royal flesh of unmarried females was forbidden to a commoner. He who had enjoyed must be destroyed. He could not be allowed to live and tell the tale. The princess had made one exception to the rule.

"'If', she instructed the eunuchs, 'any of them ever shouts his defiance of death and declares that a night in my arms is worth the sacrifice, spare his life. Such a spirit should be preserved, not suffocated.'

"Every morning she would inquire anxiously, but none of them ever did. This made her sad, but she lived a long time and in her old age spent a great deal of time in *tekkes*, where ecstasy is not dependent on physical contact."

I was greatly moved by this story, Stone Woman, or so I thought. Now I think it was the story-teller who affected me.

"Did the princess have a name?" I asked.

"She was called Nilofer."

It was a warm night and, perhaps, the moon had touched us both, so that when Selim moved closer and stroked my cheeks, I did not resist. When he felt my breasts I made a half-hearted attempt to restrain his ardour, but I wished him to go further. I kissed his eyes and his lips and undressed him. After I had made love to him we washed ourselves in the sea. He was inexperienced, but it did not matter to me. I had not been intimate with a man for nearly a year and the warmth alone had comforted me.

We did not speak for a long time. I stroked his hair as he rested his head in my lap. His first sentence was a whisper.

"Will Petrossian take me out on a boat tonight and drown me?"

I laughed as I hugged him.

"No. In order to do that it would be necessary to castrate him first. Only eunuchs can carry out such an assignment."

"I thought he was a eunuch. It is said in the kitchen that your family has castrated him in spirit if not in flesh."

When I suggested that it was time for me to leave, Stone Woman, he held me in a tight embrace and aroused my passion. This time we did not wash because the night was almost over and there was no time to dry ourselves. Am I a lost woman, Stone Woman? What if he has left me with a child? Will the passion I felt for him lead to love? ’

My words froze on my lips as I heard the noise of rustling.

"You have embarked on the road to unhappiness, my child."

"Who's there?"

My mother emerged from behind the stones. I wept as I screamed at her. "This is a sanctuary, Mother. You have defiled it by your presence. It was cruel of you to eavesdrop."

"I had come to speak to the Stone Woman myself, child, when I heard your voice. How could I walk away without hearing your story? When you were children, you would hide and listen to all of us. Now it is our turn. You must not complain. My reasons are not so different. You're such a secretive girl. You never told me about the Greek teacher – and look where it has led you. I know that life with him has made you morose and you were always such a cheerful child. I am starved of information concerning your life, Nilofer. I'm glad I heard your story even though it was an accident. Come with me."

She put her arm around my shoulders and took me to her room. I sat on the floor so she could massage my head as she did when I was a child. Neither of us spoke for a long time. The reassuring sound of her hands rubbing my scalp had the soothing effect of a balm. As I began to recover my composure I realised, to my astonishment, that she was not in the least angry with me.

"I always wanted you to be happy. When you ran away with the school teacher, I was sad only because I would have liked to celebrate the wedding of my only child. I missed the music and the feasting and the dancing. I would have liked to send you off to your husband in some style. That was a mother's unrealised dream. Once I had recovered from my disappointment nothing else mattered except your happiness. If you were happy, what right did I have to be sad? But you weren't happy, were you, Nilofer? That was the impression Halil brought back with him after his first meeting with you and that stick, Dmitri."

My mother wished to talk of the past. My thinking was concentrated on the present. I wanted to know exactly where Selim was at this moment. I wanted to know what he was thinking. I wondered whether he had told anyone about us. Was he regretting his audacity? As these thoughts raced through my head, my heartbeat quickened in unison, but the impatient expression on my mother's face was beginning to disfigure her features. It could not be ignored any longer. She would not permit me to move on until I had satisfied her. Perhaps it was more than mere curiosity. Perhaps it was a concern for the children and for my future. Perhaps it had something to do with her own life and frustrated hopes.

"Answer me, Nilofer. What went wrong?"

This was a question I had often asked myself over the last five years. My feelings poured out like a waterfall and almost overwhelmed my mother. I told her that what I had thought of as love had been nothing but the romantic fantasies of an immature mind. Dmitri had offered an escape from the closed world of our family and I had foolishly made the leap with him. I spoke of how I felt my mind beginning to atrophy in the house in Istanbul. I was imprisoned by its routines, stifled by its traditions, crushed by the weight of its history. I was overwhelmed by a desire to experience the real world. Our summer house and the sea represented freedom. Ever since I was three years old I had always loved being here. Dmitri just happened to pass by at the right time. It could have been anyone.

I told her of how all this had become very clear to me even before I had become pregnant with Emineh. Her birth had marked a point of no return. After that I found him physically repulsive and intellectually unsatisfying. He began to resent what he called my superior ways and our relationship disintegrated. I thought perhaps that a period of absence might change my mind, but after a week here with Orhan I knew it was over. I could never go back to Konya and share his hideous bed.

"And now, Mother, you have compelled me to invite him here for Orhan's sake and so that we can see my Emineh. He kept her as a hostage, you know. To make sure I returned. Perhaps he will not come, but if he does he must return alone. My children will stay here with us."

"The boy is attached to him, Nilofer. He has been a good father to both his children. Poor man. I feel sorry for him. What a misfortune to have you as a wife. He needed someone submissive and a good cook. Like me, you are neither. Meanwhile you are satisfying your needs with the help of a young barber. If Iskander Pasha finds out he'll have another stroke. First a teacher, now a barber. What next?"

"Selim may be a barber by descent, Mother, but his intelligence transcends that of most of this family."

"Stop this at once. You used exactly the same words with exactly the same stubborn look on your face ten years ago, when you decided to elope with that school teacher. At least learn from your own mistakes, my child. Selim does not pose a serious problem. A handsome purse from one of your brothers might seal his mouth. I don't want him boasting or mentioning your name in the coffee houses. He should be sent back immediately to Istanbul. And don't you dare tell me that you will return with him. You have two children to think of now."

"I will not permit Selim to be insulted by you or anyone else in this family, Mother! The very idea of offering him money fills me with nausea."

"Really? Surely the nausea you feel is induced by a fear that he might accept our offer. Whichever it is, I would rather you were sick than sorry, Nilofer."

My anger was about to explode but I managed to contain myself. "I am not a child any longer. Ten years seems a lifetime away. I accept my head is in a whirl, but I am not about to do anything foolish or impulsive. Let us remain calm and think of the future."

"How strange that you should use that particular phrase. You sounded just like your grandmother Beatrice. She was always a great believer in remaining calm and imagining a prosperous future."

I looked over my mother's shoulder and saw the familiar portrait of Grand-mother Beatrice on the mantelpiece. It had been painted the year after she married Grandfather and if her features had not been exaggerated by the painter, as was often the case in those days since painters always wanted to please in order to be employed again, she must have been a very striking woman, much more so than her own daughter, my mother Sara. The same Sara was looking at me intently as I thought of her past.

Before this day, I had never found a chance to speak with my mother as an equal. Before I ran away with Dmitri we were hardly ever alone and, in any case, I had been too young to be taken seriously. I had heard vague rumours that my mother was unhappy when she first married Iskander Pasha, but Zeynep denied that this was so and told me not to believe anything I heard in the kitchen.

Everything had changed since then, and as the mother of two children, my status had suddenly risen, at least as far as my mother was concerned. I asked her a question I had been saving for over ten years.

"Were you forced to marry him?"

To my surprise she hugged me and began to weep. Tears, which must have been stored there for many years, poured out in a torrent. It was my turn to hold her close and comfort her.

"I told the Stone Woman everything all those years ago. Nobody told you?"

I shook my head.

"Perhaps I was really alone. There were no eavesdroppers that day."

"You don't have to tell me now, Mother. There will be other occasions."

But she wanted to talk about herself. It was as if listening to me talking to the Stone Woman had unblocked something deep in her heart.

' If only my father had not been a court physician, my whole life would have taken a different course. Because like his father and grandfather before him he attended the Sultan and the royal family, it was considered a mark of prestige for lesser nobles to employ him as well. I suppose he was also good at his work, though he often used to quote his grandfather returning from the palace and remarking that the task of a good physician was not just to heal the body, which was often difficult, but to comfort the mind, which was always possible. My father thought that this commonplace was very profound and he repeated it often when we had guests, so that Mother and I would look at each other when we saw it coming and silently mouth the words.

Iskander Pasha, a great believer in maintaining traditions, had employed your grandfather as the family physician. Even so, had it not been for an accident of fate, my future might not have been determined so hastily. One day Iskander Pasha's coachman collided with another coach. Your father was slightly hurt. I think a piece of wood grazed his forehead and he began to bleed. The frightened coachman drove straight to our house and asked for my father. He was out on a visit and my mother insisted that Iskander Pasha be brought into the house so that one of my father's assistants could disinfect and dress the wound. This was not an uncommon occurrence in those days. I was with my mother when your father entered our house. After he had been bandaged my mother, aware of the fact that he had been recently appointed as the Sultan's ambassador to Paris, offered him some refreshments. He was about to refuse when he caught sight of me. A woman can always tell when a man looks at her in that particular fashion. He stayed and broke bread with us. He was still there when my father returned an hour later and he was invited to stay to dinner. To our amazement he accepted the invitation. He was in a charming mood, breaking into French and German and impressing us with his knowledge of Paris and Berlin. My father, to be honest, was flattered that such an important dignitary from such a distinguished family had spent four hours in our house.

As the coffee was served, Father was about to enlighten Iskander Pasha on the task of a good physician, when to our delight and surprise, Iskander Pasha stole the moment from him. He had heard the story before. My father was crestfallen till Iskander Pasha confided that it was the Sultan who had first relayed to him this immortal saying. A smile took over my father's face. It was so ingratiating and so servile and eager to please that I really felt my stomach turn. I had no choice but to leave the table. I rushed to the bathroom and vomited everything. Strong premonitions can have that effect on one's body.

When I returned, my face pale and drained, Iskander Pasha had made his farewells and left. I was relieved, for during the meal he had kept looking at me in a fashion that made me nervous and fearful. I was not in the least interested in him and I remember that night when I was in bed I kept repeating to myself: "Treat him like a closed door which must never be opened. If you push it even a tiny bit in order to peep through the crack you will sink into oblivion." This was not difficult to achieve, since he had not succeeded in arousing my curiosity to the slightest degree. Remember that I was not yet twenty and your father, twice my age and more, already appeared to me like an old man . . . ’

At this stage I interrupted her. I was irritated that she was exhibiting such complete apathy towards my father. After all, he was neither stupid nor ugly and I did love him, despite his many imperfections. I was in a hurry to reach the root of the problem.

"Before you continue to explain your indifference to my father, let me ask you something. Were you in love with another man at the time?"

"Yes," she replied with a fierceness that took me aback, "I was in love with Suleman. He was my own age. We shared each other's emotions, desires and dreams. There was a harmony between us, which went so deep, so deep, that it felt like the wellspring that is the source of life. Do you want to hear about him, Nilofer, or will you feel disloyal to your poor, crippled father, lying speechless next door? Be honest."

I was touched by the depth of her emotions and even more so by the fact that she could still feel all this after thirty years in this household. My feelings seemed so transient when compared to what she must have suffered. I was overcome by love for her and I leaned over and kissed her face, wiping away the single, salty tear that was crawling down her left cheek.

"I want to hear everything, Mother. Everything."

' Suleman was a distant cousin of my mother. His family, like ours, had moved to Istanbul from Cordoba in the fifteenth century, when we were expelled by the Catholics. My father came from a family of physicians who claimed kinship with Maimonides. My mother's family were merchants and traders. They were made welcome here. The Ottomans gave us refuge and employment. Suleman's forebears moved away and settled in Damascus, but without ever losing contact with the family in Istanbul. Since they were traders they travelled a great deal and, as a consequence, contact was never broken. The marriage of my parents, which was a happy one, had been arranged through the exchange of letters.

Suleman wanted to be a physician. He was tired of Damascus. He found it far too provincial and he wanted to be close to Europe. His father wrote to mine and, naturally, Suleman was invited to stay with us indefinitely. My father had agreed to procure his entry into the medical school in Istanbul. I was eighteen years of age at the time. He was a year older. It was as if the sun had entered our house.

All my friends had brothers and sisters and I had always felt odd that I was an only child. Mother could not conceive again after my birth, which had been difficult. She said that if Father had not been present, the midwife would have been incapable of stemming the flow of blood and she would have died. Strange that I, too, have only produced a single flower, which has fruited so beautifully. I was truly relieved when you produced Orhan and Emineh. I felt the old curse had been broken.

Suleman was like the older brother I never had and certainly my parents treated him like a son. There were no restrictions. I took him everywhere, both in the coach and on foot. I showed him the hidden delights of our city. Visitors from the West look at Sinan's mosques and sigh with admiration. They are bewitched by the palaces and they marvel at the rituals of the Court, but few of them ever penetrate the inner life of our city. The loves we share with a city are always secret, adolescent day-dreams, especially if that city is wide open like Istanbul, but I felt like keeping nothing secret from Suleman even though I had known him for less than two weeks. The affinities between us were deep, but there were also differences. I was wilful and headstrong. He was emotional and tender-hearted, but also insecure in many ways.

We would often dress like Westerners and take tea in a hotel and speak in French to the waiters. It was only when we heard them wondering in Turkish whether we were brother and sister or a newly married couple on their honeymoon that I replied in pure Stambouline, just to observe their amazed expressions. They were the happiest days of my life, Nilofer. The innocence that precedes true love can never be repeated. When it vanishes, it has gone for ever.

Everything seemed magical when Suleman and I were together. We would sit in a café sipping coffee in Europe as we observed the sunset drowning Asia across the Golden Horn. We could speak with each other about everything and anything. There were no taboos. Nothing was sacred. It was not simply that we exchanged reminiscences or discussed the more peculiar episodes in the history of our respective families. From the very beginning there was something much more intimate. It was as if we had never been without each other. And we laughed, Nilofer. I have never laughed so much in my life before or since that time.

Till I met Suleman, nobody had shown any real interest in me. I was the daughter of the house and, no doubt, I would soon be married off and that would be the end of my story. My father, in particular, was so busy looking after the health of his more illustrious patients that he had very little time for me.

Suleman was the first and last person to ask me what I wanted of life. He did not laugh when I confessed my deepest fantasies. He encouraged me when I said that I wanted to be a novelist like Balzac. He gave me his undivided attention. He never attempted to impose his will on mine – not that he would have succeeded if he had ever tried. At moments like this, it is sufficient simply to love life. Everything else will follow, or so I dreamed. It would be just as beautiful as now. This was not to be.

One evening, Suleman and I found ourselves alone at home. My parents, attired in all their finery, had left to attend a wedding feast at the palace. The servants had been permitted a free evening. At first, we amused ourselves by playing duets from Mozart's opera *Don Giovanni* on the piano. Then we ate. It was only later, when our conversation had reached a natural pause that I felt slightly tense in his company. My heartbeat quickened its pace. He left the room and returned with a sheaf of papers. It was on that evening he first showed me those three sketches he had made. If I shut my eyes now I can see them very clearly.

"I never knew you were an artist," was all I could say as I attempted to mask my confusion and remain aloof, calm and sophisticated at the same time.

"Nor did I," he replied.

The first sketch was a tender reproduction of my face, the second was the same face, but this time in sharp profile. I hated this one because he had exaggerated my nose, drawn it too thick, like a shapeless cucumber, but before I could remonstrate, he showed me the third . . . O, the third, Nilofer, the third. It was how he imagined my unclothed body. His hands trembled as he held it up for me. I was thunderstruck by his audacity but also very alarmed by his accuracy. Many months later he confessed that he had spied on me bathing one afternoon, but by then we had reached a new stage of intimacy and nothing else mattered. ’

Sara paused. The memories had stirred old passions and she was upset. She poured herself some water from the jug near her bed. I saw her now in a completely different light. I still could not believe that she had permitted Suleman to make love to her. If that were the case, why had they not run away together? He could have taken her with him. But why should it have reached that stage in the first place? Had my grandparents forbidden her to marry Suleman? Why?

"I can hear all the questions going through your mind, child. You want to know the exact degree of intimacy we enjoyed. Why we didn't marry or run away like you and that Greek with ugly eyes. As you know, I have never spoken of these matters to any living person. It is not easy speaking of such things to one's children. There is always an innate desire to conceal, but I feel like telling you everything. There is too much secrecy in our world, and concealment usually hurts more than the truth.

"If I was dead and buried and one day, by accident, you heard this story from one of Suleman's brood, you might or might not have believed it, but you would be upset at your ignorance. You might think badly of me. You are the only treasure I have left in this world. I want you to know so that one day you can tell Orhan and Emineh about their grandmother. Who knows but that it might even help them live a better life. Press my feet, child. I'm beginning to feel tense and tired."

I had never pressed her feet before, but, over the years, I had observed so many maidservants at work on them for hours at a time that the task posed no mysteries for me. I pressed each toe in turn, then moved to the soles, kneading them gently with my knuckles. Slowly, I felt Sara beginning to relax again.

' Suleman and I fell into each other's arms so naturally that evening it did not feel as if it was the first time. It had always been intended. The passion that we had hidden from ourselves poured out of us. We did make love then and on many other days. Sometimes our longing for each other became so great that we would rush out of the house in search of safe spots, but these were not easy to uncover. Often we had no other alternative but to hire a covered boat, oblivious to the world as the boatman, pretending to be blind, took us first to one continent and then another. This was always risky because the boats were often used for these purposes by the lower classes and I was always nervous lest one of our maids, who had confided in me regarding her adventures on a boat, should catch sight of us. In fact, that was how I knew that love-boats existed in the first place.

My mother Beatrice was beginning to look at me with suspicion. "There is something different about the way you walk, Sara. Something has happened to give you a new confidence. It is almost as if you have been fulfilled as a woman."

The day after I reported this remark to Suleman, we informed my mother that we wished to be married. Suleman had already written to his parents informing them of this decision. I thought my mother would be pleased that I loved someone from her side of the family. I thought this would reassure her. My father was always grumbling that he did not have enough money for a dowry. Even though this was not the case, I was relieved that no such expenditure would be necessary.

Your grandmother's doe-like eyes narrowed and her lips tightened when she heard the news. "I feared this might happen," she said, "but I hoped your affection for each other was that of a brother and sister, especially since you are an only child. That is why I agreed so happily that he should come and live with us for as long as he wished. How foolish I was, how blind not to see what was happening before my eyes and in my house. This marriage is impossible, Sara. I know this sounds cruel, but both of you must face the weight of reality."

We were shocked. We looked at her in disbelief. What reality was she speaking of, and what did it have to do with our love for each other? She refused to speak any further till my father returned home after his visits. She left the room saying that they would both speak to us after the evening meal. Suleman and I sat holding hands and looking at each other in bewilderment. He thought that the hostility could be related to his relative poverty; my parents would probably want me to live in style. I did not think this could be true, for Suleman was learning my father's trade and it would be natural for him to inherit the practice which the family had built up so carefully over two centuries.

In fact, Father had already begun to reveal some of the secret prescriptions for treatments that had travelled with us from Spain long, long ago. They had been written and copied in big books bound in black leather, which long use had faded years ago. I remember Suleman's excitement when he was first shown one of these books. My father had assumed that Suleman would succeed him and therefore I did not think that lack of money could be the problem.

When he finally returned home that night, I heard Mother whispering anxiously as she dragged him into her room. We ate the evening meal in total silence. I knew they weren't angry because occasionally both of them would look at us affectionately, but with sorrowful eyes. It was my father who spoke that night and explained the reasons that lay behind their opposition.

It made no sense to me. He spoke of a mysterious disease that had developed in Suleman's branch of the family after centuries of intermarriages. Since my mother belonged to that family there was a serious danger that our children would be born with severe deformities and afflictions and die young. It had happened too often for the risk to be undertaken lightly.

Suleman's face had paled as he heard my father speak. He knew that this disease had claimed the life of one of his own cousins several years ago, but surely, he pleaded, the blood relationship between my mother and his was so distant that the chances of our children suffering must be equally remote. My father rose and left the room. When he returned it was with another bound volume. This contained our family tree. He showed us that the great-great-great grandmothers of my mother and Suleman's mother had been sisters. The link was far too strong to take any risk. He was moved by our love for each other and he embraced Suleman with genuine affection, but shook his head in despair.

"It will only bring you unhappiness, Sara. However much you resent your mother and me for this, I cannot as your father and as a physician permit both of you to destroy your lives."

I began to weep and left the room. Suleman stayed behind and talked with them for a long time. I had no idea what they said to each other.

Neither of us could sleep. I went into his room later that night and found him sitting cross-legged on his bed. He was weeping silently. We made love to calm ourselves. I told him very firmly that I was prepared to take the risk and that if my parents objected we could run away. But the sight of the family tree had shaken him. He described his cousin's death at the age of seven. He did not wish our child to die in that fashion.

I pleaded with him, Nilofer. I threatened I would take my own life if he dared to leave me. Nothing would shake him. He left the next day.

I was desolate. I went searching for him everywhere. I visited the cafés we used to frequent. I went to the boatmen to ask if they had seen him, but there was no trace at all. My parents denied all knowledge of where he might have gone, though, later, my father admitted he had given him a purse to help him on his way. I never stopped mourning for Suleman. Nothing else mattered to me any more. Life could go on or it might stop. It was a matter of complete indifference to me.

It was ten days after Suleman had deserted me that my father returned home one evening with an offer of marriage from Iskander Pasha. I was to be his second wife. This, too, did not bother me a great deal. I remember saying to my mother: "Here, at least, there is no danger of any affliction." I was told I would have to convert to the faith of my husband and acquire a new name. This change of identity was the only thing that amused me at the time. It would not be Sara who would enter Iskander Pasha's bed, but Hatije. I was named after the first wife of the Prophet Memed, peace be upon him.

I was married in the house in Istanbul. There were no festivities since I was only the third wife. The first, as you know, had died giving birth to Salman. This was also convenient since I was not in the mood for any celebrations. Iskander Pasha was very kind and, mercifully, he soon departed for Paris with Petrossian and Hasan

Baba, but not me. This, too, suited me greatly. Naturally, before his departure he had entered my bed and convinced me that he was a man. I did not particularly enjoy the experience, Nilofer. It did not even comfort me. The wounds created by Suleman's betrayal were still bleeding. You were born eight and a half months later. ❜

Something in my mother's tone had told me that this was not the end of her story. An unusually complacent smile had crossed her face when she mentioned my birth.

"Sara!" I said to her sharply. "You promised the whole truth."

"Can't you guess?"

I shook my head.

"You were the proof that my parents were wrong. Suleman's cowardice was totally unjustified. That made me really angry. My sadness began to disappear. He was a traitor. My love began to drain away and I was filled with contempt for him. You were the healthiest and most beautiful child I had ever seen."

"What are you saying, Mother? You're sick! You're mad! This is just your imagination. You wanted it to be so, but it is not so. Iskander Pasha *is* my father!"

I began to cry. She hugged me, but I pushed her away. My first reaction was disgust. I felt my whole life had been taken away from me. I sat there and stared at her. When I spoke, it was in a whisper.

"Are you sure?"

"Yes, my child. If I had not been pregnant, I would never have married Iskander Pasha. If I had told my parents they would have attempted to get rid of you. Never forget your grandfather's profession. He had some experience in removing unwanted infants."

"But why didn't you tell Suleman?"

"I only discovered my condition the week after he left. I would have told him the next day, but he had gone."

"How can you be sure?"

She went to a cupboard and brought out a box I had never seen before. It contained a photograph of both of them. They looked so happy. My mother covered Suleman's nose and lips. The eyes were exactly the same as mine.

"You never told your parents?"

She shook her head.

"Why?"

"They would have been very upset. They were fond of Suleman. I was their only child and I did not wish them to feel that, with the best of motives, they had wrecked my life."

"And you never told him?"

"No. When he wrote to me, you were already eight years old. His letter was brief, its tone distant and cold. It had been designed as a cruel farewell. It informed me of three important developments in his life. He was a successful painter. He was happily married. He had three children. How could I ever hope to compete with such bliss? The effect of his message was to kill off all my dreams. I wished then that the boat that had taken him to New York had encountered a storm and I wished that all the passengers in it had survived except him. He should have fallen off the edge and never been recovered. I would rather he had died. It would have stopped him writing these stupid letters.

"I had thought that one day, before death claimed either of us, I would visit him in New York. I wanted so much to see him again, Nilofer. Just once. After his letter I felt futile and betrayed. But there was one consolation he could never take away from me. I had you, the child of our love. In order to survive, he had to rebuild his shattered life, construct an inner wall that could not be breached and obliterate all memories of the love we had once given each other. All I had to do was to look into your eyes and be reminded once again of happiness. I pitied him."

Silence. Neither of us could speak. I kissed her hands. She stroked my face and kissed my eyes. I had never felt so close to her in my whole life. I wanted to be alone to think of all she had told me. I had to decide the course of my life. It could not be determined by this household.

I took my leave of Sara and went to my own room. It was strange to think that none of them were related to me any longer. Salman and Halil were not my brothers. Zeynep was not my sister. Iskander Pasha was not my father. How absurd my world had become. I felt tears beginning to make their way to my eyes.

"Why are you crying?" Orhan's voice brought me back to reality. "Are you missing Emineh?"

I nodded, grateful to him for providing me with an excuse, and dried my face. Orhan was cheerful.

"Tomorrow, Hasan Baba will cut my hair himself. He says he cannot return without making sure that my hair is properly cut. Then he will have cut the hair of four generations in our family."

I smiled inwardly. Our family? The words held a new meaning for me.

Orhan had been filled with such excitement when he met his uncles and his grandfather that the truth suddenly made me fearful. Orhan and Iskander Pasha communicated with each other on paper every day. Both of them felt useful. Orhan felt he was helping his grandfather and Iskander Pasha had begun to teach the child the French alphabet. How could I ever tell my son that we had no right to be here, that his real grandfather was a painter in New York, that we belonged to a different world? I looked out at the sea. It was silent today as it shimmered in the dazzling light of a July afternoon. Its calmness helped to settle me.

I lay down on my bed and shut my eyes. I was pleased that Mother had told me the truth. Orhan's presence had made me feel that life would go on as before. I might not be related by blood, but this was my family. These were people I loved and would always love – despite the past, despite the future. I heard Orhan laughing outside my window. I got up to see the cause of the merriment.

It was Selim. The sight of him aroused me. I knew then that I would want him for a long time.

EIGHT

The day of the family photograph; Iskander Pasha insists on being photographed alone next to an empty chair; the story of Ahmet Pasha and how he pretended to be the Sultan

It was a languid morning. There was no breeze and the sun was hot. We were sitting under the shade of a walnut tree on the front terrace. Hasan Baba had finished cutting Orhan's hair and a maidservant was removing the pieces from the ground. Hasan Baba had chosen a style that was fifty years out of date, a style he had used when my father and uncles were young boys, and he had ignored my instructions and cut Orhan's hair far too short, but the approval he sought was not mine. He knew that Iskander Pasha would appreciate his work.

A photographer was due to arrive from Istanbul later that day to photograph the entire family. It had been an annual ritual, discontinued when Salman and Halil left home. Usually the photograph was taken on a feast day in the old courtyard of our house in Istanbul. This was the first time a photographer had been permitted to violate the privacy of our summer sanctuary. The chairs had already been laid out in exactly the same pattern as in Istanbul, except that we were fewer in number. Uncle Kemal's family had not been invited here, whereas it was usually difficult to exclude them in Istanbul.

Petrossian, following Iskander Pasha's instructions, was organising the place names so that when the time came each of us would know where to sit. I shuddered at the thought of a family gathering, but Orhan was delighted. He was greatly looking forward to the occasion and had, for once, meekly accepted my mother's insistence that he must bathe, wash his hair and wear the suit specially made for him, together with the *fez*. He was to be dressed like a little pasha. Nor would he be alone. Everyone had been instructed to dress formally. At breakfast that morning, Salman had made us all laugh by asking Uncle Memed whether he and the Baron, too, would be wearing the *fez*. Both men had looked at him coldly and refused to reply.

I was about to ask Hasan Baba to tell me of the time he had spent with Iskander Pasha in Paris, when the deep, beautiful voice of a singer chanting a Sufi verse came towards us as if from the sky.

Let us drink our fill from the wine of thy lips
Let us drink to the satisfaction of lovers
Let the hearts that have suffered too much separation become
intoxicated and bewildered;
Let their love overflow like the seven seas
Let us drink till their hearts are covered in moonlight
Let us drink till in their bliss, in their bliss, in their bliss, the lovers
experience
Allah, wa Allah, wa Allah!

Hasan Baba's frail and battered body began to change before my eyes. His eyes developed a shine and he began to sway in perfect harmony with the song of ecstasy. Suddenly the voice stopped. It had come from the direction of the garden below my father's terrace, which was invisible from the front terrace where we were seated enjoying the morning breezes and inhaling the scent of the pines.

"Who was the singer? I had no idea that we had a *dervish* in the servants' quarters."

"That was Selim, my grandson, *hanim effendi*."

I was amazed. "Are you sure?"

Hasan Baba nodded eagerly. "Selim must be tired today. He has been cutting their hair since breakfast. First it was your brothers, then Memed Pasha and the Baron. Now your father's hair is being trimmed. All this in readiness for one stupid photograph."

"But could he be singing while cutting my father's hair?" I was surprised, given the decorum normally associated with any ritual involving Iskander Pasha.

"Why not? There are many things you do not know about your father. He was a Sufi in his youth. He frequented some of the more dubious meeting houses where ecstasy had little relation to Allah. He must have instructed Selim to sing this particular verse. Perhaps it reminds him of the time he first saw Zakiye, the mother of Salman Pasha.

"I have known your father since the day he was born, but never in such a state as he was that winter when he first saw her at a meeting house. They inhaled some very potent herbs and began to whirl together. Afterwards, in a state of ecstatic exhaustion, they fell on the floor and rested. It was then that she sang the verse that we just heard again, but this time in the voice of my grandson. Iskander Pasha's heart experienced a turbulence he had never known before. His love grew by the day and there were times I thought he would lose his sanity altogether. I was with him a great deal at the time. I tried to calm him. I offered to take him to Konya for a festival. I suggested we come to this house so that he could, at least, reflect on his state of mind and, at a distance, from the object of his love. He refused to leave Istanbul. Zakiye was moved by her young admirer's passion, but I don't think she could ever reciprocate his love. He refused to rest till he had obtained permission from his parents to marry her."

I had never heard this story, not even from Zeynep, who usually knew everything of this nature. Perhaps Zakiye's death had rendered all gossip redundant.

"Why did he need such permission, Hasan Baba? And why not from Zakiye's parents?"

The old man sighed. "Oh my child, you may be a mother of two children, but you are still foreign to the ways of our world. Zakiye was attached to that particular meeting house. It had a disreputable name. She had no parents."

Despite myself I could not help being slightly shocked by this information. "Hasan Baba, are you telling me that Salman's mother was a prostitute?"

"Which debased creature mentioned money or the sale of human flesh?" he asked in a raised voice. "Zakiye believed in the joys of ecstatic union. It was her way of communicating with Allah. You look surprised? There were and there remain many others like her, including Selim's own mother, and she is still alive! Please refrain from disrupting the flow of my story with foolish questions. You may have already forgotten your previous question, but permit me a reply.

"Now, at least, you understand why Iskander Pasha had to ask his parents before he could marry Zakiye. They became very angry with him. They refused to take the matter seriously. They imagined that it was a case of lust, not love. They suggested that your father take Petrossian and travel to Paris and Florence. It was his turn to refuse.

"One night, Iskander Pasha left home and became a *dervish*. His mother was shaken by the news. She found it difficult to bear the loss. He had always been her favourite son. She weakened first and later it was she who convinced his father. Iskander Pasha was thrilled. I saw happiness dancing in his eyes, but none of us had foreseen the next problem.

"Zakiye refused his offer of marriage. It had made her angry. She told me she had no desire to become a rich man's keep. She saw no reason why, after an existence free of restrictions, she should now suffer imprisonment for the rest of her life in your Istanbul house. What happened, I suppose, was inevitable: money. The elders of the meeting house were bribed by Iskander Pasha. These were men who had looked after her as a foundling. They had educated her, taught her to sing and dance and how to achieve union with her Maker. Now they instructed her that in the larger interests of their order, she must marry Iskander Pasha and do his bidding. 'He is the son of an important notable, close to the Palace. Just think how you will be able to help us once you are his wife. You were left outside our meeting house the day you were born. We raised you as our own. Now it is your duty to obey us. You must do as we ask of you.' She was unconvinced, but followed the instructions of the elders as she had done all her life.

"And that is how the wedding took place. It was not a quiet celebration. The feasting lasted for three whole days with a great deal of singing and dancing. It must have been the last time Zakiye danced with other men and women. She seemed happy enough and it's difficult to know how it would have ended had fate not decided a cruel punishment. Within months she was pregnant and then, as you know, tragedy struck. She died giving birth to Salman Pasha.

"After her death, I observed Iskander Pasha's entire character undergo a complete change. He was devastated. He reminded me of a tree struck by lightning. A tree has no option but to die. Iskander Pasha found he could only live by reinventing himself. He remade himself in the image of his father. He became distant and aloof, very conscious of his status in society, strict with all his children and especially hard on poor, motherless Salman Pasha. Your father changed into the person you have known all your life. It was the only way he could accept that she had gone for ever. The way he had once been with her, he could not be with anyone else.

"Once, when we were in Paris and I was shaving him amidst all the finery of his residence, he was thinking of her. Knowing him as I did, I always knew when he wished to be shaved in total silence. I had not spoken a single word that day when he suddenly grabbed the towel off my shoulder, wiped the remaining soap off his face and broke the silence: 'You know, Hasan, do you not, that the man who loved Zakiye died with her? I have no knowledge of this man any more.'

"Tears poured down my face. I told him: 'I know that, Iskander Pasha. I have always known, but I do not believe that the young man I knew is dead. I think he is buried deep inside you and will, one day, return to himself.' What he said was only part of the truth. She still lived in him and to that extent his old self, too, was alive. There was another occasion in Paris which I had forgotten till now. Our memory is a strange gift is it not, Nilofer *hanim*? He had returned home late one night from some burdensome official reception. He always hated these gatherings. Petrossian had already retired and Iskander Pasha was undressing himself. I was in the next room reading when I heard him sobbing. I rushed to comfort him and found him clutching a book close to his heart. He said nothing, but handed me the book and pointed to a verse which I have never forgotten. It was from a sonnet by Michelangelo, the Italian who should have built us a bridge across the Bosporus. Should I recite the verse? Let me see if it will return to me."

He paused and went deep into his head. Then his face relaxed. "I think it was like this, but I may have forgotten some lines. After he had made me read this he asked with a sad smile: 'Hasan, do you think Michelangelo was a Sufi?'

Now give me back that time when love was held
On a loose rein, making my passion free.
Return that calm, angelic face to me,
That countenance which every virtue filled.
My soul has almost reached the other side
And makes a shield against your kindly dart.
Charred wood will never make a new fire burn.

"Today he asked Selim to sing her favourite song. She must be very strong in him at this moment."

I thought that even though Iskander Pasha was no longer my real father, the knowledge had not changed my feelings for him. I still loved him as a father. Hasan Baba's story drew me even closer to the man my mother had married in such a hurry all those years ago. I wondered whether my mother knew this story and what she felt. Both of them had loved deeply and both had lost, in different circumstances, the most precious thing in their lives. Zakiye was dead and so, in a different way, was Suleman. Why had this shared experience not brought them closer together? My thoughts shifted to Selim.

"How did he learn to sing so beautifully, Hasan Baba?"

The old man was pleased by my compliment. What would he think if he knew what we had done? I was sure that whatever his reaction, it would not be one of either surprise or shock.

"Selim's father, my oldest child, is a *bektashi*. It was he who taught him to sing when he was a little boy. My son, may Allah curse him, did not wish to be a barber." The old man began to laugh, revealing a frighteningly empty mouth. He had lost every single tooth and I had to avert my gaze.

"Perhaps," he continued, "that was his real reason for joining a Sufi order, which encourages its devotees to grow their hair long. He wanted Selim to follow in his path, but this I would not allow. He did not treat the boy well and I decided to raise him myself. Selim grew up in my house and I trained him to be a barber, but the boy, as you see, is talented. He would be good at any craft."

It was my turn to smile. Selim's grandfather might be a barber, but his father was a Sufi.

"Were you surprised when your son deserted your profession?"

The old man stroked the forest of white stubble that covered his chin and became thoughtful. "I was disappointed, but not surprised. We have a tradition in our family of being both barbers and *dervishes*. In the old times, long before the Ottomans reached Istanbul, my family lived in Ankara. It was a period when there was no prince ruling over us. We made our own decisions. In those days we were craftsmen engaged in the making of swords and knives. We belonged to the order of Karmatians. Have you ever heard of that name?"

I acknowledged my ignorance, pleading my lack of a formal education. The tutors who had taught me everything I knew had never mentioned the Karmatians.

"You would be even more ignorant if you had been to a *medresseh*," he responded. "That honourable and kind lady who is your mother probably taught you more than all the beards put together. Do you think they teach their pupils about the Karmatians? They would rather choke in their beards than speak of a past that was pure."

Unknown to us, Uncle Memed and the Baron had overheard the last exchange.

"I never knew you were descended from Karmatians, Hasan," said Memed.

"Have you heard of them, Uncle?" I inquired with the most innocent expression I could muster.

"Yes, but very little. The subject interests me. May we join you? Please carry on, Hasan."

"I'm an old man now, Memed Pasha, so forgive my ravings. The matters of which I speak were handed down in our family from generation to generation. They are not of great interest to enlightened men like yourself and Baron Pasha."

"Nonsense," thundered the Baron. "It is we who are ignorant. We await enlightenment."

Hasan Baba was flattered and his tone changed. With me it had been friendly and relaxed. In the presence of the two men it became formal and affected.

"The Karmatian brotherhood in Angora, which we now call Ankara, was so strong that it ran the town on its own. It did not feel the need for a ruler. The brotherhood consisted of different *ahis*, or craft guilds. Each had its own meeting place, but we also had central meeting houses where there was much feasting and prayers, as well as discussions of the problems of the city and how we could heal the sick and feed those without food and punish the bandits who lived on the fringes of the city and stole money and clothes from travellers. Visitors were put up in the meeting houses, which also served as inns. We swore an oath to serve the seven virtues, abhor the seven vices, open seven doors and close seven doors."

The Baron was now fully engrossed. "What were the vices and the virtues?"

"That I do not know Baron Pasha, but I know that we Karmatians, while tolerating women, tended to remain unmarried ourselves. I know that butchers, surgeons, atheists, tax-gatherers and money-lenders were never permitted to enter a meeting house. They were some of the vices."

"What about astrologers?" asked Memed.

"Another vice. They were hated even more than the atheists and the money-lenders," said the old man with anger, as if he had been present when an astrologer had attempted to gain entry to a meeting house. "Astrologers were the executioners of rational thought and for that reason it was agreed by all the meeting houses on one occasion that some of these rascals, who misled the ignorant, should be publicly executed in the square in Ankara. It is said that the Karmatians jeered as they were led to meet their fate. 'How is it', they taunted the condemned men, 'that you failed to foresee your own future? Were you gazing at the wrong stars?'"

"I do not approve of that, Hasan," declared the Baron. "The enemies of rational thought can only be defeated by rational thought. Executing those men changed nothing. They multiplied like locusts throughout the Empire."

Hasan Baba was slightly embarrassed at having been carried away by his story. I tried to help him with a friendly question. "And the virtues you spoke of. What were they?"

"The drinking of wine, the inhaling of herbs, the state of ecstasy, daily prayers and the cleansing of infidels. The Karmatians were the fathers and the mothers of all the different Sufi orders that exist today. They were the first *ghazis* in this part of the world. They were prepared to fight and die for Allah and the glory of his Prophet. The Ottomans could not have succeeded without them. Later, much later, when the capital was in Bursa, the meeting houses were disbanded and attached to mosques. That was the beginning of our end.

"My family changed its craft. We dispensed with swords and instead began to produce razors and, later, scissors. We decided it was best that we perfected their use and so we became barbers. My forebears entered Constantinople with the Conqueror. They were part of the Sultan's retinue."

Memed and the Baron exchanged smiles and, having expressed their warm appreciation of Hasan, took their leave as they embarked on their daily and much-discussed ritual, which consisted of a brisk walk along the cliffs every day, an hour before lunch was served.

Hasan Baba remained seated and my mind moved away from him. He must have felt this because he, too, rose and walked away. I began to think of Selim. How odd that I had not recognised his voice as the singer. He must have seen me sitting here with his grandfather. The song was his unique way of making his presence felt.

"Did you like my song, princess?"

He was standing there in front of me in a pose of fake humility so that if we were observed from a distance it would appear that he was there as a servant. He even pretended to clear the table.

"I did like your song, nightingale, but your voice was so different. Where do you hide it during the night? Don't stand here any longer making a fool of yourself. I will meet you tonight in the orchard, when the shadow of the moon has covered the Stone Woman."

"Which orchard?"

"The orange grove, you fool."

"It's too wet at night. I prefer the fields of lavender."

"There is no protection there."

There was mischief in his eyes. "Why should we not experience bliss in the sight of Allah?"

I laughed despite myself. "The orange grove. A stream flows through it and the music of the water soothes me. Do as I say and now go away."

He left, taking with him the tray with the used cups of tea and bowing slightly in my direction with the fake humility that most servants in our house had by now perfected. This time I managed to control a smile.

As I walked towards the house I noticed that Hasan Baba was still there, standing close to the front entrance. He had seen everything, but he could not have heard us. He gave me a strange look. Had he detected the familiarity in Selim's body language or could he lip-read? I smiled serenely as I walked past him, and went straight to the bathroom where the maids had been waiting patiently to wash, dry and plait my hair in time for lunch.

It was now three o'clock in the afternoon. Iskander Pasha, accompanied by Giulio Bragadini, the photographer, who had joined us for lunch, and followed by Petrossian, strolled out of the house and cast a slow, thoughtful glance over all the details of the arrangement for the photograph. The large wooden box with a black cloth hanging over it was what they called a camera.

Bragadini was, as usual, over-dressed for the occasion. He was attired in a black Stambouline and a matching, expensive silk hat, and his plump face wore a self-important expression. He was very pleased with himself. His family were Venetians who had settled in Istanbul hundreds of years ago and painted the portraits of princesses and noblemen. Successive Grand Viziers had not deemed the work of the Bragadini family to be of a quality high enough for them to be given permission to paint the Sultan.

It had been declared on many occasions, and in public, that they were not masters in the tradition of Leonardo or Michelangelo or even Bellini, but were, in reality, gifted merchants who had learnt the art of painting as a trade. Giulio's grandfather, Giovanni, the last of the painters and the first of the photographers, had replied to these slurs on his family honour, though never in public, with the response that the only reason why the Bragadinis had never been permitted to paint a Sultan was that they had consistently refused to bribe the relevant courtiers. This was a case, Uncle Memed had once remarked, of both sides being right at the same time.

Despite all the arguments, the Bragadinis prospered. With the invention of the camera, their long battle for imperial recognition came to an end. They obtained the exclusive privilege of photographing the Sultan and being appointed the official photographers to the Court.

Four chairs were laid out. The first of the photographs consisted of the family alone and was simply organised. My mother sat on Iskander Pasha's left as he faced the camera and Uncle Memed on his right, with the Baron seated next to him. Zeynep, Halil, Salman and I stood behind them and little Orhan, looking every inch a Pasha, sat between the feet of his grandfather and great-uncle. Giulio was now in complete control of the operation. From a distance, behind the camera, all the servants, marshalled in their feast-day clothes for the occasion by Petrossian, stood and stared at us, the gardeners solemn and the maids trying to control their giggles as they muttered obscenities. The Baron, for some reason, had always been a special target for their venom. The ritual words, always uttered on occasions of this sort where the family and the servants were together, were spoken by Uncle Memed, who walked to where the retainers were gathered, smiled and said: "Allah be praised. It seems that festive looks are all the fashion." The Baron nearly choked with disgust at this totally meaningless display of formality.

The first photograph taken, we were all seated in chairs with Orhan in the centre and behind us came Petrossian, flanked by Rustem the Bosnian, who was the principal chef and controller of the kitchen and, next to him, Luka the

Albanian, the head gardener, and Hasan Baba. This photograph, too, passed off without incident. Then a couple of benches were placed behind Petrossian's row and everyone clambered aboard them. The noise increased till my mother stood up and raised her hand, demanding silence. The ordeal could not last much longer.

As the participants in the photograph disbanded and returned to their posts, Iskander Pasha sent for Giulio Bragadini. He showed him a note. The photographer appeared to be puzzled. Petrossian and I both hurried forward to help Father. Giulio showed me the piece of paper. On it was written: "Now please take a photograph of me alone with Zakiye." I signalled in the direction of Hasan Baba. He understood immediately. He removed all the chairs except two. He told Giulio not to ask unnecessary questions, but to take the photograph. Petrossian shepherded the servants out of the garden. The family stayed behind. Father looked pleased, but he rushed indoors, indicating he would be back very soon. He could not have gone to relieve himself since he often did so in the garden.

Fifteen minutes later everyone gasped in astonishment. Iskander Pasha had returned dressed in the clothes of a *dervish*. None of us spoke. Giulio appeared to be delighted. He seated Iskander Pasha and tried to remove the empty chair lying next to him, but received such a ferocious scowl that he fluttered away to his camera. Iskander Pasha refused to look at the camera. He insisted on smiling at the non-existent occupant of the empty chair, adjacent to his own and that is how he was photographed by Giulio Bragadini.

Afterwards nothing was said. We all acted as if it had been the most normal behaviour imaginable. Our reaction was wise. Some time later, that strange photograph, the outcome of a nostalgic mysticism that had seized Iskander Pasha that day, would travel the world and appear in most of the books on early photography. It would also, and this fact subsequently caused a great deal of merriment within our family, immortalise the name of Giulio Bragadini. The fame that his forebears had been denied by the old Sultans had finally been achieved as a result of a sudden whim on the part of a sad old man who had lost his power of speech. I was told that Giulio gave a public lecture in Paris on that photograph, explaining to his admiring listeners the many hours of planning and forethought that had been required to achieve the perfect texture and composition. News of his latest portraits often appeared in the artistic columns of the European press, but we must not be diverted. The fantasies of the Bragadinis have no real place in this story and I must not run ahead of my time. The past is difficult enough.

Everything had now been cleared. The events of the afternoon had become distant, but the change in Iskander Pasha could not be ignored. He decided that he did not wish us to visit his room after the evening meal.

"I do not crave your attention," he wrote in his note, which was circulated to each of us in turn. "I yearn for solitude. You are all free to stay or return to your families."

Uncle Memed had convened a family conclave to discuss the matter. All the participants of the photograph excepting Orhan and Iskander Pasha were present. We had invited Hasan Baba to join us for coffee. Who would be the first to speak? We looked at each other, offering silent encouragement to whoever wanted to begin. Unsurprisingly it was the Baron who spoke first.

"The worst reaction on our part would be an over-reaction. Knowing the history of this family, I thought his behaviour eccentric, but not a real cause for concern on our part. He was overcome by longing for Zakiye *hanim* and decided to honour her memory in our presence. I found it quite touching."

Hasan Baba had been nodding vigorously while the Baron spoke. "I do not wish to offend anyone present, but to me Iskander Pasha's behaviour is reassuring. He loved Zakiye *hanim* more than everything else in this world put together. He never stopped thinking of her. Salman Pasha suffered as a result since he was held to be the cause of her death. My advice is to be patient. I think, far from being mad, he has decided to become sane again."

My mother usually remained silent on these occasions, but not today. "In the past he often spoke of Salman's mother. He told me he could never love again. Charred wood, he used to say, can never be relit. I understood him perfectly. However, as we all know, he has always been a very private person. It is not his emotions that worry me, but his desire to display them in this fashion. Where will it all end?"

Salman cleared his throat. "I agree with my Aunt Hatije. His initial hostility to me is of little concern now. Naturally, I, too, wished I had seen my mother, though from what I have heard it is perfectly possible that she might have packed me in a bundle and run away from Istanbul. Hasan Baba knows this well. My mother shared the nomadic instinct of the early Ottomans. She was never happy in one place. It is pointless speculating about such matters. What worries me is the streak of insanity that runs through our family. Uncle Memed, when we were children you often spoke of one of our great-great-great-uncles whose insanity was legendary. The same blood courses through our veins."

Memed began to laugh. "Great-great-great-uncle Ahmet. Well, he was very special. Even the Sultan smiled at his escapades. How many of you here know the story? Only Salman? This is odd. Perhaps the rest of you were shielded from it for your own sakes.

"Ahmet Pasha was a warrior. He had participated in numerous wars and was renowned for his foolhardiness which, alas, is usually referred to as courage. When he grew tired of fighting he began to write poetry. Some of it must still exist somewhere. His poems were far removed from war. He wrote exclusively of the natural beauty of animals. Birds, deer, fish, geese, dogs, cats, turtles, horses, elephants and ants all formed part of his anthology. He celebrated their innocence and wrote of how dependent man was on each of them. It is said that the Sultan began to laugh while Ahmet Pasha was reading an ode to the snail. He laughed so much that the courtiers cleared the chamber. Our great forebear was enraged by this behaviour. As we know, our family has a tendency to take itself very seriously. We can produce paintings that embarrass, poetry that pains the ear, love letters that destroy passion, but death to him who dares criticise our work. I suppose this attitude mirrors that of the palace where the Sultan is always above criticism. It is this dullness and inertia that has killed the Empire and retarded our development. It has done the same to our wretched family. We, too, have seen our faculties decline for a few hundred years. Pardon me, children, I am beginning to sound like the Baron."

We laughed, since we had always regarded the two men as interchangeable. It was rare to find them in disagreement. The Baron, as if to prove this point, stroked his moustache and took over the story.

"We will be here all night if Memed continues at this pace. Ahmet Pasha was so angry that he never went to pay his respects to the Sultan again. Instead he recalled two dozen veteran *sipahis* who had served with him and told them to prepare for a new war. They were bemused, but they were very fond of him and whatever doubts they might have entertained were settled when he sent a purse each to their families. He armed them and dressed them in the special uniform of the Sultan's bodyguards. He dressed himself like the Sultan and ordered a new coach modelled on that of his ruler. He began to travel the country in this style and everywhere he went people assumed he was the Sultan. They followed him in large flocks when he went to pray in the local mosque on Friday, because they thought that Allah was more likely to listen to them if they prayed with the Caliph of Islam. When Ahmet Pasha addressed his subjects he denounced hypocrisy and corruption. They say that in three villages he had the collector of taxes executed by the *sipahis*. It was news of this that panicked the Grand Vizier. Till now the Sultan had been greatly amused by Ahmet Pasha's antics and instructed the Vizier to leave him alone. As news of the executions spread, however, it created a wave of expectation throughout the Empire. The Sultan sent a messenger to Ahmet Pasha, summoning him to the palace.

"Your great forebear responded in great style. He asked the messenger to wait while he composed a letter to the Sultan. Then he dismissed the retainers for the day and said farewell to his *sipahis*. When the house was empty he hanged himself. The letter was read by the Vizier and destroyed. It never reached the person for whom it had been intended. A great pity. It would have been the first time the Sultan heard the truth. Was my summary accurate, Hasan Baba?"

The old man nodded. "To this day Ahmet Pasha is remembered in those villages. When it became known that he was not the Sultan, some began to ask 'why not?', while others went so far as to question the need for a Sultan. So even in the case of Ahmet Pasha the madness was not without a purpose. A version of the letter began to circulate in many cities. People used Ahmet Pasha's sacrifice to speak their own grievances. If he was mad, we need many more like him now. Everything is crumbling nowadays. We are heading towards the abyss. We need a Bismarck Pasha!" And pleased with his own joke and his knowledge of the outside world, the old man cackled with delight. We contained our mirth.

Halil decided it was time to close the day. "Enough of all this talk. You could be arrested for treason and shot, Hasan Baba. I am not at all convinced that our father is either deranged or heading in that direction. There is something new. He's embarked on a new stage of his life. His inner world is in complete turmoil. All we can do is try and help him as much as he will let us, so that we can ensure that he lives in peace."

As we disbanded, I accompanied my mother to her bedchamber.

"Did you ever talk to him about Suleman?"

"Often."

I was surprised. "And?"

"He was always very sympathetic. He understood."

"And did he ever talk to you of Salman's mother?"

"Yes, but not very often. He did so only when the pain he felt at her loss became overwhelming. Then he would come and I would stroke his head and let him talk of her till calm returned. We both knew that neither of us could love like that again and this realisation had drawn us closer to each other."

"Do you think he knows that I am . . ."

My mother placed her hand on my mouth. "Shh. He never asked. I never told him. This doesn't mean that he is ignorant. I simply don't know. Even if he did know, his affection for you would not alter in the slightest. He has never been possessive of me in the least. What are you intending to do about Selim? It seems he is not really a barber at all, but a singer."

"I will speak of him some other time, Mother. We have had enough surprises for one day."

NINE

Nilofer and Selim learn to know each other and she realises that her emotions are out of control

I panicked when I first looked out of the window that night. It was past midnight. Dark, ugly clouds had disfigured the sky. Behind them I could see the very faint outline of the full moon. A summer breeze was blowing across the sea and might yet clear the sky. The chimes of the big clock in the entrance hall had woken me up about half an hour earlier. How would Selim determine the time of our tryst?

My room was in a wing of the old house which, in the past, had been used to entertain princes and noblemen. It looked out in the direction of the mountains and the road, which led to the entrance. When we were children, Zeynep and I would quarrel over who had this room, because Salman had told us that when the Grand Vizier came to stay, this was where the captain of the janissaries slept so he could keep an eye on arrivals and departures. Later Salman confessed he had been teasing, but the room remained invested with military authority: his joke made sense.

The Baron and Uncle Memed were in the old royal suite below me, but here on the top floor I was alone. Orhan, by special request, slept in his grandmother's dressing room. I was trembling slightly as I wrapped a shawl round myself and left my room. The last time I had left the house clandestinely was to meet Dmitri in the orange grove. Why had I insisted on meeting Selim at the same spot? Was it to drive out the past or to debase the present?

I left the house by a side entrance. Selim had been unnerved by the moon's absence and had decided to wait for me in the garden. We held hands in complete silence as we walked in the direction of the orange grove. I was slowly getting used to the darkness. Selim was smiling. It was the innocence that appealed to me. I did not want to take him to the orange grove. Perhaps we could go to the cave overlooking the Stone Woman. If she saw everything I would not need to repeat it to her, but there were snakes and lizards in that cave and fear of them would undoubtedly throttle my passion. He sensed my hesitation.

"What's the matter?" he asked in a whisper, which sounded really loud.

"Nothing," I answered. "The breeze has cooled the ground and I'm feeling slightly cold. I thought it would be warmer."

And then I knew what had to be done.

"Come with me," I said to him as I started walking back towards the house.

It was his turn to tremble. "Nilofer," he said, "this is madness."

I did not reply. We reached the side-door and he stopped, refusing to move forward. I pinched him hard on his buttock, which made him laugh, and pushed him through the door. We climbed the stairs, trying hard not to laugh even though the situation was anything but funny. I entered my bedchamber and pulled him in behind me.

"Now, my nightingale," I said in a normal voice, "should we retire to bed, or has the danger muted the excitement?"

"I want to marry you."

"Don't be foolish. I'm married to someone else."

"I want you to have my children."

"I've got two and they're enough."

"Just one more, then . . . just for me."

Outside the breeze had done its work. The sky had cleared and the room was bathed in moonlight. I threw down my clothes and undressed Selim. We began to explore each other's bodies.

"Is this what the *dervishes* have taught you?" I whispered in his ear.

"No, but should I tell you what they did teach me?"

"Yes."

He sat up in the bed, unconcerned that he was naked. Without ceasing to caress my body, he began to sway a little and started to mutter some Sufi invocation.

"If they ask: what is there on your head, your eyebrow, your nose, your breast, the answer must be: on my head is the Crown of high estate, in my eyebrow is the Pen of Power, in my nose is the fragrance of paradise and on my breast the Koran of wisdom."

"I could not lie, Selim. My reply would be different. I would have to say: on my head the burden of being a woman, the eyebrow we could agree on, but in my nose there would be the smell of poverty and on my breasts the hands of Selim."

After we had taken our fill of each other, I asked him about his mother. He was surprised at my interest.

"She lives with us in my grandfather's home. My father, as Hasan Baba has told you, is lost to our world. He lives what he preaches and we see him, but rarely. My mother was once part of that world. The order to which my father is attached does not permit women to whirl and dance. Their role is simply to prepare the food and supply the needs of the *dervish*. My mother was given permission to leave after she had agreed to marry my father. You should hear her talk of what happens when they go into a trance.

"Can I ask you a question?"

I nodded.

"They say that your marriage is finished."

"Do they? Who are they?"

"The maids who serve your mother."

"They're not far wrong, but they gossip without knowing the whole truth and they share the prejudices against Greeks. Listen, Selim, my husband has been a good father to his children and, for that reason, I will never humiliate him. We are separated now and once the summer is over, I will return to Istanbul. Orhan and Emineh must be educated in a proper school. I will let my husband see the children whenever he wishes and he will always have a bed in our house, but will never share mine again. I think he will accept these conditions. A messenger was sent to Konya with my letter and he should be returning soon." I asked him of his future and he laughed.

"When Hasan Baba leaves this world I will sell my barber's shop. I could do it now, but it would upset the old man a great deal. Our family has, after all, been cutting the hair of yours for many centuries. How can we stop now? Hasan Baba has still not forgiven my father for betraying our profession. I will wait."

"You could become a world-famous singer. You could sing in the operas of Donizetti Pasha. You could . . ."

"No! I have no desire to sell my voice. Let it give pleasure to everyone. I will continue to sing at our own festivals and in the streets when the mood takes me, but what I would really like to be is a photographer, like the Signor Bragadini."

"But why?"

"I've surprised you, haven't I? I've surprised Nilofer with the green eyes and the beautiful nipples. Why? Answer me truthfully. Is it that you could not imagine a future for me other than that dictated by my past and my origins? Do you think only Italians can be photographers? This new art is beyond the reach of a poor boy from Anatolia?"

"Are you angry?"

He laughed and kissed me on the lips for the first time. I admired his confidence. How could he be so self-assured, so oblivious to the impediments that lay ahead of him, especially in our world, which was still closed to people like him? Perhaps he had inherited his optimism from his mother. Perhaps she had inculcated him with the belief that everything was possible. All that was needed was determination and inner strength. As if to prove that this was the case he spoke again.

"I know that one day we will be together. I feel this in my blood. Your Uncle Memed has already recommended me as an assistant to Signor Bragadini, which is what he says I will have to call him. One day I will be famous and then you will come with me. Is this impossible?"

"No," I lied. "Why should it be impossible?"

"Because I come from a poor family and you are the daughter of a Pasha."

If only he knew the truth. Perhaps I would tell him one day. I decided to change the subject.

"I'm three years older than you."

"Still not old enough to be Mother," he laughed.

"I am sure you will find many beautiful young maidens ready to fall in your arms the minute they have heard your voice."

"That would not be a new experience for me."

He said this in such a serious voice that we both burst out laughing. Even near the sea, the first time we made love, I had not felt that he was a novice. What puzzled me was the degree of sophistication that he had acquired.

"Did you learn to read at home or in a *medresseh*?"

"Why do you ask, princess? Are you surprised that I am not a yokel?"

"No. Intelligence has nothing to do with a formal education. But I get the feeling you are both inside and at the same time removed from our culture."

"Now you're saying that I'm not simply a singer of Sufi verses, but someone with an imagination of my own. Perhaps someone who might even one day become a photographer and a more talented one than Signor Bragadini."

"Why are you so sensitive?"

"Because I still sleep in the servants' quarters and that fact colours your picture of me."

"Tonight you've slept in this house. In my bed."

"Wrong again, princess. It is now too late to sleep."

"You still haven't answered my question."

"I learnt to read our language in a *medresseh,* but I learnt to read French from my grandfather and to speak it from a French diplomat whose hair I cut regularly and who shares my admiration for the work of Monsieur Balzac."

"My favourite is *Lost Illusions*."

He began to recover his clothes and dressed quickly.

"Sometimes French novels can become a terrible distraction. I would recommend the work of a philosopher. Auguste Comte. He has much to offer this country. He could stop our future from becoming a bottomless pit." Selim slipped out of the door without the sentimentality of a last embrace.

I covered myself and rushed to the window. The very faint first light of dawn had begun to change the colour of the sky. Selim was walking across the garden. He must have felt my gaze because he suddenly turned around and looked up in my direction. I blew him a kiss. He smiled and walked away.

I had always thought Selim's emotions might get out of control, that he might start to sing underneath my window, deliberately embarrassing me in front of the family. His serenity surprised me. I realised I was the one in an agitated state. An image of his naked body flashed through my mind and I began to feel weak with pleasure.

TEN

A Greek tragedy in Konya; Emineh arrives at the house; Nilofer is enchanted by Iskander Pasha

I awakened to the noise of wailing women. At first I had thought it was part of my dream, but the sound became louder and louder and my dream had been free of any disaster. What catastrophe had occurred? Had someone died? I jumped out of bed, slipping yesterday's discarded clothes over my half-asleep body. My first thought was that something terrible had happened to Iskander Pasha.

I rushed down the stairs and into the vast, virtually unfurnished and rarely used reception room to find it filled with sad faces. My mother was weeping as she hugged Emineh and Orhan. Something had happened to Dmitri.

Emineh ran towards me. I lifted her off the ground. She did not say a word, just put her arms round my neck and sobbed. I walked towards Orhan. His face, too, was wet with tears, but he stepped back when I tried to include him in my embrace. He gave me an angry look.

"Perhaps," he said in a broken voice, "if we had stayed in Konya, they would not have dared to kill my father."

"What happened?" I asked nobody in particular as the tears began to flood my face. My mother placed a finger on her lips. This was not the time.

Emineh clung to me even tighter. I took her upstairs to my room. She had been travelling all night and was exhausted. I stroked and kissed her cheeks and I laid her on the bed.

"Would you like some water?"

She nodded, but in the short time it had taken me to lift the jug, pour out the water, fill a glass and return to the bed, she was already fast asleep. Gently, I took off her dusty shoes and removed the socks from her feet. I covered her with a light quilt and sat down beside her to feast my eyes. I had not seen her for a whole month. Her face grew calm, and I was about to go downstairs when my mother appeared in the doorway. Seeing Emineh asleep she signalled I should join her.

We went into the adjoining room, which had not been dusted for at least a hundred years, and sat on the bed, after we had removed the covers.

"Where is Orhan?"

"Your friend Selim has taken him for a walk by the sea. The boy likes him. I suppose that is a good thing."

"Mother!" I almost shouted at her. "This is not the moment. What happened? Will someone please tell me what happened to poor Dmitri?"

It was a sad story. There had been trouble in Konya. Its purpose was to drive the remaining Greeks out of the city. The instigators had been under the influence of the Young Turks, who saw all Greeks as the agents of Britain, Russia and France. These were the people who wanted to recreate a pure and modern empire. There had been few enough Greeks in Konya in the first place, if one compared the town to Smyrna and Istanbul, but the supporters of the Young Turks wanted to create an impression. Messengers were despatched to each Greek household warning them that if they did not take their belongings and leave town, their houses would be taken over and the rest of their property confiscated. Everyone had left, except Dmitri. He refused to part with his books.

The messenger arrived with my letter the very next day. He read it carefully and then took Emineh to the house of a Turkish neighbour. He embraced her and kissed her eyes and then her forehead. Then he sat down and wrote a reply. He handed it to the messenger, but told him that he should wait till the next morning and return with Emineh. The neighbours pleaded with him to take the child and bring her to me, but he refused.

That night they came into the house silently and slit his throat. His books were untouched. Dmitri was the only casualty. My mother handed me his letter. I wept again as I broke the seal. It was difficult to imagine that he had gone for ever. My love for him, if it had ever existed, had not been very deep, but he was a decent man and, as I never tired of telling my family, he had been a loving father. The thought of my children made me cry out aloud. My mother clasped me to her chest and stroked my head till I had recovered. After drinking some water I read the letter from Konya.

My dear wife,
I have reached the end of the road. The future threatens and the past has already condemned me. The rogues of the town, who now dress themselves in the garb of Young Turks, claim to be supporters of reform and modern ideas. In reality they are nothing more than criminals who wish to occupy our houses and increase their own status in society. As you know this is a modest house, but my family has lived here for over a hundred years. I feel a strong sense of attachment to this town and this locality. I refuse to be swept out of here like a piece of filthy rubbish. If they actually attempt to carry out their threats, I will look the assassin straight in the eye, so that he can remember the face of at least one of his victims. I fear for the future, Nilofer. The omens are not good. They who are driving us out will destroy much that has been good in the Empire.

I do not wish you to regard yourself as responsible for my decision in any way. I realised a long time ago that we were not well suited to each other. I was the frog who remained a frog and you were always a princess. I always felt that if you had not been of such a proud disposition, you would have returned home long before Orhan was born. I think you realised at a very early stage that our marriage was a mistake but could not admit this to your parents. Your pride condemned you to a life with me, which must have been unbearable. I always felt this to be the case, but could never bring myself to say it to your face. It hurt too much.

I know that, like me, you are proud of the children we produced. I'm very sad that I will not be able to follow the story of their lives as they grow older or one day hold their children in my arms, but I know they will be safe with you. If it is not too much to ask, speak to them sometimes about their father. When they are old enough to understand, please explain to them that their father died with his dignity intact. He refused to live in the shadow of fear.

I once began to tell Orhan the story of Galileo, but stopped because he was too young to appreciate the dilemma. Galileo held the truths he had discovered to be of very great significance, but as soon as they endangered his life he recanted with the greatest ease. He felt that whether the earth or the sun revolved around each other was not worth his life. He may also have felt that it was more important for him to live and work so that his students could spread the truth. He was probably right to make that choice. I am but a humble school teacher. My refusal to submit is a political act. Tell Orhan and Emineh that I'm sorry, but there was truly no other way for me.

Dmitri

As I went to wash the tears off my face my mother began to read the letter. It was noble of him to absolve me of all responsibility, but I knew that if I had loved him he would never have given his life away so easily. Orhan's anger was justified. If I had stayed behind in Konya none of this would have happened. He had taken the decision to die without consulting anyone else. It was an act that could only be carried out within the silence of the heart. The mind could not be allowed to interfere. If his emotional life, in other words the hurt he felt at my decision to withdraw from it completely, had not become too much for him, he would still have been alive. He did not want to admit this to himself or the children, but I knew it was the truth. He found the daily pain of life unbearable and suffering it was useless since hope itself was dead. Nothing he could do would have brought me back to him. Suddenly an awful thought crossed my mind and I screamed, bringing my mother rushing to my side.

"What if it was my letter to him that pushed him into oblivion?"

"Don't think such things, Nilofer. From his letter it is clear that he acted in this fashion because of his beliefs."

"You never knew him, Mother. That is not so. He decided to die because life without me was not worth living."

"Don't torment yourself, child. Think of the children. They must believe in that letter. It was his wish and there is a nobility of purpose there which I admire."

"You always used to call him a skinny, ugly Greek school teacher, Mother."

"He was that too, but ugly people can sometimes be noble."

Despite the sadness, I burst out laughing. I was sobered by a knock on the door, fearful that it might be one of the children, but it was Petrossian.

"Iskander Pasha wishes to see you, *hanim effendi*."

I went to his room, but it was empty. Iskander Pasha was sitting at his desk in the old library. It was a beautiful old room, with wooden panels on the wall and bookshelves that almost touched the high ceiling. Most of the literature was in Turkish, Arabic, Persian, German and French. The classic works of our own culture mingled easily with the encyclopaedias of the French Enlightenment. When he was a tutor here, the Baron had helped to modernise the collection. French novels, German poetry and philosophy had filled the two empty shelves closest to the ceiling.

Hasan Baba had often told us that three Korans in the library dated back to the ninth century and their value was inestimable. This was where we were summoned for punishments as children, which may have had the effect of discouraging us from reading. The library was engulfed in sunshine today, making it seem warm and friendly.

Iskander Pasha was writing in a thick leather-bound volume, a diary in which he made an entry every single day and, since our evening story-telling had been discontinued, the number of entries had multiplied. It had become part of the new routine after his stroke. He could now walk without a stick and his body showed no signs of any disability. He turned around as I entered and rose from his desk to greet me. He held his arms out wide and I fell into them as the tears began to fall again. He stroked my face and kissed me on the head. I could not remember when he had last treated me with such open affection. The fear that he was on the edge of sanity seemed to have been completely misplaced. If anything, the entire episode of the photograph had brought his submerged humanity back to the surface.

His speaking notebook, as Petrossian had named it, was in the pocket of his dressing gown. He took my arm as we walked back to his room. As we sat, side by side, on the divan, he took out the little book. In it he had written: "My little Nilofer, who has been widowed, I want you to know that I have always loved you. Nothing mattered."

"Did you always know?"

He smiled and nodded.

"But how?"

He wrote: "You had green eyes and red hair, unlike your mother and unlike everyone else in our family for as long as I can remember. I knew for sure when you laughed as a child. It was a very nice laugh and it made your mother very happy. I was sure it reminded her of her lost lover. I did not mind in the least. You were a beautiful child and I was proud to act as your father. You have made one big mistake in your life so far, but, despite what I once thought of him, I'm very sorry that the schoolmaster Dmitri died in such circumstances. Ottoman civilisation has collapsed. Those who seek to fill the vacuum imagine they can make up in violence what they lack in culture. Talk to Halil about this one day. I think he underestimates the problem."

I talked to Iskander Pasha that evening for many hours, and for the first time I felt that he was treating me as an equal. I told him that I had been somewhat disoriented when Mother revealed to me who my real father was, but that after a few days the knowledge had ceased to matter. He wrote in reply that the importance people attached to blood relationships had a great deal to do with the laws of inheritance and not very much with genuine affection. In this regard, he joked, our Sultans have been remarkably unsentimental, ordering that their male children, bar their chosen successor, be strangled to death with a silken cord – the choice of silk being important so that the royal neck was not sullied by cheap cloth before it was broken, but even more importantly so that no royal blood was spilt by common executioners.

I asked whether everyone in the family knew of my origins. He shrugged his shoulders indifferently and wrote that he had not discussed the matter with anyone and when Halil and Zeynep's mother had raised the suspicion with him on her deathbed, he had not even bothered to reply. He then insisted that we had exhausted the subject of my birth and he never wished to discuss it with me again. I was *his* daughter and nothing else mattered.

In a bold attempt to change the subject I posed a totally unrelated question. "Have you ever read any book by Auguste Comte?"

The question seemed to really shake him. He wrote in an agitated way: "Why? Why do you ask?"

"Someone asked me."

"Who?" he wrote.

"I think it may have been Selim."

His eyes softened immediately. "I have read something by him, but Hasan Baba became a complete devotee for a short time, when we were in Paris. He forgot the Sufis and embraced rationalism. He even began to dress in the style of a French plebeian. It all wore off after we returned to Istanbul. This Empire has a strange way of sweeping aside all the refined thoughts in our heads as if they were mere cobwebs. The clergy have made sure that Istanbul thrives on ignorance. We will talk of him tomorrow. The Baron might have a great deal to say on the subject. Organise a conclave after dinner. Let us discuss something serious for a change and tell Petrossian to make sure that Hasan and his grandson are present. I am so proud of the way in which you have taken over the running of this house. Your mother must be relieved."

I was filled with a very deep love for him, a love I had not felt before. The remote figure I had known all my life and whose wrath I had so often feared had vanished. In his place there was a warm, generous man with a depth of understanding that must always have been there. We are all capable of wearing the mask, but underneath we remain what we are even if we do not wish others to glimpse that reality. I was sure that Iskander Pasha had returned to his true self. Perhaps he had found inner peace at last. I sat there for a short while, looking at him in silence. Then I kissed his hands and left the room.

I went in search of my orphaned children. I was about to leave the house and look for them in the garden when I heard the sound of Emineh's laughter. Both of them were in my mother Sara's room. A maid was teaching Emineh the tricks that can be played with a piece of string and a pair of hands. Sara herself had her hair tied back and covered in henna paste. It was a sight I knew well. Orhan was looking out of the window.

"I think we should leave your grandmother alone while she tries to colour her hair so it can match mine. Come with me."

Both of them followed me out without complaint. Emineh held my hand tight as we walked out of the house. I took them to the small, shaded terrace underneath the balcony of Iskander Pasha's room. There was a blazing sun. There was no breeze and the sea, motionless and silent as in a painting, was smothered under a haze caused by the dazzling heat. The discordant cry of seagulls was the only noise I recall on that very still afternoon.

My disoriented children and I sat down on a bench. Orhan's anger had evaporated. He had let me put my arm around him and did not complain when I kissed his cheeks. For a long time we did not speak. We were together and nothing else mattered. We just sat and looked at the sea.

It was difficult to breach the silence. Young children experience the death of a parent or grandparent in different ways. It is so remote from them that they find it difficult to comprehend its finality. I remember when the mother of Zeynep and Halil died. She had always been nice to me, treating me in much the same way as she did her own two children. We were all upset when she died so suddenly, but I don't remember any of us crying. It had seemed unreal. I know that I would have liked Iskander Pasha or Sara or Petrossian or any grown-up to talk about it, to tell us what had happened and why, but they never did, assuming, perhaps, that because the feelings of children are still undeveloped they can be left to heal on their own.

I began to talk to my children. I told them what a loving father Dmitri had been and because of that I would always cherish his memory. I spoke of the letter he had written me and told them they could read it whenever they wished, but they might understand it better in a few years' time. I did not lie or exaggerate. I did not wish to be insincere even in the slightest degree. It is not easy to discuss the death of a father with young children. Orhan noticed I was about to cry and he sought to divert me.

"Selim says that the men who killed Father are ruffians, worse than animals. He says they will soon be found and punished. Is that true, Mother?"

"I don't know, child. I doubt it myself. We are living in very uncertain times. The old order we have known all our lives is dying. The Sultan is no longer powerful and the Empire of which Petrossian speaks has itself become a fairy-tale now. Everything is being taken away and nothing is ready to take its place. It is this that turns many ordinary people into madmen and assassins. They do not know what lies ahead and they find it convenient to blame everyone except those who are to blame. They cannot do anything about the Sultan or the Great Powers who are dismantling our country. In the face of the real enemy they are powerless. Killing a few Greeks makes them feel better. Whatever happens to those who killed him won't bring your father back to life. Do you understand me, Orhan?"

"Of course I do. I'm not stupid. What will happen to father's books? Did the ruffians burn them all?"

"We know that all his books are safe, including all those notebooks in which he used to scribble so much and the copies of all his reports on the schools he inspected. Everything is intact. It shall be kept for both of you."

"Where will we live now?" asked Emineh.

"In Istanbul, in a house which neither of you has seen. That's where I grew up."

"Is it as big as this house?"

"No, Emineh, no!" I held her close to me. "Much smaller, but don't worry. It's large enough for both of you to have your own room."

Hasan Baba was approaching us and Orhan began to giggle.

"Emineh." He looked at his sister with a mischievous grin. "Just wait and see what I do. I'll make this old man laugh and you can see that he hasn't got any teeth at all."

"Then how does he eat?" asked Emineh.

Hasan Baba was dressed in a clean pair of trousers and a loose shirt. He had shaved and his bald head was, uncharacteristically, covered by a black cloth cap. I had never seen it on him before, but it was vaguely familiar. It made the children smile.

"It looks like the cap we saw on that funny performing monkey in Konya. Remember, Emineh?"

Orhan's memory was accurate. The children burst out laughing. I controlled my own laughter with some difficulty.

"Allah bless you, grandchildren and daughter of Iskander Pasha," the old man began to wail. "Allah will protect you. What a tragedy has befallen our household. Rogues and ruffians are assembling in all our cities. Where will it end?"

The condolences over, he patted both children on the head.

"Hasan Baba," Orhan said with a completely straight face, "tell us the story of the Grand Vizier with square testicles."

I pretended I had not heard the remark, but it did make the old man laugh and Emineh gasped in awe at his empty mouth. Both children ran away to laugh in private.

I was pleased to be alone with the old man. I told him of my conversation with Iskander Pasha earlier that day and how surprised I had been by his warmth and openness. Naturally I did not mention the subject of my own father. Hasan Baba smiled and nodded sagely.

"He was always like this as a child and a young man. The death of Zakiye *hanim* changed everything. In the Ottoman lands he played the part of a strong nobleman well. It was the same when he acted the strong father who tolerated no insubordination and whose daily routines were fixed and irreversible. What I can't understand is how he could carry on like this for such a long time. I know it often tired him. Sometimes when I was shaving him, which I did every morning as you probably recall, he would look at me and wink. That's all. No smile. Not say anything I might repeat in the kitchen and which would get back to the house, but just wink. That was the only message he sent to the outside world.

"It was different when we were in Paris. He was much more like his old self then and even though he had to dress in his robes and turban on official occasions, underneath it all he was the *dervish*, constantly mocking their ignorance, but drinking in the knowledge. We all did that – and not just knowledge. The wine cellar in the Ottoman embassy in Paris was considered to be the best in Europe. Those French women fawned over him as if he were a beautiful stallion. They would feign innocence and ask after the Sultan: 'Excellency, is it true that the Grand Seignior still keeps a harem with twenty women?' Iskander Pasha would stretch himself as high as he could, fold his arms and reply in a deep voice: 'Twenty, madame. That is even less than the size of my own harem. The Sultan, may his reign last long and may Allah give him strength to fornicate every day, has three hundred and twenty-six women to serve his needs. A new one for each day except during the month of fasting, when he prefers young boys from the Yemen.' They would pretend to scream and faint, but this was only a cover to conceal the turbulence and anticipatory excitement that lay underneath their long dresses. Forgive me, Nilofer *hanim*. I forgot myself."

I smiled. "Hasan Baba, you are of a certain age and wisdom and you must always say what you wish in my presence or that of anyone else in this family. I do not like formality or ceremony any more than the real Iskander Pasha does. What you're saying is that he was his true self only when he was abroad, but was transformed into a totally different person at home. Did this not cause some mental imbalance?"

The old man became pensive.

"I had never thought about that before, but perhaps it did and perhaps that incident with the photograph was the first manifestation of this imbalance. Allah help us. Allah protect us. Everything is reaching its conclusion."

ELEVEN

Sara recounts her dream to the Stone Woman, igniting other memories and a few bitternesses

'Last night I saw Suleman in a dream again after almost twenty years, Stone Woman. Do you remember when I first came here? I was still young. I was nursing a wounded hurt and my child at the same time. Nilofer was about seven or eight months old. I remember coming here and weeping at your feet. I know you have no feet, but if they had existed they would have been where I wept that day. I thought I heard you speak. A voice asked me what was wrong and I remember saying: "The one I love has gone far away." And then your voice said something very sad and beautiful: "Love is the longing of the flute for the bed from which the reed was torn. Try and forget." I did try, but I never could forget. However, I did become accustomed to his absence. Time can never completely heal our inner wounds, but it softens the pain.

All my love was diverted to our child, Nilofer. As she grew older, she would laugh just like Suleman used to laugh when we were on our own. A deep, throaty, abandoned laugh. I cannot believe he laughs like that with anyone else, but I'm probably deluding myself. People who have been betrayed in love often fall prey to self-deception.

The dream I had last night was not a nice dream, Stone Woman, and it would not stop. It went on for most of the night, or so it seemed to me. When it finally woke me up, I was in a state of great agitation. My body was covered with sweat. My throat was completely parched and I consumed a whole jug of water.

My Suleman looked so different in the dream, Stone Woman, that I could not bear the sight of him. His hair had gone white and his slim body, which I used to love for its feminine softness, had hardened. He was now bloated and ugly. That was the first shock. He was naked in bed with a very young woman. She could not have more than twenty-four or twenty-five years old. She must have been one of his models, because there was a canvas not far from the bed and even in my dream I noticed that the breasts matched. I did not object to the model at all. I preferred him to be with anyone but his wife.

Then two other women entered the room in my dream. I suppose the fat ugly woman must have been his wife and the other one her friend or sister. They screamed at the naked pair. His wife took a paint brush and began to whip Suleman. Her friend suddenly produced a bottle and began to pour liquid on the model. The poor young thing screamed in anguish. I can still hear her and see her disfigured face. She was blinded in one eye and ran out of the room naked. While all this was happening Suleman lay helpless. He did not help the woman or try and stop the other two from harming her. It was when they moved towards him with knives in their hands that he shouted my name three times: "Sara! Sara! Sara!" At this point I sat up in bed trembling. It was not yet dawn.

I have never been superstitious or believed in signs or omens, Stone Woman, but this was so real. You know me well. We have spoken often since I first came here though I admit I have avoided you for the last few years. But this dream has become a load on my heart. It is a premonition. I feel he is in trouble or perhaps even close to death. As you know, I never forgot Suleman, but I was very disappointed in him and, deep down I can't rid myself of the feeling that my father paid him a very large sum of money to help him establish himself in New York and give me up.

Poor Suleman. He was always a deeply insecure man. His own parents had, in their different ways, abandoned him. He longed to be part of a family and always wanted to please and be praised in return. He was never like that with me, but this craving for some form of recognition was embedded in his character.

If he had stayed on in Istanbul for another year and not rushed to New York and married the first woman who made eyes at him, I would have told him that we had a beautiful daughter and that all the fears regarding our children had been unfounded. If he loved me still I would have asked Iskander Pasha for my freedom and run away with Suleman to Damascus or anywhere else where we could start a new life. My parents would have found the scandal unbearable and Father might have lost a few wealthy patients, but none of that would have affected my decision in any way.

My love for him used to be so strong, but he chose to run away. He said the very thought of life without me in Istanbul was unbearable, that he would die rather than see me in public with another man, but all this proves is that the roots of his love did not go very deep. He said he could not stay in the Ottoman lands for wherever one was in the decaying Empire, one always dreamt of Istanbul. With the kind help of my father he decided on New York.

We have some family there, but they are so well integrated that they look down on those of us who settled here. We are too backward for them, but not for the letters of credit from the firm of my maternal uncle. Our wealth, however, is perfectly acceptable. How much did my father pay Suleman? I never wanted to know at the time, but now this question has begun to nag me. It won't go away. His papers are still there in the house.

For a long time I avoided my own childhood home. My pain was so great, Stone Woman. I used to weep and pray for an inner strength that would help me forget, but whenever I went home I would hear his voice whispering to me: "Sara, are we alone? Are they all out? Should we go to your room or mine?" I last went when my father died. It was the first time I did not hear Suleman's whisper in my ear.

Several months later, my mother showed me the letter she had received from him. In it he had made no mention of me, not even as a courtesy. Perhaps his conscience troubles him. Guilt, my daughter Nilofer tells me, can become both a self-protective and a self-deceptive emotion. Incapable of mentioning me, he wrote instead of his high regard for my father and how he would never forget the kindnesses he had been shown by our family. Kindnesses. I felt overcome by nausea. Towards the end of the letter he wrote that he was sure my mother would be pleased to hear that his wife was pregnant again. My mother may well have been pleased. She has never got over the fact that I was their only child and that she failed to produce a son to carry on my father's healing tradition. As you can imagine, Stone Woman, my feelings on reading this were not warm. The sow, I remember thinking to myself. How many little pigs will she produce before she dies? My one Nilofer is worth all of them ten times over.

I will return to my home when this strange summer is finally over, Stone Woman. I will read all the letters. I want to know the exact number of silver pieces he took to forget me. Did he give my father a receipt for the kindnesses? Mother is, alas, getting too old to remember anything. Her memory has almost gone. Sometimes she doesn't recognise me. What should I do, Stone Woman? I need to know that he is well. I cannot stay calm until I find out. I will write to my Uncle Sifrah in Istanbul to see if he can send a telegram immediately. Suleman has, in the past, done some work for their branch in New York and my uncle will find out if all is well or whether my fears are well founded.

Dreams are funny things. Why did such a dream ever enter my head? Why do we dream what we dream? Is there a simple answer, or is it what my father used to call an insoluble problem? I remember him saying to the guests at one of his dinner parties that there was a doctor in Paris and, I think, in Vienna who were both doing a lot of work on dreams. Have you ever heard of the Viennese doctor, Stone Woman? I can't quite remember his name.

This dream may have changed more than I can imagine.

For a long time when Iskander Pasha used to come to me at night, I would shut my eyes and think it was still Suleman. I could not do this all the time because Iskander Pasha is a big man and bearing his weight was very different, but at the point when union dissolves into pure pleasure the image in my mind was that of my lost lover from Damascus. In that way I could enjoy the experience, but still love my Suleman. Iskander Pasha's visits became less and less frequent, till a few weeks ago. Once again the image of Suleman entered my head, but now I have a very real problem. This dream has ruined everything. I can never imagine the old Suleman ever again. The cruel image of the dream has taken over. Perhaps I will now have to think of Iskander Pasha and him alone? The prospect is not as unpleasing as it might have been before. Something has changed in him. ’

TWELVE

Memed and the Baron have an argument on Islamic history in which Memed is worsted; Iskander Pasha recovers his power of speech, but prefers to thank Auguste Comte rather than Allah

"I'm really surprised by your lack of knowledge on this critically important aspect of the history of your religion and culture."

The Baron sounded irate. The three of us were in the library, waiting for the others to arrive. Iskander Pasha, who had summoned the conclave, had decided to take a walk after dinner. It was beautiful and balmy outside, and with the windows of the library wide open the scents of the night were overpowering.

When I entered the room Uncle Memed and the Baron had been shouting at each other. They ignored my arrival, but lowered their voices. They were dressed today in cream-coloured shirts and white trousers, though Uncle Memed had, unlike his friend, responded to the weather and dispensed with his silk cravat.

"Well?" continued the Baron. "Do you still insist that the Ommayads and Abbasids were simply rival factions engaged in a power struggle and nothing more?"

"Yes," replied Memed in a very stiff voice. "*Your* knowledge of Islam is taken from books, Baron. *Mine* is first-hand."

"I see it all now. Everything is suddenly illuminated," the Baron responded facetiously. "You were actually present yourself in Damascus during the eighth century. I can see you with your quill and parchment, noting down what the leaders of the rival factions were saying of each other and meticulously counting the number of dead bodies on the streets."

"*Reductio ad absurdum* will not work in this case, Baron. Mock away if you like, but elevating the Ommayads and the Abbasids to the level of the world-spirit will simply not work. Feuerbach would have spanked you for resorting to sarcasm when argument failed."

The Baron tapped his stick angrily on the wooden floor. "It is not your naïveté that amazes me, Memed, it is your obstinacy and arrogance. When knowledge of a particular subject has eluded you and an old and valued friend is attempting to dispel the clouds of ignorance that have descended on your raised eyebrow, you should, at least, do him the courtesy of hearing out his whole argument. It will help. Once you have been enlightened then, of course, you are free to disagree."

Now it was Uncle Memed's turn to sulk. "Have it your way, Baron. You always do."

The Baron ignored the petulant tone. "Listen, Memed. They were rival factions. Of course they were, but what was the reality that underlay their hostility to each other? Power? Yes, but why? Let us not forget that thousands of lives were lost in this civil war. I see the entire struggle as one between the declining forces of the Arabs, who had monopolised Islam since the death of your prophet, and the, how should I put it, more cosmopolitan forces of Islam. Why were the Ommayad dynasty extinguished so mercilessly? Every surviving male except one was destroyed. I grant you that Abderrahman's escape was a miracle of the imagination. He was an unusually gifted political leader and showed great initiative in heading for Spain. Once he was safe in Cordoba, the populace acclaimed him as the Caliph. But it was the acclaim of the soldiers that was decisive and they were loyal because they were Arabs. We agree? Good. I will continue.

"The battle for the Caliphate in the Arab heartland was between a Damascus-based Arab oligarchy represented by the Ommayads and the Abbasids who were backed by the Persians, the Turks, including your own ancestors my dear friend, the Kurds, the Caucasians, the Arameans and the Armenians and so on. These were the new converts, but their numbers were many and the arrogant refusal of the Ommayads to recognise this numerical superiority and share power in the greater interest of Islam, meant they had to be wiped out. A new legitimacy was needed because Islam had become a world religion. Arab vanity would not tolerate a compromise."

Uncle Memed's nose twitched slightly as he rewarded the Baron with a condescending smile. "Interesting, though, isn't it, that the Cordoba Caliphate under the sway of the vain and short-sighted Arabs was far more advanced in many ways than your cosmopolitan Abbasids? The Ommayads in Spain were far more tolerant and far less susceptible to any nonsense on the part of the clergy. The Andalusian philosophers were continually being denounced in Baghdad as heretics. Scholars were discouraged from reading their books."

"Very true," replied the Baron, "but the conditions in al-Andalus were very different. The Ommayads confronted Christiandom. They were fighting on the borderlands of the two civilisations. They needed their philosophers to help them win new converts to Islam. There it could not simply be done under the shadow of the sword. The situation demanded intellectual triumphs. I am extremely partial, as you know, to the Andalusian philosophers. Without them the Renaissance in Europe might have taken a different form. But understand that they were allowed to develop their brilliant minds only because they were faced with a powerful intellectual enemy in the Catholic Church. When the Bishops decided that the enemy could not be overwhelmed by argument they backed a Holy War and the Pope gave

Europe the Inquisition. All this proves, Memed, is that new ideas develop best when they are engaged in struggle against orthodoxy. The synthesis is usually original and exciting.

"The Catholic scholars were careful when they subjected Islamic culture to an *auto-da-fé* in Granada in the fifteenth century. They removed the manuals of medicine and other learned books, which they needed for their own survival, from the fire. Have I convinced you, my dear old thing?"

Uncle Memed looked at his friend and raised an eyebrow. I had always envied him this capacity. It was an art, he explained, that could not be taught.

"You may not have convinced me completely, Baron, but you have certainly compelled me to think."

"It is these small victories that enrich one's life," muttered the Baron as my father, flanked on either side by Halil and Salman, entered the room.

Father and sons were followed by grandfather and grandson. Hasan Baba and Selim must have been waiting outside for my father to return before they entered the library. Hasan Baba could not overcome years of habit and still maintained the posture of a retainer. Selim suffered from no such inhibitions. He walked in with his head naturally erect. My heart quickened its pace as I saw him. He smiled. My eyes softened. I looked around the room casually to see if anyone had noticed. Father had taken his customary position in the armchair closest to the window. Petrossian entered with a large jug filled with the fresh juice of oranges. Glances were exchanged between the Baron and Memed, who could not believe that they were being deprived of alcohol for the evening. Their worries were premature. Petrossian's grandson walked in with the champagne and wine glasses that I had never seen before in the house. The sight cheered the two friends.

"Well, Iskander," began Uncle Memed, "why have we been summoned this evening? What delights await us today?"

My father did not reply. He waved his stick in the direction of Halil.

"It was my idea that we meet tonight." Halil's soft voice compelled Hasan

Baba, who was getting more and more deaf with each passing day, to move close to the speaker and cup his good ear in the direction of the sound. "For the last few days I have been discussing matters of some importance with my father and brother. They concern the future of our Empire."

"What future?" the Baron interrupted. "If we're going to speak frankly let us confront reality."

Halil smiled. "Baron Pasha! You have stolen my words. It is because the Empire has no future that we need to speak and not simply that, but to act. I am a simple soldier. I am not a philosopher of history or a political thinker, but even I have come to realise that if we do nothing, if we simply sit still and watch our country being devoured, everything will be lost. Our people will wake up one morning and find themselves, like our Sultan, enslaved by Britain, France, Russia and the new Germany. It is our good fortune that these powers are not in agreement. Each needs us alive in order to prevent its rival from eating us whole. There is deep unrest in the army. The young officers want to act now. They wish to depose the Sultan and establish a republic."

He paused to see if anyone had reacted. Memed clapped his hands in delight.

"It has to be done, Halil, but we are already a hundred years too late. We should have learnt from the French much sooner."

Hasan Baba frowned and shook his head. "No good will come of it. It is not possible for a fly to lift an eagle and dash it to the ground."

Selim disagreed. It was the only time he spoke that evening. "Halil Pasha speaks the truth. It is *we* who are the eagle, Hasan Baba. The Sultan and his corrupt courtiers are the fly. They are the parasites who have clipped our wings and lived off us for centuries. Now we want our wings back and there is no height that we cannot reach."

My brothers smiled. I simply felt like kissing his lips.

"I agree with young Selim," said Salman, whom I had not seen with such shining and alert eyes since he had first arrived here. "I agree with Uncle

Memed that we should have acted a hundred years ago. But let us not forget that the French, too, have been playing musical chairs with their history. They execute the King and crown Napoleon. The English and Austrians topple Napoleon and the French restore their King. Another revolution gives us another republic and then we get an imitation Napoleon, who calls himself the Third, and so the circus goes on. When we act – and act we must – let us do so in such a way that there can never be a restoration. These cursed Sultans have let us decay for far too long. Let them take their jewel boxes and go and live on the French Riviera."

Iskander Pasha had been listening intently to the discussion. He tapped his stick gently on the floor to demand attention and then, to the amazement of everyone present, he began to speak, low and stuttering. But it was speech! It had returned. We all rose spontaneously, amazement and happiness written on each face, and moved towards him. Tears shone in Hasan Baba's eyes as he threw his arms around Iskander Pasha.

"Allah be praised. This is nothing less than a miracle. How could this happen?"

"The human body remains a mystery," said the Baron. "If he could walk again, I suppose we should not be surprised that he can talk again. This calls for a real celebration."

Iskander Pasha told us all to sit down. Hearing him speak again was unreal. I found it difficult to contain my happiness. The first thing I will do tomorrow, I told myself, is bring Emineh to him so she can hear his voice.

"Please," he said in a slightly hoarse voice, "I did think of remaining silent and announcing the return of my speech tomorrow, because what we speak of tonight is much more important than our individual lives. Let us continue. The question we confront is not the Sultan or the Caliphate. All that is over. What will we put in its place and will we have a place or will they carve us into tiny slices and share us out? My speech returned a couple of days ago when Nilofer asked me whether I had heard of Auguste Comte. I was relieved to hear that she had heard the name from young Selim, who I knew could only have got it from Hasan. After Nilofer left the room, my lips repeated the name Auguste Comte and to my astonishment I realised I could speak. It was Comte, you see, and not Allah. So, my dear Hasan, from now on I want you to say 'Comte be praised' or 'There is only one Comte and he is Comte and we are all his prophets.'"

Everyone laughed, including Hasan Baba, though he could not resist muttering dire warnings. "The first thing you do with your recovered tongue is to speak blasphemies. Careful lest it be taken away from you again."

"Speaking of tongues, Father," said Salman with a glint in his eye, "do you recall the remark attributed to Yusuf Pasha, the glorious builder of this beautiful house?"

Iskander Pasha shook his head.

"One day, he was visited by a group of courtiers from Istanbul. They had brought him gifts and honeyed words fell off their tongues with great facility. Yusuf Pasha knew they had come to spy on behalf of the Sultan. The Ruler of the World wanted to know whether his old friend had truly repented so that his exile could be ended. The courtiers, who feared our ancestor's influence, wanted to prevent such a calamity. At first, Yusuf Pasha refused to receive them, but after many entreaties he agreed that they should be allowed into his library, this same room where we have all assembled today. He looked at them sternly and warned them that if they did not repeat his exact words to the Sultan, he would ensure that they were all punished. The courtiers trembled a little, but nodded obsequiously. Then he told them: 'Your visit today has been very welcome, but I have an important piece of advice for you. If you value the life of our Sultan and Caliph, act on it the moment you return. As you all know, I revere and love the Sultan since we grew up together. I am seriously worried about his health. Since your tongues spend so much time up the Sultan's posterior, I am worried that you might infect him with some dangerous disease. I have discussed the matter with my physician and he insists that courtiers in your important positions must have their tongues circumcised without any further delay.'"

I have never seen Iskander Pasha laugh in such an abandoned fashion as he did that night on hearing Salman's joke. Even the Baron, momentarily, lost his poise.

Salman, too, had changed. Like his father, he appeared to be a very different person these days. When he had first arrived here he gave the impression of suffering from a deep inner despair. His whole being had been infected by a cynicism of the coarsest variety. His father's affliction and recovery had rekindled something in him or perhaps it had been his long discussions with Halil or perhaps both had played some part in his recovery. Whatever the cause, the result was a joy. Yesterday he had spent the whole afternoon playing with my children, without once mentioning his own.

The Baron cleared his throat and the room became silent again.

"Iskander has posed your officers an important question, Halil. After the Sultan, what and where? I fear you will lose everything. Ultimately you might be left with Istanbul and Anatolia. Do you agree? Are you prepared to accept a truncated but compact country?"

"No!" said Halil. "We will not lose the Hijaz or Syria. Egypt has already gone. Our Albanian viceroy, Mohammed Ali, saw to that and his Beys control the cities, but the British navy controls the sea and he who controls trade determines how new countries are made. We must keep Damascus at all costs."

"History does not believe in 'musts', my dear man," replied the Baron. "A lot will depend on the British. I think they want it all. The whole region is a route to their most prized possession, India. There, too, the wretched Mughal Emperors failed to lay stable foundations. The story is not as dissimilar to the situation here as one might think. This weakness in statecraft lies at the heart of your religion. We shall see whether or not you retain the Hijaz and Damascus. The tribes will go with whoever offers them more money and less trouble. Your real problem lies in Istanbul, the heart of what is left of the Empire. If no history happens where you are, you forget what history is. You lose all sense of direction. Look at Italy and Germany in the long period before they were unified. That is the fate I foresee for the Ottoman Empire unless you act."

"The only way to save something is through progress and order," said Halil. "That is why the writings of Comte are of interest to us. He advocated a rationalist society without religion playing any role in the functions of the state."

"True enough," said Uncle Memed, "but if I remember well he wanted to create a secular religion, which for me is a contradiction. True, he called it a religion of humanity, but he wanted a Church with rituals and a priesthood of scientists. Hasan Baba's Karmatian forebears were more advanced in some ways, despite their attachment to our religion. Comte did have some good ideas, but he was also a tiny bit deranged."

The Baron chuckled in agreement. "Comte's three favourite secular saints for his new Church were Julius Caesar, Joan of Arc and Dante: the first a tyrant, the second a deluded peasant woman who wanted to be a soldier and the third a great poet. I'm glad Comte appreciated the *Commedia*, but surely we cannot be expected to take this fellow seriously. Like all talented charlatans he attracted many followers, but much of what he wrote was well-intentioned gibberish."

"He also said that one day society would be ruled by banks and the whole of Europe united into a western republic ruled by bankers," Memed added contemptuously. "What could he have been thinking of when he wrote all this rubbish?"

"The pair of you are far too dismissive," said Iskander Pasha. "When I was in Paris, Hasan and I used to disguise ourselves and attend radical gatherings. Comte was very much the fashion. He was seen as a true follower of the Enlightenment. Many people come up with ideas for providing an alternative to religion. Robespierre tried something, did he not? The Mughal King Akbar attempted a new religion in India, of all places. Long before him, in the fourteenth century, our own Sultan Bayezid the First wanted to achieve a union of Islam, Judaism and Christianity. His sons were named Musa, Isa and Memed. When he tried to win over Pope Nicholas to this idea they tried to convert him to Christianity. He then realised his dream was impossible and gave up altogether."

"Yes," said the Baron, "and wasn't it Sultan Bayezid the First who claimed descent from King Priam of Troy?"

"Baron," laughed Iskander Pasha, "before we go any further in discussing the whims of men who ruled us for many centuries, let me ask you two questions. If we act and build a new republic, will Prussia be an ally or an enemy?"

"You mean Germany and, yes, it would be an ally, if only to stop you becoming a bridgehead for our ever-ambitious English friends, who strive hard to deny us our share of trade. They believe the world belongs to them, which is a fatal illusion as all Empires discover sooner or later. There is something else in your favour. Our young Kaiser Wilhelm the Second is a neurotic mystic. For that reason alone he might have been inclined towards Istanbul, but he is also a great enthusiast for the religious and warlike mania exhibited in the operas of a dreadful man named Wagner, who writes bad music and dresses equally badly in a ridiculous beret and a velvet jacket. Our young Emperor has a feverish brain, which gives him too many sleepless nights. He dreams of himself as Parsifal. I think he will wage war against someone. The choice of enemies is not limitless. Will he strike his Russian cousin first or his British cousin? When this war is waged, he will need allies. Does that answer your question? Good."

Memed began to chuckle. "I do not share the Baron's dislike for the music of Wagner. Its structure appeals to me, though I accept it is far more demanding than the simple tunes of these well-meaning but not highly intelligent

Italians. Puccini, Verdi and dear Donizetti Pasha are pleasing enough, but the structure of Wagner's music makes you think. If the Baron were serious he would—"

The Baron looked at his friend with total contempt and raised his hand to silence him. "Some other time, Memed. Now, what is the nature of your second inquiry, Iskander Pasha?"

"You have been mocking our fondness for Comte and I greatly appreciate your scepticism. We all have our weaknesses, my dear Baron. What appeals to us in Comte is not his list of secular saints, but his unyielding rationalism. It is the clergy that provided our Sultans with the moral power to impede progress for so long. It is pointless decapitating a single head, when the beast we confront is double-headed. Halil, you see, has a real problem. Some of his subordinates are very hot-headed. The situation demands that they are taught the art of patience. But in order to calm them, one must have a master-plan with some chance of success. He has come to us for help because next week he will be visited here by six of these young firebrands. Our choices have moved beyond the luxury of a relaxed intellectual debate within the confines of this library. The lives of others depend on what advice we offer my son. He was very happy when he became a general, but he never realised that one day his men might call on him to wage a war against the enemy at home, including the very people who had made him a general. My father would have advised him either to turn in the traitors or resign his post and rest for a few months in Alexandria. Some years ago, in my role as a responsible father and a pillar of the state I, too, might have said something similar, but those times have gone, Baron. Now do you understand what is at stake?"

The Baron became pensive. He had realised that this had not been intended as an evening of clever talk where his rapier intelligence could outwit all of us. Halil stressed the urgency of what his father had just said.

"If not Comte, then who? Hegel?"

"No, no. Definitely not Hegel." His tone had changed. He was no longer trying to impress, but had become reflective. "I think the man of the hour for your officers is someone they will never even have heard of, let alone read. I am thinking of an Italian by the name of Niccolò Machiavelli. He is the great thinker of politics and statecraft. You need him badly at this moment."

"How ridiculous you are, Baron," said Memed. "Of course we've heard of Machiavelli. There was a vigorous exchange between the Ottomans and Renaissance Italy. Did you know that the Sultan had asked Leonardo and Michelangelo to design a bridge across the Bosporus?"

"This is a serious discussion, Memed." The Baron's tone was frosty. "Let us leave diversions, however pleasant, for another day. If nothing changes here soon you might even lose your beloved Bosporus. Many people may well have heard of Machiavelli, but how many have read him, how many have understood what he was really writing about all those years ago? Anyone here excepting me? No, I thought not, and I'm not surprised. I would have been one of you had I not been a pupil of Hegel's successors. I only read Machiavelli because Hegel wrote of him with such respect in his celebrated 1802 text 'On the German Constitution'. It was that essay by Hegel that made me want to read the object of such unstinting admiration."

"We will study closely whatever books have to be read, Baron," said Halil with impatience. "What you need is to explain: why this Italian and why now?"

"This evening has become too heavy for me," said Memed. "I'm not sure I can stay awake for the lecture on Machiavelli that the Baron is preparing to deliver. Halil's men are preparing a revolution and all we offer them is ideas."

The Baron glared at him. "Perhaps you should retire to bed in your crimson silk pyjamas and dream of Michelangelo hovering over the Bosporus, Memed, while I stay here with Halil to help save your country. Without a goal based on ideas, all radical action is meaningless."

Nobody left the room. I exchanged glances with Selim, who had been completely engrossed by the discussion this evening.

"I'm sure I forced Memed and Iskander to read Hegel's essay when I was a young tutor in their Istanbul house all those centuries ago. Can either of you remember the opening sentence?"

Memed looked away in disgust. Iskander Pasha raised his hand as if he were in class.

"Good," said the Baron. "Iskander?"

"*Deutschland ist kein Staat mehr.*"

"Excellent," said the Baron, imagining he was a tutor once again. "That's correct. *Deutschland ist kein Staat mehr.* Germany is a state no longer. The Ottoman Empire is a state no longer. Italy was a state no longer. A new state was necessary to move forward. Machiavelli's prince is the state. This great and original Italian philosopher of politics observes the reality of Italy as it is and not as some imagine it. What he sees is a split and divided country, permanently vulnerable to attack by foreign powers. Not exactly the same, but not so different from the split and divided Empire, confronting an assault by foreign states. Machiavelli's greatness lies in this fact: he does not resort to the past, to antiquity, to plan a new future. He sees it all in the present and understands that something new is required . . ."

And the Baron continued in this vein for a whole hour.

When the discussion ended it was close to midnight. Everyone had been transfixed, except Hasan Baba, who had fallen asleep, and me. I knew I had to stay awake because this was a moment of some importance. History was being made in my presence. But there was also another restraint on my natural inclinations. If I shut my eyes I would no longer be able to see Selim.

This house, isolated and beautiful, had suddenly, unexpectedly, become part of a larger world. We could no longer hide ourselves from the ugliness of the reality that confronted us outside. One phrase that the Baron had continually used from Machiavelli – "it is an evil not to call evil an evil" – had reverberated in my head the whole evening. Sometimes when the Baron moved on to a more abstract level, this little phrase kept returning to me. It could apply to anything, not simply the world of politics.

Later that night I was in a light sleep when I heard the door open. Uncertain whether or not I was dreaming, I saw a familiar figure undress and slip into my bed. At first I thought it was still a dream, but the hard object that gently prodded me below the stomach was only too real. Selim had entered me, turning some inconsequential dream into an existence that was pure bliss.

THIRTEEN

Salman meditates on love and talks of the tragedy that blemished his life; his cruel betrayal by Mariam, the daughter of the Copt diamond merchant Hamid Bey in Alexandria

'Am I really the first man to appear before you, Stone Woman? When I told my sister Zeynep that I needed to speak with you she became openly hostile and contemptuous: "Why are you desecrating what has been a sanctuary for the women of this house?"

I had to remind her firmly that, as children, it was not the girls alone who hid behind the rocks to eavesdrop on our guilt-stricken mothers and aunts and servants. Halil and I were always here as well. On hearing this she smiled and relented a little and, as a result, I come to you, after almost twenty-five years, with the reluctant permission of my sister.

If you thought that this light-hearted return to your side indicated that I was once again the carefree boy of my youth, you would be wrong. I am tormented, Stone Woman. Over the last five years my soul has experienced far too many dark nights.

Hasan Baba always taught us that without the experience of darkness one can never properly appreciate the light, but there is another side to this profundity. What if the darkness never goes and light becomes a distant memory? I have heard that in parts of the world where the sun almost disappears during the winter, there are many people who find it unbearable and take their own lives. The same is true of the inner darkness that can sometimes smother the soul.

Since you have never heard my story, I suppose I should begin at the beginning. I will not dwell too long on my mother, who died bringing me into this world. Others must have mentioned her to you and told of how her death transformed my father completely. To avoid thinking of her, he became a person who could never have thought of her or been attracted by someone like her. Each of us has an instinct for masquerade and self-transformation. It gives some pleasure to know we are capable of it and it helps to deceive prying eyes. My father, unfortunately, took the self-deception so far that he almost began to believe in his new identity. I was the one who suffered the most. For Iskander Pasha, I must have become a dual reminder of her and the unwitting cause of her death. What my brother and sisters don't know is that often when he saw me alone as a child, he would lift me off the ground and kiss my cheeks with great feeling. I always knew he loved me, but another side of him wished to punish me and as I grew older, so did my acts of defiance against the petty tyrannies of his household, and our relations deteriorated. From the age of fourteen onwards I wanted to run away from this family. I envied my mother, who had been brought up without a family, and grew up as a freer spirit than any of us.

The moment I was presented with an opportunity, I left Istanbul and after travelling for a year, I ended up in Alexandria. I had spent many months in Jerusalem, Damascus and Cairo, but none of them appealed as a residence. Jerusalem was too religious and the other cities, despite their charms, were far too noisy and too remote from the sea. I was bemoaning the loss of the sea one day, when an arrogant young Bey said to me: "If our delicate little flower from Istanbul wilts without a sea breeze why does he not go and live in Iskanderiya? Personally, I can't bear it for more than two weeks each summer, but there's no accounting for Ottoman tastes. Go and live in our house as long as you like, Salman Pasha, and if you like the city then find yourself a place to live."

That was how I happened to settle down in a city that bore my father's name. Is it possible to fall in love with a place, Stone Woman? It is. I did. I used to walk for hours each day, till I came to know every corner of Alexandria. To escape the noise of the morning, I would walk away from the city and find refuge near the sea. I had seen a tiny cove on one of my walks and this became my very own and special retreat. I would come here for the early part of the day, before the sun made it impossible to look up at the sky. My only friend in those days was a copy of Verlaine. I would gaze at the sea, dream of happiness, think about my life and sometimes find amusement in writing bad poetry. One of the easiest things in the world, Stone Woman, is to write bad poetry. Has anyone ever told you that before?

The important thing was that I found what I had craved for all these years. I was on my own. Solitude, I discovered, is essential for the mind to gauge its own strength. It is true that a solitary existence has its drawbacks. The satisfaction we feel at not being injured by contact with others is sometimes negated by the sadness that can overcome us because we have only ourselves. This is again very different from the solitude that was forced on me some years later. The sense of loss I suffered made my life a continuous agony of loneliness. Even in the company of my friends, to say nothing of strangers, I felt completely alone.

My money supply was beginning to contract. As always, my Uncle Kemal responded generously. Before I left he had made me promise that if I was in financial difficulty, I was always to approach him and not worry my father. This suited me perfectly. I sent Uncle Kemal a telegram, thanking our stars that the Empire had agreed to install the telegraph system. A few weeks later one of his ships touched port at Alexandria. The captain called on me with a small, sealed packet. I thanked him, offered him some coffee and asked if he knew my uncle's plans. To my amazement he informed me that Uncle Kemal was preparing to visit Japan and set up an office in Tokyo.

The minute he left, I quickly undid the packet and found, to my delight, a medium-sized, uncut stone nestling in cotton wool. I did wonder then why Uncle Kemal was so fond of me. I had never attempted to cultivate his affection. He had three daughters, each uglier and more stupid than the other, so perhaps I was a surrogate son. There had been other hints, but I had made it very clear to his wife, my aunt, that I was not in the least interested in any of her daughters as a possible wife. My uncle had laughed on being told this.

There was also a letter of credit to my uncle's bankers in Cairo and a note for me which recommended that I should use the diamond as surety and not, under any circumstances, sell it without first consulting him. He had sent me the name of "a small, but very reliable" diamond merchant in Alexandria, with whom he had often "done business. He is a Copt, very trustworthy and an old family friend. Go to him if ever you're in trouble". He had told me of this person before I left Istanbul, but since I had no plans at that time to visit Alexandria, I had not shown any interest. When I finally did reach here I remembered my uncle's friend, but I had forgotten his name and felt that if I sent for his address from my old office, it might burden me with tiresome social responsibilities. I remained aloof. I could let nothing breach my solitude. Nothing except the shortage of funds.

The journey to the house could be delayed no longer. I went there one day straight from the beach and a fairy princess opened the door. She burst out laughing at the sight of me. I had sand on my clothes and hair, sandals on my feet and a tattered copy of Verlaine in my hand. "Have I come to the right house?" I stammered, unable to stop my eyes from travelling her entire body. "Does Hamid Bey live here?"

She nodded and invited me into the house. She had deep black hair, an olive complexion and small eyes, which made me wonder whether her mother was Japanese. She was wearing a European-style dress, which revealed the lower parts of her legs, but what had delighted me the most was her laugh and the fact that her feet were bare.

"You caught us by surprise," she said. "My father is taking a bath at the moment. Are you Salman Pasha? We were expecting you one of these days. Can I offer you a drink? I hope you will join us for lunch. If you will excuse me, however, I must go and change my dress. Please feel at home."

It was my turn to laugh. She disappeared without asking me to explain the cause of my amusement. Do you know why I laughed, Stone Woman? Their house could not have be more unlike home. In Istanbul we lived in the eighteenth century, and here, in Yusuf Pasha's summer palace by the sea, time lost all meaning. The house in Alexandria was very much ahead of its time. I had never seen such elegant furniture in Istanbul, not even in the house of the Bragadinis. They, too, preferred to live in the past, but here was the latest furniture from Italy. In the hall there was a large Chinese chest. Everything was new. As I was admiring the decorations on the walls,

Hamid Bey came down the stairs in a white silk suit and greeted me warmly. He must have been approaching sixty, but was extremely well preserved and surprisingly slender, unlike my father and uncles who were all on the portly side.

I thought it might be best to get our business over with before lunch. I showed him the gift from my uncle. He took it to his desk and inspected it under a microscope. "It is a very good stone. I assume you wish to use it to raise some money for whatever project you are preparing at the moment?" My only project was to enjoy life to the full and it was for that I needed the money, so I nodded and smiled. "I trust Kemal Pasha more than my own brother. You did not need to show me the stone. How much do you need to borrow?" Without thinking I named a figure. He told me to return the next day and collect the money.

When his daughter came down for lunch a transformation had taken place. She looked demure, was far less relaxed and more traditionally attired in a yellow tunic that touched the floor and leather sandals, which, to my great annoyance, hid her naked feet. Her face, if anything, appeared stern. I hoped it was only her father's presence that was responsible for the change.

"This is my daughter, Mariam. She has managed the affairs of this house ever since her mother's absence."

Nothing more was said of the mother and it was not till many months later that Mariam told me the whole story. Our conversation during lunch was polite. My Arabic not being as fluent as that of Hamid Bey and Mariam and their Turkish being non-existent, I lapsed into French. The pleasure on her face was visible. She never had the opportunity to practise and perfect her knowledge of the language and was excited by the fact that I spoke it so well.

Stone Woman, I know that nothing surprises or shocks you. That is why so many have sat in your presence over centuries and spoken to their heart's content.

On that very first day, while I was having lunch at her father's table and as his honoured guest, I fell for this creature. Love can never be planned like a book of accounts. You cannot say to yourself: this person meets all the conditions I have laid down for falling in love. She has features that are attractive. She is well-spoken, but will not speak out of turn. She has a reasonable dowry. She will bear me healthy children. I will, therefore, proceed to fall in love with her.

I have known merchants who measure love as they do their trade; physicians who feel their own pulse to make sure they are in love; philosophers who constantly doubt their own love; gardeners who think love grows like a fruit and egotists who can never love anyone else. Don't misunderstand me, Stone Woman. I am not saying that love does not grow, deepen and become stronger with each passing year. That is all true, but for that to happen it is important how it begins. In my book there is only one true beginning. All others are false. Love must strike one like lightning. That is what happened to me eight years ago on that pleasant summer afternoon as the sea breezes wafted through the house of the Copt merchant, Hamid Bey. Mariam had barely turned eighteen. I was approaching my thirty-second year.

I returned the next day to collect my money. An old woman with a cross hanging ominously from her wrinkled neck opened the door and informed me in a very formal voice that Hamid Bey had left for Cairo on business. He would be away for several days. He had left an envelope, which she would now hand to me, and would I please return in ten days' time, when her master would be back in the city. The old crone must have seen the disappointment on my face, for it registered a degree of pleasure on her own. I stood there, paralysed and despondent.

Before I could think of saying anything, Mariam came running into the house from the terrace, slightly out of breath, but, Heaven be praised, bare-footed. My heart melted at the sight of her feet.

She shouted at the old woman, "I told you to send for me when Salman Pasha arrived." The retainer shrugged her shoulders in disgust and left the room.

Mariam turned to me. "Ignore her, Salman Pasha. She is over-protective and impolite. She's been in my father's family for centuries and really enjoys being discourteous. She hated my mother. Should we go and sit on the terrace? Would you like a fresh lime drink? Have you brought any French books with you? Why are you laughing?"

I do not have the strength to live through the entire experience again, not even for you, Stone Woman. Some of the memories are so pure and sweet that they would make me weep. I would become weak and love her again and all would be lost. It would be like falling into the abyss, but never hitting the ground – the worst possible nightmare. I am determined, whatever the cost, to avoid such a calamity. For that reason and that alone I will quicken the pace of this narrative.

Hamid Bey's stay in Cairo was extended beyond a week. Mariam and I would meet every day, but never after sunset. The crone with the cross had expressly forbidden that, and Mariam felt it foolish and unnecessary to defy the restriction. Wherever we were in that large house, I began to feel we were being watched, and Mariam began to feel the same. We were being suffocated. I told her of my secret cove. Her eyes grew large at the thought of an adventure. She would send for Maria, for that is what the crone had been christened, instruct her to make us some coffee and while she was in the kitchen, we would run away from the house like thieves with our French books firmly tucked under our arms. Mariam, too, fell in love with the little cove, where we were completely alone.

We declared our love for each other on that day. She, too, admitted that the sight of me with sand on my hair had touched her greatly though she was sure it must have been the sight of Verlaine that had created the lightning effect. We kissed and caressed each other. We discarded our clothes and swam in the sea. We dried ourselves and read aloud to each other. I delighted in each part of her body described in this verse from Verlaine's love poem, "Spring":

Beauteous thighs, upright breasts,
The back, the loins and belly, feast
For the eyes and prying hands
And for the lips and all the senses?

The poem excited us even more, but I did not possess her, even though she was prepared to sacrifice her virginity and I was by now in the grip of a white-hot passion. I ached for her. My testicles were hurting, desperate for the fluid to be released, but I resisted her. Why? Because making love to her would have been a violation of her father's hospitality. Strange, isn't it, Stone Woman, how old traditions and habits become so deeply embedded in our minds and how difficult it is to uproot them? She was enraged when I confessed this to her and began to curse all Pashas and Pashadoms and declared herself to be a free citizen in the Republic of Love. She became cruel in her mockery. She also made me laugh a great deal. I had never met anyone like her.

When Hamid Bey returned to Alexandria, and before Maria could pour poison in his ears, I asked for Mariam's hand in marriage. I told

Hamid Bey I wanted nothing else. I was not interested in a dowry. We would be married and live on our own. I had thought he might ask me to wait a year or, at least, six months and in some other city to determine whether my affection was real or transient, but he had no such doubts. "I felt from the first day you lunched with us that Mariam and you were ideally matched. You have my blessing. As you know I am a Copt. I would like the wedding to be in church. When you take her to Istanbul you can have another ceremony."

My heart was so filled with joy that I laughed. "Hamid Bey, I would marry her anywhere. As you know, I am not a believer. The actual ceremony is of no consequence to me."

Hamid Bey did not wish to delay the matter any further. I had no desire to inform any member of my family, with the exception of Uncle Kemal. The telegram I despatched to his office was firm on one point. I told him that the news was for him *alone*. I did not wish to receive messages from anyone in Istanbul. He sent me a telegram of congratulations and wrote that he accepted my request for secrecy, but in return he insisted that the house I was buying must be a joint wedding gift from Hamid Bey and himself. Stone Woman, I accepted their kindness. After all, it was a house they were offering me, not a camel herd. I did, however, firmly turn down the offer of Maria as our housekeeper. Some sacrifices are simply unacceptable.

Within two weeks Mariam and I were together. These were times of real happiness for both of us, but now when I look back even on that early period I remember episodes that at the time seemed insignificant or even childish.

All of us have different aspects to our character, Stone Woman. It would be unnatural if this was not so, but Mariam was a deeply contradictory woman. In a way I think she really would have preferred Hamid Bey to deny us permission to marry. In her eyes that would have been a test of my love. Would I have run away with her to some other part of the world? My affirmative responses had little real effect on her because it was something that could never be proved. At other times she would say: "I hate it when you're too happy with me. I prefer you when you're sad." I never fully understood why and when I questioned her about this later she denied she had ever said anything of the sort.

It was a long time after the festivities that she explained why Hamid Bey had been in such a hurry. He knew that if there had been a long engagement, it would have been difficult, if not impossible, to prevent her mother's attendance.

Her mother, Arabella, was the daughter of an English plantation owner and his Chinese mistress, who lived in the British colony of Malaya. Her father, who was unmarried, recognised her and she had grown up in the plantation house, but without her mother, who saw her once or twice a week. Later she was sent to study in Britain. Mariam loved and hated her mother. The words in which she told me the story reflected this duality.

On her way back home from London Arabella was overcome by an urge to see the pyramids at Giza. The ship's captain telegraphed Singapore and her father agreed. She disembarked at Alexandria. Her father had friends here and had informed them that his headstrong child was on her way. An old couple (now dead) had arrived at the pier to receive her. She was always a spoilt child and took everything for granted. In her photograph she appears to be an Englishwoman. In real life her complexion was slightly darker, but she never wanted to be mistaken for a hybrid. That's why what happened in Egypt astonished everyone.

Hamid Bey had sighted her at a private dinner, where she confessed her desire to see the Sphinx. He offered to organise her tour and a chaperone. But he was smitten with her and followed her everywhere. Hamid Bey is still a striking man. Twenty years ago, he must have been irresistible. She was flattered by his attention, amused by his jokes, impressed by his wealth and attracted by his body. He proposed. She accepted. Her father sent numerous telegrams forbidding the match, but she was of age and in a defiant mood. Her hosts told her she could not possibly marry an Egyptian. She walked out of their house, declaring that she was half-Chinese and proud of the fact. Everyone knew, of course, but it was never mentioned since everything about her appeared to be English.

Another small problem arose. Hamid Bey comes from a Copt family which traces its descent back over a thousand years. They were already upset that he was defiling the purity of his family by marrying an Englishwoman, but his mother was close to tears when Hamid Bey proudly told his mother that he, too, would have been doubtful if Arabella had been completely English, but the fact she was half Chinese had greatly reassured him.

For Mariam's grandmother, the Chinese did not exist except as figures that appeared on the screens she sometimes bought from Italian furniture shops. She probably thought that the whole Chinese race was a comic invention. Hamid Bey got very angry. He screamed at his mother. Then he calmed down and gave her a lecture on Chinese civilisation. They had invented the compass, gunpowder, printing, and so on.

They were married quickly. Mariam was born. Her mother was bored. Hamid Bey was travelling a great deal in those days. She led an aimless life. She read little, was not really interested in Egypt or its history and soon began to resent the fact that she was no longer invited to European homes. Soon she started seeing a new set of people. They were non-official Europeans and they met at one club in particular, but usually at each other's houses to drink gin and play cards. One day she met an Englishman on his way to India. She left her husband and daughter without even a note. Mariam was eleven years old at the time. Her mother wrote to her once saying that she had never really loved Hamid and that true passion was a wonderful experience, which she hoped Mariam would discover one day. Mariam did not see her again, though the two exchanged letters and Arabella sent money every month. She went on to have two more children, whose photographs Mariam has never asked to see, for fear of upsetting Hamid Bey.

It was unbearable for her to witness the decline in her father. He became a mere shadow. They would eat together, discuss books, meet friends, but the joy had gone out of his life. Arabella's room was left just as it had been on the day she left. Her clothes remained in the cupboard for many years. That dress Mariam wore the first time she and I met, which I liked so much, belonged to Arabella. Later Mariam emptied the room, gave most of her mother's things away, kept a few for herself and transformed it into a library. She told her father that books were the one item that would never remind him of his wife. He smiled.

Then he went with Uncle Kemal Pasha on a long journey to Japan. He returned a different man. Mariam had no idea what happened or what he experienced, but he became more like his old self. They began to entertain in their house again. Once she tried to speak with him about her mother. His face became lined with pain and he whispered that she had died a long time ago. Mariam never raised the subject again.

The aspect of this story that struck me as peculiar, Stone Woman, did not concern Hamid Bey. His feelings were natural. The only surprise in his case is that he never married again. What puzzled me was Mariam's own reaction to her mother. In her tone there was always a mixture of anger and admiration. She had been abandoned. That made her angry. But her mother had put love and passion before all else and Mariam had forced herself to admire this side of her mother. I suppose it was the only way she could deal with the betrayal.

The thought that a woman who had done this to her only child was selfish beyond redemption was something that occurred to her but it was always put out of her mind. The result was a deep ambivalence in Mariam's own character. She developed a real fear of commitment. The experience of losing her mother at a young age had wounded her deeply and the scars never disappeared. To me, who had never known a mother, it was incredible that in all our time together she never once evinced the slightest desire to see her mother again. I was more curious than she was and offered to take her to India, but she was angry with me for the suggestion. It would, she said, be an act of betraying her father and he had suffered more than enough in a single lifetime.

After a year and a half she had still not conceived and this made her very unhappy. She wanted children for more reasons than a normal woman in her position. Her own family and children would help her forget what her mother had done to her, and she became so desperate that it began to affect our relationship.

One day she said, "Perhaps it is your seed that is defective. I should find another man." She would start crying after she made remarks of this nature, hug me warmly and plead forgiveness. I was not angry at that time, Stone Woman, just sad. To find a woman whom you love so much that she becomes part of your very being and you learn to share everything – joys, sorrows, victories, defeats, good times and bad – is this not rare for men as well as women?

She became pregnant in our third year together and then again the following year. I have rarely seen her so happy. She became absorbed in the children and would take them to visit Hamid Bey every week, sometimes spending the whole day in the big house. Her interest in me had diminished considerably. I remember on one occasion when Uncle Kemal was passing through Alexandria and stayed as our guest, she became extremely irrational when he kissed the children and gave them each a tiny little purse with a gold coin. It was when he began to speak to them with great affection and as a great-uncle that I first noticed her face. When Uncle Kemal said, "Your grandfather Iskander Baba will be so pleased to see you one day", I saw Mariam's face darken with anger and she left the room in a rage. I was genuinely amazed. It was inexplicable.

After Uncle Kemal left I tried to discuss her behaviour with her, but my remarks only provoked a tirade against my family. She spoke of why she did not want her children to be taken over by the Pashas of Istanbul; of how there was degeneration and madness in my family and she manufactured numerous other complaints. Given the extent of my own alienation from the family, I found her conduct pathetic and unreasonable.

Even at this stage I made excuses for her irrationality. I convinced myself that she was merely being extra possessive because having lost her mother, she was now fearful of losing the children. Who knows how long I would have continued deluding myself, Stone Woman? But fate took pity on me.

One day, while taking my afternoon walk by the sea, I was approached by a European woman dressed in black and wearing a hat with an attached veil. She was clearly distressed and asked if I was "Signor Salman Pasha, the son-in-law of Hamid Bey". I acknowledged my identity, whereupon she insisted on speaking with me urgently and immediately. I asked her to accompany me to a less crowded section of the promenade. We sat down and she began to sob. The memory still upsets me and I will not dwell on it too long, but she told me the truth, Stone Woman, even though I only half-believed her at the time. I may sound calm now as I talk to you about all this, but at the time what she told me made me want to die. The sky and the sea went dark. The people walking in front of us became shadows. My mind became numb. The Italian lady told me that I was not the father of our children. Her husband was their real father. It emerged that she was married to the son of the furniture-maker who supplied the needs of the rich in Cairo and Alexandria. The furniture in Hamid Bey's house had been made by them and I now remembered the young man, Marco, who had measured our villa and who visited our house often till the job was done.

His wife described in every painful detail how Mariam had seduced Marco away from her. She knew because she had taken her suspicions to her father-in-law, who had expressed amazement, but instructed an old carpenter to follow his son discreetly. They used to meet in the early afternoon in my little secret cove, where Mariam and I had first tasted each other. I screamed aloud on hearing this detail. She must have been far gone in her depravity that she took such a risk, knowing that I often went there to read and write. Was she hoping I would see her?

Marco's father had forced him to confess this and every other detail. He had been sent first to the confessional and then despatched to work in his uncle's shop in Genoa as a penance. His wife told me that she and her two young daughters were preparing to join him within a month. He now pretended to be remorseful and claimed it was Mariam who had taken the initiative and enchanted him. He had become a slave to her passion. He did not see her before he left, but he told his father that she wanted him to give her another child. Marco's wife referred to Mariam as a loose and crazy woman and said she had come to me with the truth because she had heard that I was also suffering. I doubt that this was her real motive, but I took my leave of her and wished her well in the future.

I have no recollection of what I did after that encounter. When I reached home it was past midnight. I went into my room and sank on the bed. She was in her room but not asleep. Will it shock you, Stone Woman, if I say that my love for her was so strong that even at this stage I was prepared to forgive her? It was, after all, my seed that had failed to sprout. I told myself that if she was so desperate for children, what else could she have done? She came into my room wearing my old grey silk dressing gown and asked why I had been out so late. I looked at her face and found myself overcome with rage. I wanted to hit her, but I controlled my anger.

"Mariam, I knew we had employed the best furniture-makers in town to supply us with tables and chairs and beds. I had no idea that you had asked their carpenter, Marco, to furnish you with children as well."

She was shaken, Stone Woman. Her face became pale and she began to tremble. I spoke to her again. "If only you could see your lying, hypocritical face in the mirror! Are you trembling with fear and guilt? Good! Before I finish with you . . ."

I stopped because she had begun to weep. The sight of her tears had always touched me deeply. I walked to her and began to stroke her face. She reacted to my touch as if I were a leper. Her face was transformed completely. I no longer recognised her as the woman I loved. A strange, scornful smile appeared on her face, a smile of triumph. She was actually pleased at the sight of my misery, glad that I had been humiliated and betrayed. She looked at me with real loathing and said, "My true feelings for you have long been those of disgust and contempt. It is not just that your seed was infertile, but your love had become a punishment for me. I needed to free myself from you and the restraints of this life."

I did not sleep that night. Her pitiless cruelty left me with no choice. I thought of the two beautiful children I adored. It was difficult to think of them as not belonging to me. I was tempted to see their little trusting faces for the last time, but I resisted the urge. I packed a little *valise* and walked out of the house at the first sign of dawn.

The streets were empty. The only noise was that of the seagulls scavenging for food. The beautiful sky was red at the edges and slowly turning pink. I couldn't help contrasting the beauty of nature with the ugliness of what Mariam had done to my life. I walked to Hamid Bey's house. Maria the crone opened the door, clutching her rosary. For the first time she looked at me with sympathy and patted my back as I entered the hall. Perhaps the pain etched on my face attracted her sympathy. Perhaps she knew. Hamid Bey came down the stairs, took one look at me and realised what had happened. He embraced me warmly and asked Maria to bring us some coffee.

I sat down on a large sofa, whose frame had probably been constructed by Marco, and told Hamid Bey the whole story, just as I am telling you, Stone Woman. I hid nothing. I did not spare his feelings. I did not care that she was his daughter. I was bitter and angry. He heard me in complete silence and then said, "She has turned out just like her mother. Leave Alexandria today, my son, and think of Mariam as dead. It will take a few years, but you will recover. I will make sure all your affairs are in order. I do not know what will become of Mariam, but she remains my child and I will provide for her. Perhaps she will move back here with her children. Let that not concern you any longer. Consider yourself free of any responsibilities and re-make your life somewhere else, Salman Pasha."

And with these words he embraced me once again. There was sadness in his eyes as we parted and he muttered a few words almost as if to himself: "She who was the wife of a prince has become the keep of a carpenter."

I left Alexandria the next day on a boat bound for the East. I spent a year in Tokyo, which was so different from our world that it distracted me from the pain and grief I had left behind in Alexandria. The mind has a capacity to relegate unwanted baggage to its most secret recesses. I was never fully cured. Memories of those early days of happiness sometimes came flooding back and I fought hard to drive them away by recalling the ugliness of the last week or the cruel words that she had deployed to kill our love.

My Uncle Kemal was also in that part of the world, expanding his fleet of merchant ships, opening new offices in Tokyo and Shanghai and seeking solace in the arms of his numerous mistresses. I had met one of them in Tokyo. He had decided that there should be no secrets between us and introduced me to her. She was beautiful and, on the surface, submissive in her exquisitely embroidered red silk kimono.

She had prepared a meal for us and I was, frankly, horrified when she sat cross-legged with us on the floor, but did not touch her food till she had fed my Uncle Kemal. She did so with some delicacy. The fish never escaped from the little sticks as she dipped it in a tasty sauce and popped it into my uncle's mouth. I could see why he spent so much time in the East. He had never been happy with his wife. How could such a good-looking man with a passion for finery and a strong sensuality have married a woman with no redeeming qualities? He could never understand why I was puzzled by his choice and would say, with a touch of irritation, "Do you think I would have agreed to the marriage if her dowry had not been able to finance my shipping company? I always loved boats and the sea. So I thought if I had to marry this midget and fertilise her with my sperm, I must make sure the means of escape was always nearby. There are times, Salman, when one is forced to sacrifice long-term happiness in favour of short-term gain. What is really annoying is that all my daughters have inherited their mother's shape, size and stupidity. It will require three very generous dowries to have them removed from the house. I mean, can you imagine anyone, and I really mean anyone, falling in love with any of them? The pity is that I love Istanbul more than your other uncle and your father. Iskander loves Paris. Memed is besotted with Berlin. I have remained faithful to my Istanbul, but the beauty of the city has become associated in my mind with the never-ending ugliness that greets me at home. So I escape and, as you can see, I am happy here. I prefer Tokyo to Shanghai. Here I can submerge myself in the landscape. Shanghai is too noisy and too filthy. I never feel safe in its streets."

I was keen to visit China, Stone Woman, and for many reasons, but Uncle Kemal suggested I return to Istanbul. "They worry about you," he said. "They imagine you are still in Egypt. I think you need them a little now. Solitude cannot help you any more. You can always come back to me later. You have always been like a son to me, but now we have also become friends and this is a rare pleasure at this stage of one's life."

I followed his advice and returned to Istanbul. I was there when my father suffered a stroke and I rushed here with Halil. Remember Halil when he was little? Full of mischief. Who would have thought he would be a general?

When I first came here I was gripped by a severe depression and unable to focus on anything, but the clouds have lifted at last, Stone Woman. My father and I have never been as close as we are now. I love Nilofer's children and soon I will tell her my story so that she knows why I do not speak of "my children". And as for General Halil Pasha, what can I say? He, of all people, has reawakened my youthful interest in politics and history. We are on the verge of big changes, Stone Woman. Everything could be different. The inertia that has always marked our lives could be swept away by a tidal wave of reform. It is in times like these that one realises that there are other joys in this world apart from those of love and union with the beloved.

All will change, Stone Woman, and it will change soon, but I hope you will always remain to provide comfort for those who find it difficult to tolerate pain in silence. ’

FOURTEEN

Nilofer is overcome by longing for Selim and decides to marry him; the Baron refuses to discuss Stendhal on love

News that Iskander Pasha's speech had miraculously returned and he was speaking again without impediment had reached Istanbul. Letters and messages from friends and officials began to arrive here at an alarming rate. Some saw in his recovery the invisible but omnipresent goodness of Allah. Others felt it was a strong omen.

The Grand Vizier himself despatched a special messenger with a letter congratulating Iskander Pasha on his recovery and inviting him, on behalf of the Sultan, to attend an audience at the palace as soon as he returned to the capital. The letter ended with the following sentence: "You will no doubt be amused to hear that the Austrians are running into serious trouble in Serbia. When I informed His Majesty, he smiled and remarked, 'May Allah help those ungodly Serbs to drive the Emperor's soldiers back to Vienna.' I told him that you would appreciate this remark and he very graciously gave me permission to repeat it to you."

After we had all read the letter in turn, Salman rose to his feet and began to mimic the Vizier's servility with exaggerated and slightly vulgar gestures, common to sycophants the world over, while all the time he kept repeating the last sentence over and over again. Everyone present began to laugh, with the exception of poor Zeynep. Her husband worked at the palace as a secretary and was, everyone supposed, loyal to his masters. Even if he had been secretly disgusted with what was taking place he had not informed his wife. Zeynep had been growing more and more alarmed by the goings-on in this house. I think that is why she decided to leave immediately for Istanbul – or it may have been that she was missing her children and felt that since Iskander Pasha had recovered fully, there was no need for her to remain here any longer.

She left the next day after an emotional farewell. She hugged Halil with extra warmth, whispering words of warning in his ear and advising caution in whatever he had undertaken. Out of all of us Zeynep was the easiest to please. She was happy with her husband, whom we all regarded as dull beyond endurance and whose premature baldness was a source of great amusement to my father. She was happy with her children and her home and she was even tolerant of her mother-in-law, regarded widely as one of the most poisonous women in Istanbul. Her malicious lies were so well known that her name had become a byword for mendacity in the bazaar. Shopkeepers hated her because she continued to haggle long after they had reached their lowest price. Even my brother Halil, the mildest of men, was heard to remark that he would contribute generously to make up a heavy purse in order to hire a few bandits to kidnap and lose her in Albania. To his horror and my father's delight news of this remark, too, spread in the city and Halil received three letters from the richest shopkeepers offering to pay any amount of money if he would take on the responsibility of organising the actual abduction. Zeynep knew all this, but preferred to maintain a discreet and slightly sad silence. She knew that if she had joined us, life at home would become unbearable. She had to face this woman every single day.

I was preoccupied with my own problems. While the children were beginning to recover from the shock of their father's death, helped by the love of my mother, Halil and, even more, my lovely brother Salman, I had become very deeply involved with Selim. I had never known anything like this before and there were times when I was frightened by the intensity of the relationship. Frightened not by him, but myself and how dependent on him I had become. I longed for his presence. I yearned for his passion. There were days when we could not meet and I would think of him all the time. Sometimes, to reassure myself that I was in control of the situation, I would neglect him quite callously and we would squabble. He would get very upset and the anguish lengthened his face. It may sound cruel on my part, but sometimes I preferred to see him sad rather than happy. It was the only way I could assert my power over him. He could never understand that my behaviour was intended to test myself and not him. Was I really in love with him or was it simply his sensual presence? I was sure his love for me was real, even though I had no idea where it would lead us and how it would end. I had never swum in such a sea of love before and I was frightened that I might drown.

The children alone were capable of distracting my attention. They had to be loved, looked after and settled in bed every night. At these moments nothing else mattered to me. Orhan and Emineh were the two most important things in my life. But the minute I left their presence, Selim would instantly enter my head and I would be overpowered by longing.

He had already been here for three weeks and Hasan Baba had begun to grumble and moan and had berated him for leaving his shop in Istanbul untended. Selim would argue that the children were freshly orphaned and Orhan, in particular, needed his company. This was true. Orhan had become very attached to Selim and the two of them would go for a long walk every day, while my mother and her maids fussed over Emineh, doing and redoing her hair in several different styles and showing her the mirror to get her approval. But Hasan Baba was not convinced and threatened to request Iskander Pasha to instruct Selim to return to Istanbul.

He had told me all this a few nights ago. He had never felt any fear at the prospect of being discovered. It did not bother him at all. He would laugh at the thought and tell me that if ever we were caught *in flagrante,* there would be no choice for me but to marry him. I was not yet convinced that this was the best solution. Orhan and Emineh might react badly. My mother might withhold her permission. The romance of elopement begins to fade when there are children involved.

What could I do in this situation? I knew from my own experience with the unfortunate Dmitri as well as the experiences of a number of my women friends that, often, grand passion burns itself away and the couple who mistook it for a deep and lasting love realise one day that they have nothing to say and do after they have briefly enjoyed each other's bodies. The discovery discomfits them because they had always believed their love to be unique and special. They were not like other people. When they finally admit that there is nothing left, they run away from each other and the place where the love originated, as rapidly as the coachmen can drive them. All the letters written late at night but never posted are now hurriedly destroyed. If, some years later, they run into each other by accident at a wedding or funeral or in a shop buying presents for their children or lover, the only emotion they feel is one of embarrassment.

I say all these things to convince myself that this time I must not rush into anything and yet I know that it was never like this with Dmitri and that if I push Selim aside, I might be punishing myself rather than him. I doubt whether I could feel such a love for anyone again. There are times when I am bewildered by the calm he exhibits in the present situation. There are other questions which for him are more important than our love and, in a curious way, I find that reassuring.

The last time we made love, he stayed in bed afterwards discussing the dangers of a military uprising against the Sultan unless the ordinary people were aroused to defend their own interests. I did not know what he meant. The bewildered look on my face silenced him. He held me very tenderly in his arms and explained. "Nilofer, there are rich and poor in this world. The poor are many and the rich are few. Their interests have never coincided. Both rich and poor need to get rid of the Sultan, but what will happen after they succeed? Will we find another Sultan whom we will call a President, but who will wear a uniform? Or will we found a party as they have in Germany and France which fights for the poor?"

I had never thought of these matters before and I found them dull, but for him they were the subterranean dynamos that charged every fibre of his body.

For over an hour, I had been sitting outside on the terrace watching the changing colours of the sky, while my mind was whirling with ideas and possibilities. When Zeynep left that morning it had just begun to rain. Even now, though the sky remained cloudy, the tiny strip of blue that had marked the horizon since the morning had been growing by the hour. I had observed it at various intervals throughout the day. The clouds had now begun to disperse in strange shapes and the setting sun at the edge of the sea was painting them different shades of pink, red and purple. The effect was sensational, and suddenly this raw natural beauty made me want to share my life with Selim. The thought grew stronger and stronger, till I went in search of Salman. I found him strolling in the lower section of the garden, where steps lead to the sea. He, too, had been admiring the sunset. I did not pause for reflection. I told him the story of my love as we walked up and down the terraced garden. He did not interrupt me, not even once, but waited till I had finished telling everything, which I did, including the fact that Selim often entered the house in search of my bedroom and my body.

Salman smiled as he embraced my shoulders. "I think it is dangerous to continue in this fashion any longer. I will talk to Halil to see if our young friend can be recruited into the army as an officer this week. Then I shall talk to Father on your behalf and you must tell your mother at the same time. I think that through such a combined operation we could achieve instant success. But tell me something, my little one. Are you very sure this time?"

I nodded. "When we were first together it was as if a stroke of lightning had passed through our bodies at the same time."

He laughed. "I know something about this lightning. You must never let it burn you. Never forget that its effects are not always permanent. Lightning comes differently at different times. You can be unstruck by it as well."

"I know that," I replied. "But with us it becomes more and more intense every day. It is not simply the passion, Salman. We are close in so many different ways and he is genuinely fond of Orhan. There is a natural affinity between us. Is that not truly rare?"

"Yes, it is, but how can there be a natural affinity when you had no idea as to the identity of Auguste Comte?" he teased. "You might have to change your reading habits."

And then my brother told me his story. When he had finished he saw the tears pouring down my cheeks and he embraced me.

"I stopped weeping a long time ago, Nilofer. You mustn't start now. Life is full of pain and suffering, but there is always a way out. Always. Once you stop thinking that, you are doomed. I was on the edge of self-destruction. Everything appeared out of focus and I could no longer see the sharp outlines of my future. It was Hamid Bey and my Uncle Kemal who saved my life. I can never repay them for such a favour. Now I am at peace with myself and waiting impatiently for our world to change."

"Do you never think of her?"

"No."

"That frightens me, Salman. How could it all have gone away when you once loved her so much? If love is so ephemeral and transient, what hope is there for us?"

"It did not go away of its own accord. She plunged a dagger through my heart. The love simply bled away. The wounds remained for a long time, but they have healed now. When I think of that episode in my life I feel angry with myself, not her. It was I who misjudged her. You know, I have this strange instinct that she would have done this even if the children had been mine. There was a streak of pure masochism in her. I do not wish her any harm, let alone those poor children. The only person I miss in Alexandria is Hamid Bey. He is such a warm human being and I hope he has found true peace at last. Why is there so much unhappiness in our lives?"

When one is feeling happy it is not possible to answer such questions and I moved the conversation in another direction.

"Salman, there is something else I have to ask you."

He looked at me and smiled. "Today has been declared the day when family secrecy was abolished. Ask and you shall hear the truth."

"Did you know my mother Sara's story?"

A worried frown appeared on his forehead. "I know your mother Hatije's story."

"It is the same story."

"I disagree."

"Why?"

"Sara loved another man who abandoned her. Hatije is your mother and my father's wife."

"You are wrong, Salman. Sara is my mother and Hatije is your father's wife."

"We heard all that years ago, but Father loved you so much as a child that it killed the gossip instantly. A maid in the employ of Halil's mother was dismissed for spreading vile rumours. If Iskander Pasha had been unhappy, this household would have talked of you and your real father without pause and your mother's life would have been a misery. That never happened. Instead we were lucky to have a beautiful child in the house and one who looked so different. What we all loved about you as a child was your strong character. I sometimes wish Zeynep was a bit more like you. That girl has learnt to suffer in silence, which is never good for anyone. Enough family talk for one day. I will go and find our General to discuss your future. You should take yourself immediately to the library and study some Comte. It can only enhance your happiness!"

We were laughing as we walked towards the house. It had suddenly become dark, but the clouds had disappeared and stars were beginning to fill the evening sky. Outside the door, we paused for a moment to gaze at them.

Salman sighed. "One memory will always stay with me. When I was fleeing Alexandria and heading for Japan, our boat reached the line of the Equator. It was a warm night, but it was very late and all of us were in our cabins. The captain had seen the sight many times, but there must have been some poetry in his soul. He weighed anchor and ordered us on deck. Never in my life have I seen the sky as it was that night. It was truly as if we were on the edge of the world. The sky was like a sea of stars and they were rolling past us at an incredible speed. I knew then that I was going to recover. Compared to the universe our emotions are as nothing."

A few minutes later, on my own, I reflected on Salman's tragedy. There were aspects of it that would haunt me for a long time. Everything had turned out wrong for him and yet, despite the grief, he had recovered his life. He had reverted to being the thoughtful and generous person I had known as a child. His own mother had died giving birth to him. He had been unable to give his wife a child. Was his seed infertile or had something else, deeper in him, forced him to hold back? Was it a fear that the woman he loved might also die giving birth? I became desperate on his behalf. I wanted him to meet a woman who might bring some real happiness into his life. I wanted him to have at least one child of his own. I did not like the thought of my dearest brother Salman growing old and lonely. There are limits to solitude. Perhaps I was wrong. Perhaps he did not need a fixed companion. Perhaps he would take over Uncle Kemal's mantle and travel for the rest of his life, a free spirit, finding comfort wherever it became available and not thinking too much of the past or the future.

After the children were safe in bed, I went to my mother's room. I told her of my decision to marry Selim. The news did not shake her serenity.

"I knew this would happen. I hope this one works better for you, though you are still young and might yet have a third chance."

When I saw she was serious I burst out laughing. "I appreciate that your confidence in my judgement has been shaken, Mother, but please give me some credit. I would not make the same mistake twice. I have thought about it very carefully and asked myself the most searching questions. I am not drifting into this in a trance. My head and my thoughts are clear. I know I will be happy with Selim. I just know, Mother. I'm sure this time."

"I hope so, my child. You are not alone. There are two children whose lives are involved in your decision. I don't want you to be like the camel who went to demand horns and found instead the ears he already had were shorn from him."

I had never heard Sara talk like this before. "Where in heaven's name did you get that from?"

"My grandfather used it a great deal when my mother was a child. He was a Talmudic scholar and often spoke in this language. The camel was always brought into the conversation to stop my uncle taking risks and finding he had no money left. It never happened like that, of course. My Uncle Sifrah is one of the richest private bankers in Europe. The Sultan often borrows money from him."

"Then he won't be rich for too much longer, Mother. Better warn him to get his money back and move to Paris or New York."

"Why do you talk like that? It's not my business. Now tell me, Nilofer, will you talk to Iskander Pasha about Selim or should I?"

"Iskander Pasha has already been informed and has come to give his blessing." My father, wearing a broad smile, had walked into the room. He hugged me and kissed my cheeks. "This time you have made a good choice."

"Are you sure, Iskander?" asked my mother. "At least the Greek was a school teacher."

Iskander Pasha laughed. "This young man will go far if he learns to control his tongue and doesn't expect the moon to fall into his lap immediately. I am truly pleased. Hasan Baba is almost a member of the family and, as you know, I have been very close to him for many years. The news has made him weep with joy. Nilofer, you must please go downstairs. Your brothers are questioning Selim, and the Baron and Memed are already celebrating with another bottle and are waiting to congratulate you. I need to speak with your mother alone."

A full-scale discussion was in progress when I reached the library, but my entrance froze them. The Baron rose and proposed a toast to Selim and me. Hasan Baba came and kissed my head. Halil put his arms around me and whispered.

"At least we'll all be present this time."

Salman waved from the corner. Selim appeared to be embarrassed and averted his eyes from mine. His over-confident demeanour had momentarily disappeared. I had surprised him. He never really believed I would go this far so soon. Now he was confronted with a decision I had made. It was the Baron who was the first to speak.

"My dear Nilofer, we have been discussing when you two should get married. There is a great difference of opinion on this subject and a fierce argument was raging when you appeared on the scene like a Greek goddess. Memed was for October, which he says, and here I agree with him, is a beautiful month in Istanbul. Salman is indifferent. Halil prefers September since he is on military manoeuvres later in October and naturally assumes that his new Adjutant Selim will be at his side. Have you a preference?"

I assumed there might be many difficulties to negotiate before the ceremony and for that reason I had not thought of an actual date. I decided to surprise them all, including myself.

"Why not tomorrow afternoon in this very room? I will tell the children in the morning."

The Baron roared. "The girl has courage. Let us agree!"

Uncle Memed smiled. "Fine. Then, at least, I will not be disturbed at an unearthly hour every night as some young blade tries to tiptoe his way up to your bedroom. Let tonight be a night of rest and tomorrow we will dance and sing."

I felt myself blushing and looked in the large mirror to confirm that this was indeed the case. The Baron and Memed had known all along. No matter how large the house, it could not hold any secrets. Selim was standing near the window. As I joined him we looked at each other and began to laugh. Uncle Memed's voice interrupted our tiny moment of privacy.

"Have you ever read Stendhal on love, Baron?"

"No," said the Baron. "And I do not intend to do so. I'm amazed that you have wasted your time on Stendhal. He wrote too much and at too great a speed. His books were not in our house in Berlin. The only French novelists permitted in our library are Balzac and Flaubert and of the two, Flaubert is the true genius."

"What about Rimbaud and Verlaine, Baron?" inquired Salman. "Are they permitted in your library?"

"I was speaking of novelists, Salman Pasha." The Baron's tone indicated that he was not in a mood to be trifled with today. "Of course the poets you mention are present, but I find Verlaine too luscious for my taste. The English romantics, Shelley and Keats, have produced much better verse. Forgive an old man his prejudices, Salman, but we Germans are terribly spoilt. After Goethe, Schiller, Holderlin and Heine it is difficult for us to take the French versifiers too seriously. There is Pushkin, of course, and he is a totally different matter, though I do sometimes wonder how much of the music in his verse is inherited from his African forebear and how much has been inspired by that cursed primeval darkness they call Russia."

Before we could discuss Stendhal's exclusion from the Baron's library in Berlin, Iskander Pasha entered the room to ask if we had decided on a date for the wedding. He was greatly amused by the suggestion that the event was planned for the following day. When he realised we were serious he remained unruffled and turned to Hasan Baba.

"Do we need a beard to officiate or can you manage on your own, Hasan? I doubt whether anyone else present knows the words of the prayer for the occasion."

Hasan Baba's face was wreathed in smiles. "You know as well as I that our religion was not made for priests and monks. In fact they could be married without the prayer that was instituted much later. These things were invented so we could compete with the Christians. If they had priests, we needed our own. In our faith there is no divide between the spiritual and the temporal."

"That has been a big problem," said Halil.

"I do not want a debate on theology tonight," Iskander Pasha intervened rapidly to guillotine the discussion. "All I want to know is who will perform the marriage ceremony. It's a practical question. If a beard is needed we shall have to send a messenger tonight."

"I will marry these children," said Hasan Baba. "Provided we have two reliable witnesses I don't need anything else. I would suggest Iskander Pasha and General Halil Pasha as the witnesses. That will suffice."

I ran to tell Sara that we had agreed on a day and time, but she was already fast asleep and snoring gently. I went to my room in a slightly uneasy mood. I was sure of Selim, but something still bothered me. Why? I should be jubilant, singing tunes of infinite rapture, just like the celebrated birds in Sufi poetry. Everything was being done so that it accorded with my needs. I was puzzled as to why none of them had objected to Selim's pedigree. Ten years ago edicts would have been issued. Disdainful eyes would have looked at me across the breakfast table accusingly for polluting our family by marrying a barber whose family had cut our hair for centuries. What had changed them all? Was it their own life experiences and the passage of time that had mellowed them – or was it something much greater than any individual? Was it the impending collapse of the Empire and the Ottoman civilisation of which we had been a part for a very long time and without which we would be sucked into a vortex of uncertainties?

I now realised that it was the ease with which my family had agreed to the match that made me uneasy. Whatever the reason, I was pleased and my mood changed. I was looking out of the window in a slight daze when I felt two gentle hands cupping my breasts. I screamed and the hands covered my mouth.

"Selim!"

"Did you think that I would be so overpowered by sentimentality that I would really stay away tonight?"

"Yes."

"Well, you were wrong. Are you glad you were wrong?"

"Yes. But before you take your clothes off I want to know why you agreed to join the army."

"To make it easier for everyone. They can say that Nilofer is married to a young officer under Halil. It sounds better than saying: 'Nilofer is marrying our barber's grandson. Yes, he's a barber too and it will be so convenient for us because, from now on, we won't need an outsider for the circumcisions.'"

I couldn't help laughing, because he was mimicking my mother's voice perfectly, but I knew instinctively that the joke was designed to conceal the truth. He would never have agreed to join the army to help preserve our family's pride. On the contrary, he would have used the very words he put in my mother's mouth himself whenever we had company simply in order to shock their sensibilities.

"I don't believe you, Selim. I want the truth."

"The officers are planning to get rid of the Sultan, his court, the clergy, their privileges, and who knows what else will fall when we push him off his throne? There is no political party in our country like the German Social Democratic Party or the French Socialist Party. Perhaps there never will be such a party, but till one comes into existence the army is a good place for me."

"But Selim," I shouted at him, "what if there's a war? You might be killed!"

"We're too weak and poor to fight in any stupid war," he laughed. "We won't fight against our foreign enemies. If they attack, we'll surrender quietly and quickly. The war we're planning is against tradition and obscurantism at home. If we get rid of them, then we can build up our strength again."

I was relieved. If he had agreed to Halil's request simply in order to please me and appease my family, he would have become bitter sooner or later. The decision was his and taken for reasons of his own.

"Now you can take your clothes off and come to bed."

He did as I asked.

"Nilofer," he whispered as he put his arms around me, "tomorrow is an important day in both our lives and I think we should refrain from feeding our passions tonight. Let us just lie like this for some time and dream. Then I will leave so that we can both sleep well tonight. What do you think?"

I put my hand between his legs and felt an old friend rise. "I fear, Selim, that your mind is incapable of controlling your body. This is not good for a young officer."

He began to laugh as his lips sought my nipples and I mounted him.

FIFTEEN

Nilofer sends Selim to clear his head by talking to the Stone Woman; he is surprised by the experience

'My name is Selim, O Stone Woman. I am Nilofer's new husband and she has sent me here to meet you. She has told me about you, the secrets you guard, the effect you have on people, including some who are so private that they are unaware of their own problems. Is it true that for hundreds of years this was a place only women came to? I wonder why?

I know we are living in a time when everyone is unsure about the future and men also need to discuss their problems and worries. This used to be the case in the village where my father was born. Hasan Baba talks of the old days in our village, and how during the winter afternoons, men would gather once a week in a circle, blankets held tight around their shoulders, warming their hands by a fire as they spoke of their problems to each other and waited for someone to offer them sage advice. At these gatherings, they rarely spoke of their crops or the lack of water in the village or the rapacious tax-collectors, who, in lieu of money, insisted on other goods, including young women. These were not special problems. It was part of their everyday life.

The winter circles were organised to discuss personal problems and the younger men, too shy to speak in one particular winter, might none the less be emboldened to speak a few years hence. Hasan Baba says that there were very few inhibitions.

It was a mixed village with Armenians and Kurds, though we Turks were in the majority. The Armenians had some of the best land and, last year, the Kurds burnt their houses and drove them out of the village, though thankfully nobody was killed. After the Armenians had been driven out the winter gatherings came to an end. My grandfather says it disrupted the solidarity of the village and those who remained could not look each other in the eye. They had done something so terrible to their fellow-human beings that it was difficult to pretend they could solve each other's problems.

I'm really surprised that anyone comes here at all, Stone Woman. From a distance you look like the remains of a pagan goddess, but from where I am you're just a giant rock and it's very uncomfortable sitting on this stone. Hundreds of delicate and well-cushioned posteriors have sat in the same place for many years. They should have made this stone smooth and soft. It is not easy for me to speak with a stone. I have never found it necessary, but Nilofer wanted to share you with me. The only thing I would not discuss with a close friend or my grandfather is the intimacy between Nilofer and me. That is our own precious secret. It is something so beautiful that we discuss it with each other every day. If, for some reason, I could not tell her certain things, I can see you might be useful, but not now.

There is one small problem. Young Orhan was a bit taken aback when Nilofer told him about us and for the first few days after the marriage ceremony, he became quite distant. He refused to speak with me or come for a walk on the cliffs as we often did during the day. He is getting better now and I'm sure he will be fine. His behaviour is not unnatural. No child wishes to see its father replaced, even if the father is dead. And if the father is alive and tormenting his wife and children, it is difficult to be disloyal. When I was Orhan's age, I would sometimes hear my father beating my mother. I would put my fingers in my ears to banish her screams.

One day I came home unexpectedly and found my mother coupling with a stranger. Even though I knew my father was cruel, I still resented this man's presence. When he left, I became very angry with my mother. I abused her and shed many tears of rage. My mother's face was filled with terror. She thought I would tell my father. She said if ever I told my father of what I had seen, he would kill her without pity. She threatened me with fear.

I believed her, Stone Woman. My father claimed to believe in Sufi philosophy and he could certainly get intoxicated, sing the songs and dance all night, but it never affected his inner being. He may have been a *dervish*, but he was also an ignorant and a cruel man. I may have been upset at seeing my mother with another man, but that did not make me love my father. Naturally, I kept quiet and till this day I have never recalled that incident to anyone. Why have I told you?

It was at this time that my grandfather, with their approval, took me away from my parents and began to educate me in earnest. I learnt to read and write and later started to attend the *medresseh*. I have never seen my parents since that time. Eighteen years have passed and they showed not the slightest interest in me. I think of Hasan Baba as both my mother and my father.

One thing does worry me, Stone Woman. When my father learns of my marriage to the daughter of Iskander Pasha, he might decide to take advantage. He could arrive at the house on the pretext of paying his respects and seeing his new daughter-in-law, but in reality, to demand money. I have not mentioned this to Nilofer. She would laugh and treat it as inconsequential. You must understand that it is not my father's poverty I am ashamed of, but his character. He is a disgusting and evil creature and I do not wish him to come to this house or visit us in Istanbul. I have mentioned this to Hasan Baba. It troubles him as well, but he is old and helpless now. He does not offer advice, but shakes his head despairingly and looks up towards the heavens.

I think I will mention my father to Nilofer and her mother, just in case the scoundrel arrives while I am away from the capital with General Halil. In a sober mood he can appear normal and even charming, but they must be on their guard.

I'm going now, Stone Woman. I'm surprised my visit was not wasted. I did reveal a secret and it was helpful. Nilofer will be pleased. ’

SIXTEEN

The Committee for Union and Progress meets to discuss a conspiracy to overthrow the Sultan; the Baron unveils a spy; Nilofer would rather be an Ottoman than a Turk

We had become so used to each other's company over the last few weeks that it came as a slight shock when I first noticed the dust rising in the distance. The men on horseback heading in our direction were not unexpected. Halil and Selim had been awaiting their arrival with a mixture of excitement and anticipation. I rushed to inform them that their guests had been sighted and the three of us went to the front terrace to watch their arrival.

The coach contained two generals, one of whom was very short. The four young officers, one of them much younger than Selim, were on horseback. They jumped off as they ran and saluted Halil. Then my brother went down the stairs to receive his fellow generals. They saluted each other and laughed, but underneath it all even I, far removed from political intrigues, could detect the tension. Selim was introduced to the newcomers, though I observed that no names were mentioned. I led them into the house and then the dining room where breakfast was waiting to be served. Halil had insisted on total secrecy. Petrossian alone was entrusted to serve the meal. My brother did not want even the identity of the officers present to be known to anyone. The Baron and Memed were upset at being excluded, but accepted the decision with bad grace.

I, too, was about to leave when one of the officers, the youngest among them, stopped me.

"Is she your sister, General Halil?"

My brother nodded. "Yes and she is the wife of our new friend."

"Is she on our side?" asked the same officer.

I looked him straight in the eyes. "I am."

"Good," he said in a deep and very serious voice. "Then you must stay. We want to end the situation where women are considered good only for the affairs of the heart or the home or, indeed, for purposes of procreation. We want them also to become experts in organising the affairs of the state. We want to stop encouraging them in the trivial activities they have invented to keep themselves busy while we work. The only reason my wife is not with us today is that her father is seriously ill. Are we agreed?"

The others smiled and nodded. How strange, I thought to myself, that this young man with a pleasant face and a thin moustache can speak with such authority in the presence of three generals. Where does this confidence come from?

The discussion during breakfast was deliberately low-key. They kept referring to the Committee. At first I thought it was the code-name for their leader, but it soon became clear that the Committee was a secret society to which they all belonged. I was angry that Selim had not mentioned it to me before and since the young officer had made such a fuss when he insisted on my presence I felt that my voice should be heard again.

"Excuse me, gentlemen, but what is the Committee?"

The young officer looked at Selim and Halil in disbelief. "Neither of you has told her?"

Both men became sheepish and avoided my eye.

"The Committee, madame," said the officer, "is the name of the largest secret society ever created in the entire history of this Empire. It is the Committee of Union and Progress to which we all belong. It is secret, but they know we exist and their spies are everywhere. It is not restricted to soldiers, though we form the largest component within its ranks. There are many writers and officials who are members. Some of our best people operate from Paris and Salonika. Namik Kemal, whose play *Vatan* you may have seen or read, is one of our inspirers. After today, if you agree with our aims, we shall invite you to join the Committee. My wife is a very active member in Istanbul. She teaches at the Galatsaray *lycée* and is organising other like-minded women."

I told them I was honoured to be considered and they would have an answer from me by the evening. It was the older of the two generals who replied in a voice so soft and feminine that I seriously wondered whether he had been accidentally castrated. Unlike his colleague, he was not one of nature's more imposing generals. He was short, clean-shaven and possessed a paunch whose size attracted attention. Because he was different from the other officers, I took a liking to him, but something must have gone wrong at some stage in his life. He spoke in the squeaky voice of a young girl and the effect was frankly disconcerting. I found it extremely difficult to maintain a serious face while he spoke.

"We are delighted to have made your acquaintance. We must now retire to discuss certain logistical details in case there is an unforeseen emergency and we have to take action without the luxury of widespread consultation with other members. Unfortunately this discussion is exclusively for officers, but we shall be finished after lunch and would be delighted if you joined us in the afternoon."

I smiled and left the room. Outside in the garden I heaved a sigh of relief, sat down on the bench and began to laugh. I had been so taken with the morning that I had not noticed Uncle Memed comfortably seated on his favourite armchair underneath the walnut tree. He had been absorbed in a book and had initially frowned at the disturbance created by my laughter, but smiled when he saw that it was me. I was summoned with an imperious gesture of his forefinger. The Baron, who was never too far away from Uncle Memed, emerged from the other side of the tree, adjusting his *pince-nez*.

"Share your joke with Favourite Uncle."

I explained why I was laughing and Memed, who had an infectious giggle, joined in as well, which made me laugh even more. I looked at the Baron, fully expecting a brief lecture on the human voice and the conditions that caused it to change or not to change, but he had suddenly become very distracted and thoughtful.

"Baron?" asked Memed, worried by his friend's demeanour.

"An awful thought crossed my mind on hearing Nilofer's story, but it is of no consequence. Now, young lady, are you aware that your children have been taken sailing by Salman?"

"No. He never asked my permission. Neither of them can swim."

"They won't need to. Just look at the sea. It is so calm today. I have been watching them through my binoculars and they all seem perfectly happy. Here, you have a look."

I borrowed the binoculars and walked to the bottom of the garden for a better view. It was as he said. They were not far from the shore, the sea appeared benign and all was well. None the less I felt nervous at the thought of them out at sea in my absence. I had never thought of death before Dmitri was murdered. Now I am often worried. What if I die? Who will take care of them and love them as I do? Sometimes I have dreams of anxiety in which the children are in danger and I am unable to reach them in time. These dreams are so powerful that I always wake up and rush to their bedchambers to make sure they are safely asleep.

I shouted at Salman when they came back, but the children rushed to his defence. Over the last few weeks he had spent more time with them than us and I was sure he talked of Selim and how good it was that I had married again and was happy, because I noticed that Orhan had become friendly again.

Curiously enough, Emineh, who was much closer to her father than Orhan, had shown no signs of resentment or hostility. In fact her relationship with Selim, which had barely existed before, was now warm and she was losing her shyness towards him. I gave them the binoculars so they could see the sailing boat in which they had just returned go further and further out to sea. Salman took my arm as we began to walk in the garden.

"Is the conspiracy proceeding well, Nilofer? When can we look forward to our liberation?"

"I will have a better idea by this evening, but you, who are knowledgeable and have travelled so much, should join the Committee."

He shook his head firmly. "On this subject I am in agreement with my father completely. It is another reason for our closeness to each other. We both feel that the Committee is too heavily dominated by uniforms. Getting rid of the beards and the eunuchs is a big leap forward, but replacing them with uniforms might not take us as far forward as we need to be if we are ever to catch up with our rivals."

"Who else is there to effect the change? The poets?"

"Heaven be praised," he laughed. "Nilofer, you have become one of them?"

"I am thinking of it."

He talked of other fears. The last period of reform had been constructive. "Replacing the robe and the turban with the stambouline and the fez may have been symbolic, but it was a start. Most importantly, the edict of 1839 announcing the reforms was of an egalitarian character. It was also generous insofar as it offered the same opportunities to all the subjects of the Empire. Now the mood has changed. There are people in your committees who believe in purity and they, my dear sister, frighten me. I find that all talk of purity is very dangerous."

"Why?" I asked for the sake of argument. "Nobody accuses the Greeks of being dangerous when they want their purity and want to be separate from everyone else. In fact, most of Europe supports them."

"The question is," said Salman, "are we going to slit the throat of every Greek who wishes to stay here? Just like your late husband? Is every Armenian going to be driven out of his house? Petrossian's family have lived in their village for over five hundred years, just as long as the Ottomans have ruled these lands. Are we going to purify Petrossian's village? These are the new questions that need to be answered. Ask your new friends what they mean to establish after they have put Sultan Abdul Hamid on a boat and pushed him in the direction of Britain."

Salman had forced me to think seriously about these matters. I was for a complete change, but I was not for purity at all, especially if it meant driving out all the Christian subjects of the Empire. Salman was surely right about that, but it is also true that there is always chaos when Empires begin to crumble.

Would the Prophet Memed and his followers have been able to make such rapid progress if the Roman Empire had not been in a state of terminal decline? The Muslim armies had taken Spain with a few thousand soldiers. That would never have been possible if Rome had still been powerful. And our own Osman. Could he have prospered if the Eastern Empire had not begun to decay? What we had gained in the past was now being taken away from us as we began to decay. That was the way of the world. Britain and France were ahead of us as we were once ahead of the Romans and the Byzantines. There would be chaos when the Sultan fell. I did not have to be a deeply profound thinker to understand what anyone could see. The Committee was important because it might be able to control the chaos and minimise the confusion that lay ahead.

I was about to join my new friends in the library when I noticed the Baron and Uncle Memed deep in conversation with Halil, who had been shaken by something the Baron had said to him. I saw him nod earnestly as the Baron spoke and then rush back into the house.

An hour later, the Committee was in full session in the library. Halil appeared to be calm again. The general who had not spoken before cleared his throat, and we fell silent.

"We can no longer look away from our own history. Our tendency is always to boast. We constantly look backwards and say to ourselves: we who once were nothing built a great Empire for the glory of Islam. Our children are constantly being taught of our victories and, it is true, there were many in the past, but our failure to understand our own decline is why we are now at an impasse. I do not wish to speak for a long time, but let me map our decline briefly. We have now been on the retreat for two centuries.

"Our failure to take Vienna in 1683 was the turning point in our fortunes. The result of that was the Treaty of Karlowitz, which we signed exactly two hundred years ago in 1699, giving up Hungary to the Habsburgs and retreating to Belgrade. In 1774, it was Ottoman imbecility that gave the Russians the power to protect the interests of our Christian subjects. Why did the Sultan or his Vizier not ask in return for the right to protect the Russian serfs, since their treatment was an affront to our entire population?

"More defeats followed in 1792, when the French were preparing to execute their King, and then we suffered again in 1799, 1812, 1829 and then just twenty years ago when we lost Serbia, Romania and Montenegro and the Austrians even took away Bosnia and Herzegovina. The French and English navies send in their ships to the outskirts of Istanbul and threaten us with punishments unless we follow their dictates. It is the end of this Empire. We must act now to limit the scale of the disaster. We could move in army units next week and take the Sultan, but it is pointless unless we are agreed as to what we shall put in his place. That is all I wish to say for the moment."

This general had spoken very clearly and in a strong voice had said what we all knew already, but the starkness of the decline had never been so visible to me before. One question had always bothered me.

"Forgive my ignorance, General, but why were we unable to take Vienna?"

Everyone sighed in exasperation as if this was something they had been discussing all their lives and now, of all things, a woman wanted to know the answer. It was the young officer from Salonika who replied.

"As you can imagine, this is something our military historians have been discussing for a long time and there is no real agreement. The defeat of our army outside Vienna in 1683 was understandable. The Habsburgs and the Poles were in possession of new Western techniques of warfare. Our soldiers were demoralised and in a state of some discontent. I think by then it was a bit late for us. The real question is what happened when we were at the height of our strength and Sultan Suleman's armies were sweeping aside everything in front of them as they took Belgrade, Rhodes, Hungary and Transylvania but stopped at the gates of Vienna in 1529. Why did we lift that siege when the city was in our grasp? That is the real mystery. For at that time we were militarily dominant and politically in alliance with the best people in Europe: German and Dutch Protestants as well as the Jews and people of our own faith being expelled from Spain. If we had taken Vienna we might have defeated the Catholics decisively and changed the face of Europe. Think what might have happened if we had reversed the trend in Spain. The victory might have forced us to modernise ourselves two hundred years ago, along with the rest of Europe. Suleman's failure to take Vienna was the decisive moment, in my opinion. And everyone here is likely to give you a different reason for the failure. We would be here for weeks and even then we would not reach agreement. If you are seriously interested in Ottoman military history we will plan an evening in Istanbul and bring all the experts together. I think . . ."

My brother Halil interrupted the discussion. "Always the past. Always the past. It's what we usually accuse our enemies of doing. Let us discuss the future. Before we proceed, however, I have something important to report to you. There is an old family friend staying here. He was once a German tutor, but on the death of his brother, he inherited the family estates in Prussia and became a Baron. He claims that there is a person present in this room, who is spying on behalf of the palace. He knows this because he was present in Berlin when this same person negotiated a secret treaty between the Sultan and Prussia, committing us to support them in any future European conflict. In return they would help preserve the Sultan in power. This is treachery on two different levels. The first is against the interests of our country. The second is directly against the Committee. If such a person is actually present it would be useful at this stage if he could identify himself."

These remarks created a sensation. The young officers rose to their feet in anger. The general with the squeaky voice was beginning to tremble. He was looking at the floor, but everyone was looking at him. His voice cracked even further.

"This is a complete misunderstanding. It is true I went to Berlin on behalf of the Sultan, but how could I refuse without betraying our cause? I did as I was told by the Grand Vizier. Is that a crime?"

A long silence followed this remark. The other general looked at his colleague with a sad expression. "Orders have to be carried out. We know that well, but why did you not inform me at the time? I was your senior officer. And why, when you established contact with the Committee, did you not inform its members in Istanbul? I think it would be best if you told us the truth, general."

Then the young officer spoke again. "Have you given our names to anyone?"

"How could he?" The menace in Halil's voice was completely new to me. "He has never met you before, but he could have given the names of the two generals who approached him to join the Committee. Did you?"

I began to feel sorry for the man with the woman's voice. He was shaking his head in disbelief as he began to shrink and disappear in the corner of Iskander Pasha's large, faded green leather armchair. I suppose he was amazed by the coincidence of a Prussian *junker* with links to the military leaders in Berlin being here on this particular day and recognising him. Who can blame the poor general? Very few people, including some who were very close to the family, were aware that Uncle Memed and the Baron had been lovers for thirty years. Even the most brilliant spy could not have foreseen such a disaster, but, at the very least, he might have been better able to pull himself out of the morass by inventing a story that created a doubt in the minds of some of those who were present. Not this man.

Never in my life have I seen someone disintegrate so completely as did the eunuch-general on that day in the library of our summer house in August 1899. Everyone was looking at him. Nobody spoke. He was cowering in fear. Slowly a smell began to pervade the room. Our noses began to twitch. I realised then that the wretched man had soiled his trousers. I think this act disgusted his stiff-backed colleagues even more than the treachery. Halil ran out of the room and returned with Petrossian, who stepped back as the stench assaulted his senses.

"What one is, one does," said the other general in a tone of total disgust.

The eunuch-general had begun to cry. He pleaded for mercy. He sought our forgiveness. He swore on the Koran that he would tell us everything, including the names of all the spies in the Committee, provided his life was spared.

"Go and change your clothes first, you wretch," said the young officer. "You deserve to be executed for this act alone. We will determine your fate on your return. Your very presence in the army is an outrage."

Petrossian lifted him out of the room. We all rushed to breathe the fresh air of the scented garden. Usually I find the scent of jasmine too cloying. How welcome it was on that day as I inhaled its sweetness! Halil and the other general were walking together, deciding what to do with their colleague. The officers, including Selim, were in a huddle closer to the house. I was looking at the sea, unable to take in every possible angle of the events of the afternoon. Even if the eunuch-general gave us a list of the spies there would be no guarantee that he was telling the truth. He might deliberately mislead us to create more trouble within the Committee. It was difficult to think of him doing anything intelligent, given the scale of the earthquake that had shaken his life, but he might be thinking now as he cleaned himself up in the bathroom.

The generals signalled that the officers should join them. The eunuch-general's fate had already been decided and the young men were being asked for their opinion. I did not want him executed. I knew what he had done was shocking, but killing him would not help anyone. They must have read my thoughts, for Selim and Halil came to join me.

"It's his life or ours," said Halil. "If we let him live we will all have to go into exile and that will leave the Committee headless inside the army in Istanbul. We cannot let that happen. It's a military decision, Nilofer."

I was not to be convinced that easily.

"And if you kill him and bury his body somewhere, what will the man waiting anxiously for his reports begin to think? I assume he will be suspicious. He's not an insignificant person, you know. He is a general and they don't just disappear into thin air, not even in a dying Empire."

Halil nodded seriously. "The others never told him they were coming here. He did not even know that he would be meeting us. He was simply told that we had organised a meeting with two officers who had come for consultations from Salonika and that there might be a member of the Committee arriving from Paris. Nothing else. That is all he could have reported to his superior who, don't forget, is the Grand Vizier, a man with a few other problems on his mind. It is very possible he said nothing at all and decided to wait till he had met the officers. Even if he has informed the Vizier that two generals are interested in the Committee, that is something we can always deny.

We cannot take the risk of these young officers being exposed at this stage, Nilofer. It would be like destroying our future. Don't forget that the spy was present during our morning discussions as well. We evaluated our strength in different units of the army in his presence. That is the sort of information for which the palace would happily sacrifice dozens of lives. Instead we are only taking one. You must understand."

"So you are going to kill him?"

Halil and Selim looked at me, at each other and finally their gaze shifted far away, in the direction of the sea. I knew then that the poor eunuch-general would never see the sun rise again. Within an hour they had saddled their horses, summoned the coachman and left our house for ever. I knew I was seeing the eunuch-general for the last time and, despite myself, the thought saddened me. A human life was about to be truncated. I understood why he had to be despatched. I knew that it was sometimes necessary to do bad things for a good cause, but the man was so pathetic that I felt another way might have been found. Selim did not agree with me. He admitted that he, too, was unhappy, but he was convinced there was no other solution. I had seen them leave. The sentenced man had recovered some of his dignity. He walked to the carriage with his head raised, which somehow made it worse for me.

That evening's meal was dominated by a discussion of the day's events. The Baron had emerged as the unlikely hero of the whole affair. That is how Halil referred to him as he proposed a toast in the Baron's own champagne. After we had all sipped the sparkling liquid, I could not resist speaking.

"Hero, perhaps," I said, and then surprised myself. "Surely executioner would have been the more appropriate word."

There was silence. Selim glared at me.

The Baron recovered rapidly and smiled. "You are right, Nilofer, but look at it this way. If the eunuch had been spared, your brother, husband and those fine officers who were here earlier today might have lost their lives."

"Baron," I continued, "I did not mean to sound offensive. I accept what you say and perhaps what is being done probably even as we eat and drink is something that had to be done. That doesn't make it less distasteful. Can I ask you another question?"

He nodded.

"The dead man was actively engaged in the interests of both the Sultan and your Kaiser Wilhelm. It was he who signed the secret protocol between Istanbul and Berlin. Our officers may regard that as short-sighted treachery, but surely you would favour such a course."

The Baron sat up straight in his chair. "I would. But for me old family loyalties are more important than politics. The ties between our two families go back a very long way. Did you know that my great-grandfather once stayed at this very house with Memed's grandfather? That is why I agreed to come here as a tutor. So you see, my dear child, that there are more important things in life, such as personal loyalties and these, for me, always override political affiliations."

"Spoken like a true *junker* and a good friend, my dear," said Memed in a surprisingly emotional tone. "I propose another toast. To loyalty and friendship and a curse on the narrowness of politics."

This time, unlike the others, I did not raise my glass.

I had not been alone with Selim the whole day and I began to feel a pent-up, uncontrollable tenderness for him. The meal, alas, was far from over. Memed was in an ebullient mood. I had referred to the spy as a eunuch-general. This was now confirmed by Memed.

"He was castrated as a child so that he could serve in the palace as a eunuch, but with the promise of reforms in the air, his poor parents realised they had a mistake. The story reached the office of the Grand Vizier and, to his credit, he felt sorry for the child's family. The father was an Albanian water-carrier. This boy was one of six children. He was sent to a *medresseh*, but a very good one, with teachers who taught and did not just beat the pupils into submission. It is where the children of the palace servants were sent and the teachers had to be careful. When he reached his sixteenth year, the Vizier took him as an office boy and watched his mind develop. He had a prodigious memory for faces and documents. He had to read a paper only once and he could memorise most of the important details. He was transferred to the palace and became a crucial figure in the spy network of the state. He will take many secrets to his grave."

My father was surprised. "How do you know all this, Memed?"

Memed exchanged a quick glance with the Baron.

"I told him," interjected the Baron. "The eunuch developed a fondness for me and one night in Berlin, over his cups, he told me his life story. That is why I was shaken when I sensed his presence in this house today. It was his intelligence that made him so dangerous. Poor man. How was he to know that I would be here? Poor, poor, man."

We retired to the library after supper. This had been the scene of the eunuch's ignominy and there was a vacuum where once the chair had stood. Father had to be told now that his favourite chair was being cleaned and it needed to be aired for at least a day in the sun to lose its stench. He was outraged.

"May that eunuch roast in hell!"

"He will, Father," replied Halil in a cold voice. "He will."

Just as we were about to leave the table, the Baron decided to enlighten us with one of his pronouncements. "I spoke briefly to the younger officers, today. One of them strikes me as the strong leader who will be needed one day when a new state needs to be carved from the rubble of the old Empire. I recommended a reading of Machiavelli to this officer and he said something very interesting to me in return. He said he was not well educated enough in foreign languages and he would, therefore, have to wait till the Italian text was translated into Turkish. Then he said something truly remarkable, which filled me with hope. 'I think', he said with total confidence, 'in order to move forward fast we will have to change many things, included our outdated script. We will Latinise the Turkish alphabet within a year of taking power. It will make it easier for everyone to learn the languages of Europe. Perhaps then many people can read your Machiavelli.' I thought to myself then, I hope this young man succeeds in his mission. It is the vision you need to go forward."

Later that night, Selim and I made love in silence. We had been deprived of each other's company for the whole day and words were no longer sufficient to express the longing. Afterwards we talked for a very long time.

He was excited by the events of the day. He spoke of the young officer who had made what was really difficult sound possible, namely to make progressive ideas a reality. So often in the past, lofty ideas had been transformed into their opposites, when those who had proclaimed them actually came to power. This had happened in France after their Revolution, but it had happened here as well. Whenever the reformers had been made Viziers, their ideas disappeared and they were compelled to govern the Empire in the only way they knew, which was the old way.

This time, Selim felt it would all be very different. They had agreed to transform our Arabic script to Latin, abolish the powers of the clergy, make education for girls compulsory and remove the veil from their lives for ever. He gave me a detailed account of the only major disagreement that had marred the day. That too had been an argument about the past, not the future. The three generals had said that it had been necessary to crush the janissary uprising of 1826. The younger officers were inclined to be more sympathetic to the janissaries, since they felt they were now in a similar situation to the defeated cohort in that they were preparing to unleash their own mutiny against the Sultan.

"Halil got angry with us at this stage," Selim laughed. "He said we had nothing in common with the rabble that was crushed in 1826. They were degenerates who oppressed the people and had become completely corrupted.

They should have been disbanded many centuries ago and a new army created on the European model. We should have learnt from the French and the English. He said that all the janissaries would have done is to have imposed a new Sultan, more amenable to their crimes. The young officer from Salonika who seems to have made a big impact on the Baron was not in a mood to compromise. He agreed that the janissaries had too much power in the Ottoman state, but it was the only way to maintain the core of a permanent standing army. Either you have dukes and lords on the European model, whose responsibility it is to raise an army for their king, or you have the janissaries. The only other way was during popular revolutions, such as when the English created their New Model Army and the French their own version after 1789. In the end we were convinced by their arguments, but it was an interesting debate. What did you think of the officer from Salonika?"

"I thought he was from Istanbul. That is where his wife teaches."

"Yes, but he was born in Salonika and that is where he has most support."

"I was impressed."

"You were meant to be."

"Are you jealous?"

"Yes."

I was not prepared for sleep and so I returned to the subject that Salman had raised with me earlier. "Did you discuss how pure the new state would be?"

"What do you mean?"

"There are people in the Committees who openly say that we need Turkishness. They say that Ottoman culture is too cosmopolitan and that the influence we have assimilated from the Arabs, Persians and Europeans is comparable to flowers raised in the hothouse. They want native plants only to be nourished. How can this happen, Selim? In our cities and villages different communities have lived side by side for many centuries. Turks, Armenians, Greeks, Kurds, Jews and heaven knows how many smaller groups."

Selim agreed with me and insisted that Turkishness had not been discussed at all in their deliberations, though he could see that it might become an important question in the future.

"What will I be in the new republic, Selim? I am of Jewish origin. As you know I'm not a believer, but I have no desire to be described as Turkish. I prefer to be an Ottoman. I know you'll think I am infected with mysticism, but the Ottoman soul is a treasure-house of feelings. Turkishness strikes me as being soulless."

"It is a problem," he acknowledged. "We are Ottomans because we are part of an Empire. The Greeks wished to stop being Ottomans and are now Greeks. The same applies to the Serbs and the Western powers have been fuelling the Armenians to go in the same direction. In this new situation we might have no option but to become Turks."

"And the Jews of Istanbul and Salonika?"

"They will remain Jews. Why should there be a conflict?"

"And what of the Greeks who do not wish to leave Istanbul or Izmir? They would prefer to remain Ottoman, but you will either force them to be Turks or drive them into the sea. That is what my brother Salman fears might happen."

Selim did not reply. His hands had begun to wander across my body. It was a convenient but pleasant way to end our argument. I offered no resistance to the young Turk rising between his legs. My Selim would never be a eunuch-general.

SEVENTEEN

A mysterious Frenchwoman of uncertain disposition arrives unexpectedly and demands to see Iskander Pasha, who later reveals how he used to spy on a married woman in the baths in Istanbul

"A French lady has arrived to see your father, but Iskander Pasha is not at home. He has gone for a walk with Selim and the children. Will you please come down and receive her?"

Petrossian had been running up the stairs and was out of breath. It was unlike him to lose his calm over the arrival of a visitor, however unexpected.

"Have you shown her to the reception room? Offer her some refreshments. I will be down in a minute."

I hurriedly brushed my hair, examined myself in the mirror to make sure I was presentable, and descended at a dignified pace to receive the French woman. In the hall just outside the reception room, I encountered Petrossian and Hasan Baba, deep in a conspiracy. They fell silent at my approach. I had entered this room twice since I arrived here and on both occasions the reason was the same: Orhan and Emineh wanted to see every room in the house and I was forced to humour them.

This room was so large that my family rarely used it, even when there were visitors. They sat either in the garden or in the library. Yusuf Pasha had insisted on the size, despite the objections of the architect. Our ancestor had wanted a ballroom on the European model so that he could entertain his friends, including European ambassadors, in a grand style. Later, orchestras were hired from Istanbul to play for special occasions, but those days were over. The room was furnished in an opulent French style, though the summer sun had faded the rich colours. Iskander Pasha claimed that neither the fabrics nor the furniture had been touched since the house was built.

The Frenchwoman was standing by the open windows and admiring the view out towards the sea. I mustered my best French to greet her.

"Bonjour, madame."

She turned round and smiled.

"You must be Nilofer. Your father mentioned you often and described your green eyes to me in great detail. You are very beautiful."

"Thank you, madame, but I really have no idea who you are or why you are here, but whatever the reason, welcome to our house."

Her laughter was genuine. "My name is Yvette de Montmorency. My husband, or should I say my second husband, is Vicomte Paul-Henri de Montmorency. He is the new French ambassador to Istanbul. We both knew your father well when he was Ambassador of His Most Exalted Majesty in Paris. I heard you were in your summer residence and I thought I would come here and surprise you."

I smiled politely. I took an instinctive dislike to her. She was wearing a crimson dress and the layers of make-up on her face did not succeed in concealing her age. She must have been approaching her sixtieth birthday. Her corset was tied very tight because the lift of her breasts was too pronounced and, as a result, unconvincing. How could she bear the discomfort? She was of medium height and, I must admit, well preserved for her age. The rolls of fat on her neck were still under control, though the tiny hairs that had sprouted on her upper lip had been removed a bit too effectively; the resulting smoothness was false.

"Well, you certainly have surprised me, madame. My father, who is out with his grandchildren, has never mentioned you or the Vicomte. The only Comte ever mentioned in this house is Auguste Comte. Are you by any chance familiar with his works?"

She shook her head in horror. "He was not a real Comte! You know that, of course. He was a dangerous radical and the Vicomte's uncle, the late Bishop of Chartres, had to denounce his teachings in church in very strong fashion. Oh no!"

To my utter delight, something that I had been secretly wishing for was granted the moment the thought crossed my mind. The Baron and Uncle Memed walked into the room and gave us both an exaggerated, but very comical bow. I made the introductions using the Baron's full name and stressing his title. Yvette began to simper with delight. I noticed the slight rise in the Baron's temperature and left the room on the pretext of organising some refreshments.

My serenity disappeared the minute I stepped outside the door. I was assailed by a wave of giggles, which I could not control. I slumped on the stairs and tried to stop my laughter, but without success. Hasan Baba came and sat next to me on a stair. I hugged him and carried on laughing. He smiled.

"Why does she make you laugh so much?"

"Who is she, Hasan Baba? Who is she?"

He looked around to see if we were completely alone.

"Now, I am not telling you this and you never heard it from me! Blame Petrossian if you have to name anyone. Please blame him. He is so discreet. It would be good to destroy his reputation. Who is she? Let me tell you. Many years ago in Paris, for a few weeks only, she became your father's wife."

The information sobered me instantaneously. "What? I can't believe this!"

"It was nothing serious. She came to a reception at our embassy and was entranced by the Ottoman experience. Iskander Pasha did those things in great style. Once I remember he told us all to dress like *dervishes* and sing Sufi songs in the presence of the British ambassador just to avoid discussing anything serious. He said it was a special day when we could do nothing but listen to devotional songs and once a guest entered he could not leave till the singing was over. If the *dervishes* observed any person leaving the room they could rush after him and stab him with a devotional dagger. The Englishman was allowed to leave after an hour."

"That is funny, Hasan Baba, but what about this woman?"

The old man started laughing at the memory. "She refused to share his bed unless he married her. He summoned Petrossian and me to the bedroom and told me, with a wink, to marry them. Petrossian signed a piece of paper witnessing the event. I muttered some nonsense and put their hands together. Iskander Pasha told her they were now married and he asked us to leave the room, making sure I took the signed paper with me. After being pleasured for three or four weeks, he tired of her. She was divorced in our presence in the same room, but they parted on good terms. I think she realised the ceremony wasn't serious, though if we had wanted it could have been a formal marriage. A few months later he was invited to attend her wedding to some aristocrat. She had been engaged to him all the time."

"Did the lustful Turk attend?"

"Of course. He is very proper on these questions. He went dressed in full Ottoman regalia, including a ceremonial sword, with Petrossian accompanying him in the uniform of a janissary, even though the janissaries had been abolished by then."

"Why do you think she's here?"

The old man shrugged his shoulders as Orhan and Emineh burst into the house with shells of different colours, their faces rosy with exertion. My father and Selim followed a few minutes later.

"A guest awaits you in the reception room, Father.'

"Why the reception room?"

"Petrossian thought it was appropriate and I agreed."

He took off his hat and I followed him into the reception room.

She squealed with delight when she saw him. "Eeeskandeh," she purred, "you are as handsome as ever, you devil. Surprised?"

I was amazed at the calm displayed by Iskander Pasha as he walked up to her and kissed the proffered hand. Was it my imagination or had his movements become slightly Parisian? The Baron, Memed and I looked at each other and turned away, fearful we might lose our poise and disintegrate completely before we left the room.

"Welcome to my house, Yvette. I hope my brother and Nilofer have made you welcome. I'm not very surprised that you are here because I read of the Vicomte's appointment as the French ambassador. Has he presented his credentials at the palace?"

She smiled. "Oh yes, and it was wonderful. As you know, I always love ambassadors and how they have to dress. The ceremony was out of the *Nuits Arabiennes*. It was like magic. I felt like a princess."

The Baron interrupted the exchange. "Just before you arrived, Iskander, Madame de Montmorency was telling us that what we really need at the moment is a few quick wars in Europe. I did not fully grasp the meaning of what you were saying, madame, but if I understand correctly you thought this might improve the genes of those who survived. Could I have misunderstood you? Would you kindly retrace the underlying philosophical argument for us?"

The Baron's irony was completely lost on her.

"Of course I can, Monsieur le Baron, and this time you must be a good boy and listen carefully. It is my judgement that if we do not have any more wars we will be faced with very serious problems. There will be too little work for too many men. They will become criminals and begin to do dangerous things. They will be encouraged by those socialist agitators always trying to stir up trouble, like that mulatto man from Cuba. I think his name is Lafargue.

If there are too many people without work it is dangerous. People in our position will no longer be safe. In these conditions it is good, is it not, if young men from the poor classes join the army and kill each other? Those who survive will be the best and will work well after the experience. Anything is better than being killed. So they will not fight against those who are giving them work and in this way we will revive all our countries. In the old days the doctors used leeches to suck the blood out of their patients. War will do it much better. It will, in general, be a good thing. A few shells in the rue Fontaine will not alarm me unduly. It is simple, is it not?"

Three of us nodded our heads vigorously.

"Exactly, madame," said Memed. "Very simple. And now if you will excuse us, the Baron, Nilofer and I have to discuss the arrangements for a children's picnic tomorrow."

We sat in silence on a bench in the garden. I revealed what Hasan Baba had told me, which made the Baron snort.

"I thought he had better taste than that. I mean, a tart from Montmartre would have provided better value!"

"Iskander was always a bit susceptible to large bosoms," said Uncle Memed, trying to excuse his younger brother's follies. "But I agree with both of you. This woman has absolutely nothing to recommend her. Our Committee of Public Safety should act quickly and despatch her!"

We laughed. I offered the two friends a better reason for Iskander Pasha's blindness. "I don't suppose they talked much when they were together."

The Baron could not be outdone. "No," he agreed with me, "I don't think Iskander Pasha encouraged any intellectual exertions on her part."

We laughed and laughed again. Our frustration at having to suffer the French ambassador's wife had found a natural release. The two men thought that she had come here simply to make an impression, but I was not sure. I felt there was something else and hoped it was nothing that would upset Iskander Pasha. He had recovered fully from his stroke, but the physicians had all agreed he must rest for a year. They had told us to keep bad news from him unless it was essential. My instincts warned me against this woman. She was bad news.

Mercifully, she did not stay long. Before an hour had elapsed her coachmen were alerted and she left. We all stood on the steps of the terrace and waved our farewells. Iskander Pasha appeared to be in perfectly good spirits. He was clutching a notebook and some old letters held together with a ribbon.

"Well," said Memed, "what did she want?"

"Nothing," replied Father. "Nothing at all. She returned some letters and a diary I had kept for a few months when I was in Paris."

"Is that all?" I asked him.

"There is one other thing she mentioned, though it is without significance. She showed me a photograph of her oldest son. I'm afraid the next Vicomte de Montmorency will have an Ottoman complexion."

I knew she had not come here without a reason. I could hardly wait to inform Salman and Halil that they had a French half-brother.

"Is the boy here?" inquired Memed.

"No," replied his brother. "He is at the military academy in St Cyr."

"She has other children?" asked the Baron.

"Yes, two daughters, who appear to be replicas of their mother."

"Heaven help them," said Memed.

"Are your letters to her and the diary she returned for public viewing?" I teased him. "Will they be placed in the library as documents of historic importance?"

"Juvenilia of this sort should always be destroyed," he replied. "The diary, if my memory serves me, is not personal in the least. Wait a minute, Nilofer. I will read it again to decide whether or not it can be put on a shelf in my library."

I was slightly perturbed by his unruffled reaction to Yvette's revelations. Was he really as indifferent as he appeared to be? I pressed him further.

"Father, do you not have the slightest curiosity about this boy? Wouldn't you like to meet him just once?"

"No, my dear child. No." He hugged me and kissed my forehead. "Have you forgotten what I told you a few weeks ago? Blood relations do not matter to me in the least." He dragged me away from Memed and the Baron, and we walked in silence to the very edge of the garden.

"Tell me something, Nilofer. Are you sometimes curious about your real father? Would you like to see him in the flesh, just once? Be honest with me."

"Yes," I heard myself say. "Yes, I would, but not for myself. I would like to see what it was that appealed so much to my mother in her youth."

"If you like, my child," said Iskander Pasha, "we can easily arrange for you to visit New York. My brother Kemal has ships that sail there regularly. A passage could be organised for all of you without any difficulty."

I embraced him very hard at this point. "Listen. I have no desire to travel for two months to see the face of this man. You are my father. All I meant was that if he happened to be in Istanbul one day, I would be curious to see him. Not even to speak with him, but just see him. A woman's curiosity, nothing more."

He smiled and then began to laugh. I wanted to know why, but he shook his head and his hand gestures implied that it was a trivial matter. I insisted and was relieved we had moved away from the subject of real fathers and real sons.

"When you said 'a woman's curiosity' I recalled an incident from my youth. I was sixteen or seventeen at the time and had become infatuated with a married woman, who often visited our house with her husband. They were family friends. She was very beautiful, or so I thought at the time. It was a truly Byzantine face. I think she was from one of the older families of the city. I began to stare at her quite rudely and was reprimanded by my mother in private. I would follow her when she visited the shops. A few school friends would watch her house, which was not far from our own. She complained to my mother and my father warned me that unless I stopped he would be compelled to punish me severely. The threats had no impact.

"One day my best friend came to see me with important information. He had discovered that she visited the women's baths each Thursday. This information excited me greatly, and my imagination became inflamed. I was possessed by a desire to see her without any clothes, to which end I bribed the bath attendants. You look shocked, but this was quite normal at the time. Not boys of my age, of course, but young men wanting to see whether or not the body of their future wife was blemished often paid the attendants so that they could spy on the woman who interested them. They say that some women did the same thing in the men's baths, but it was less common. All these baths have their little secrets. Anyway I had my way, and it was a beautiful sight. I will spare us both the embarrassments by not describing her details. But from then onwards, Thursday became my holy day, a day of pure bliss, and the afternoons were sacrosanct. Life was proceeding well till someone told my mother – to this day I am not sure who. It was probably one of the servants. One afternoon after having watched two women massage each corner of her soft and delicate body with loving care, I walked home in a complete trance. I would have run away with her to Albania if she had so desired. As I reached our house and went in through the front door, I found my father in the hall where he had been waiting for me to return. His face was filled with anger and disgust. That was the first shock.

"'Where have you been? I want the truth!' The second shock was self-inflicted. I startled myself by the sheer scale of the lie I had invented to escape punishment. 'I was outside the palace, Ata. The Sultan is dead.' My father believed this and his mood changed. He rushed upstairs to bathe and dress so that he could go and offer prayers at the Blue Mosque. You're laughing, my child, but think of me at that age. I was petrified. I hid in my room and wondered what would happen when my father returned. I heard him coming home and began to tremble. I expected the worst, but he came and reassured me. He said it was a false rumour. Although the Sultan had become very ill last night, he was not dead. I could hardly believe my luck. Perhaps it was that incident that pushed me towards Sufi mysticism a few years later. My misdemeanour was forgotten. So you see, Nilofer, it is not only women who are curious!"

EIGHTEEN

The death of Hasan Baba, who is given a Sufi burial; the return of Kemal Pasha; Sara's anger

There was a gentle knock. Selim was fast asleep. Nothing woke him. Nothing. I was convinced he could sleep through an earthquake. I thought it might be one of the children and got of bed quickly, covered myself with a dressing gown and went to the door. It was my mother.

"You should wake him up," she whispered. "The maids have just come and told me that when they took his breakfast to his room they found poor Hasan Baba dead. I'm going to tell your father now. He will be very upset."

I had to shake Selim really hard to wake him. He was shocked by the news and began to weep.

"He lived a good life, Nilofer. It was a good life, he used to say, that is why I have lived so long. He was ninety-one a few months ago. And I know he was very old. I know he was old, but I didn't want him to die. He was never orthodox. He used to ask me which animal I liked the most and I would reply 'an eagle' and he would say to me: 'Selim, when I die I will become an eagle.' He belonged to a Sufi *tekke* that believed that if you had achieved perfection in this world you could choose the physical shape in which to return to life after death. I will miss him, Nilofer. I will miss him."

We walked out of the house and crossed the garden to the little room where his body lay. Iskander Pasha rose as he saw us and embraced Selim. Both men began to weep.

"You have lost a father and a grandfather, Selim. He is irreplaceable. I know that better than most people, but always remember, I am here if ever you need me."

Hasan Baba had asked to be buried on a mound a few hundred yards from where the Stone Woman stood. He had instructed the head gardener only a few weeks ago as to how deep they must dig and where, and since his death this morning they had been digging his grave according to his detailed instructions. Petrossian watched them, weeping. He had so many shared memories with the dead man. They had both grown up together in this household and, in the old days, travelled everywhere with Iskander Pasha. They knew more about this family than any of us did. Hasan Baba had taken many secrets with him to the grave. Petrossian was now the sole survivor. And he never talked about us to any living person.

Hasan Baba had asked to be buried just before the sun set. Everyone from our household, men and women, master and servant, was present when his body was lowered into the freshly dug grave. The earth was moist and the scent of the wild flowers and trees would have pleased him. A few people had come from the closest village, a few kilometres from the house. We all cupped our hands and spoke the funeral verses from the Koran. Selim alone remained apart from us. He did not cup his hands. He did not offer any prayers. Instead, after we had finished, Selim's voice soared like an eagle as he sang a Sufi verse to send the old man who had been his father and teacher on his way.

"I sing this one for you, Hasan Baba." Selim's broken voice made me weep. "I sing it for you, my eagle."

O Sufi, to you the mosque and the tavern were one,
The voice of the devout and the cry of the drunk were one,
The remembrance of God and the goblet of wine were one.
You gave up hypocrisy,
Because for you the throne and the beggar's stool were one.
You burned with love,
Because for you the candle and the moth were one.
Become light and see, become light and fly,
Because you and the eagle are one.

By the time Selim had finished there were no dry eyes amongst those present. Petrossian and Iskander Pasha embraced and kissed Selim. They flanked him and, taking an arm each, escorted him inside the house. I followed them into the hall, where Selim slumped on the stairs and lost control of himself. He wept silently. He hit his head against the banisters. He wept loudly, talking to Hasan Baba all the while, referring to him as 'Perfect Man'. I sat next to him and gently forced his head on to my lap, stroked his hair and forehead. How long we sat there I can no longer remember, but it was Petrossian who came and told us that the funeral feast was being served in the garden. Selim rose to his feet immediately, wiped the tears off his face and lifted me up. He was smiling.

"Now let us celebrate his life."

It was dark outside, but oil lamps had transformed the garden. Iskander Pasha had sent a coach to fetch the musicians from a village about twenty kilometres from our house. They were *dervishes* and had begun to play their instruments as if in a divine trance, which Selim told me later that evening had been inspired not by the Creator, but by *hashish*. Three lambs were roasting on spits. Cauldrons of special rice had been prepared, and trays of fruit were laid out on all the tables. Individuals were singing the praises of the dead man.

Without warning, the musicians stopped and rose. They clapped their hands to attract attention and signalled that all present should join them. We did and they began to whirl, urging us to do the same, which we did till we became giddy and fell to the ground to recover. A great deal of wine had already been consumed, but the musicians continued to whirl, till they, too, became exhausted and stopped. Instead of resting, like us, they began to play again with a renewed vigour.

It was while we were feasting that a coach drew up and a man of medium height with thick grey hair stepped out and began to breathe the sea air. Petrossian, ever watchful, had heard the noise of the wheels on the gravel. He rushed to receive the guest.

"Glad you're still here, Petrossian." The man's voice was strangely familiar. "What in the name of Allah is going on here? Is it a wedding or a funeral?"

"A funeral, Kemal Aga. Old Hasan Baba died in his sleep last night."

When did Uncle Kemal return to Istanbul? I rushed to find Salman, and we both went to greet him.

"I'm sorry to hear that, Petrossian," said Uncle Kemal. "I'll miss the old rogue, even though he used to cut my hair too short when I was a boy. He claimed he was carrying out our mother's instructions, but I'm not so sure. Salman! Good to see you again, my boy. And you're smiling again."

The two men embraced and kissed each other's cheeks.

"And you?" he said, inspecting me carefully. "Which one are you?"

I laughed at his frankness. "Nilofer."

"Of course! Can't see your green eyes. Pity they don't shine in the dark. Where are your children? I'm sorry about the Greek school teacher. Very bad news."

"She's married again," Salman informed him.

"Good," said Uncle Kemal. "I hate long waits myself. And here are my brothers."

After they had hugged each other and laughed, Uncle Kemal demanded a room, a bath and a meal.

"I was looking forward to *not* hearing you speak, Iskander. It would have made a change in my life. Trust my luck. I return and hear that you've recovered your speech. All the way back on the ship I was dreaming of how I would entertain you with my stories and how you would not be able to interrupt me with a stupid joke, but no. This was not to be. Why couldn't you have waited another week?"

The brothers laughed and escorted Uncle Kemal to his room. He was exhausted and did not come down again. Petrossian took some food and wine to his room and, no doubt, answered his questions on the state of the family. It was only when Petrossian came down that my mother asked when Kemal had returned to Istanbul.

"His ship docked at the harbour at lunch time, *hanim effendi*," said Petrossian. "He went home, ordered a coach to bring him here and did not stay at his house long enough to change his clothes."

My mother burst out laughing. "What a strange man your uncle has become! If he can't bear the sight of them, why doesn't he do something?"

"But he does, Mother Hatije." Salman had joined us in the library and now shut the windows to keep out the noise of the musicians. "He travels the whole world and avoids their company. I think he's happy with this life. He could divorce his wife, but he would still have to maintain her and his ugly daughters, so why bother? I think it suits everyone concerned."

"Is he really happy, Salman?" asked my mother.

"Which of us is really happy, Mother Hatije? I don't believe there is any such thing as real happiness. It's an invention of the poets. All our lives go through different stages and one of these is usually happiness, but does it last for ever? I do not believe so. There is permanent emotional disorder in our lives, which does not permit any settlement of the happiness question. Nilofer disapproves of my theory?"

"Selim and I are very happy together, Salman!"

"And long may you remain so, my beautiful Nilofer. I would never deny that there are exceptions to my rule, but far from contradicting what I have said they prove the exact opposite. Uncle Kemal seems to be very cheerful, which is not a good sign. It means he will start his stories at breakfast and we will still be listening to them when the evening meal is being served. I am going to bed so I can build up the necessary energy to survive tomorrow. Peace be upon you both. One more thing, Nilofer, lest I forget. Please tell Selim that his song moved me deeply. I was weeping like everyone else. He has a very fine voice. It will be wasted in the army."

I was about to go into the garden again and sit with Selim, but my mother advised me to leave him on his own tonight. She felt it was better if he bade farewell to Hasan Baba in his own way, without any restrictions. I had left sharing a goblet of wine with the musicians and had promised to go back, but Mother convinced me otherwise.

"It is likely he will stay up all night and sing again at the grave when the sun rises. Let him be. It's a beautiful night. Come with me and have some mint tea."

I was exhausted. My mother gently massaged my neck while I sipped the tea. For a long time we did not speak. She had not done this for such a long time that the touch of her hands brought all the emotions of the day to a head. I felt weak and overpowered, and tears began to wash my cheeks. My mother remained silent as she wiped the tears away and kissed me. I told her then of the offer Iskander Pasha had made regarding a trip to New York to see my real father. This surprised Sara as much as it pleased her, but she approved strongly of what he had said regarding blood relations.

"You know, Nilofer, if Suleman were to see you now he would be embarrassed. Your presence would be a permanent reminder of his cowardice. Even if he wanted to, he could never love and appreciate you as much as Iskander Pasha."

I agreed with her, but if this was the case with me, surely it could have been the same for her. Why had she not even tried to fall in love with her new husband?

"You're a great one for clever phrases, Nilofer. Look what happened when you tried to fall in love with that poor skinny Greek. You convinced yourself beautifully and, alas, him. Look at the result. You left him. He got himself killed. My babies are fatherless and now you have fallen in love again. I know, I know. This time it's the real thing. Well, I had the real thing and it let me down badly. I still think of his betrayal, you know. The other day I was thinking that even if we couldn't have a child we should still have lived together. He should not have crumbled in the face of my father's superior knowledge – which turned out to be wrong anyway – or his money. Perhaps we were not really suited to each other. My mother must have said that a hundred times each day. My Uncle Sifrah echoed her when he came to our house for his weekly lunch. All my friends repeated it after he had run away to New York. They never said that when we were happy together. Never when I told them of my adventures with Suleman. Never when they saw us together on a few rare occasions and noticed how close and natural we were with each other. It was only after it was all over, and he had deserted me like the little rat he was about to become, that everyone suddenly discovered how bad we were for each other. I knew it was rubbish, but I believed them at the time. I wanted to believe them. I had to believe them. It was the only way to rebuild my life again and move on."

I sat up cross-legged directly opposite her and looked straight into her eyes.

"Don't do that, Nilofer. It reminds me of him."

She was in an impossible mood, but I persisted. "Listen, I know what you felt about him and why you're still angry, almost thirty years later, but that is not what I am asking you. You still talk as if it happened yesterday. The wounds can't possibly still be hurting, Mother. I was asking you something else. Five or ten or twenty years after I was born, you could still have tried and made Iskander Pasha love you. He's such a lovely person and—"

"Stop it, Nilofer! I've had enough of this nonsense. My husband is a good and generous man and I am attached to him. There is no tension in our relationship, but nor is there much passion. Neither of us wants anything else. So spare me your matchmaking at this stage of my life and concentrate on your own happiness. Sometimes I think there is too much romance in you. You are too impulsive. Too instinctive. You don't think before you act."

I began to laugh at her. "And where do you think I inherited that from? Not him! It couldn't be him, because he accepted Grandfather's gold pieces – and I'm sure it was gold, not silver – and deserted you and every instinct in his own body. Isn't that correct, Mother? Whom do you think I take after? You, or that rat?"

She did not laugh as I had hoped. She smiled. "Go to bed now, child. You're very tired."

NINETEEN

The fragments of Kemal Pasha's life and his ambition to create the world's largest steamship company; Nilofer reflects on happiness and the meaning of life; the death of Mariam

"No, it was not as you say, Iskander."

We were still at the breakfast table and the three brothers who, I had to remember, had not been around the same table since their father's death nearly thirty years ago, were dominating the conversation. Petrossian stood in the corner, listening to every word and permitting the odd smile to lighten his face.

My father had just suggested that Uncle Kemal had been such a self-sufficient and solitary person even as a child that their father had been impressed and thought he might become a great thinker or philosopher. Kemal Pasha denied this assertion. "I suppose that was one possible interpretation. The reality was otherwise. I learnt to depend on myself from an early age not because I was morose or preferred my own company, but because Memed and you demanded so much attention from everyone all the time. I remember our mother saying to me on one occasion how nice it would have been if I had been born a girl, so that she could have dressed me in her clothes and jewellery. It was her way of wishing she had paid me more attention."

Memed smiled affectionately. "My memory is somewhat different. I remember being reprimanded quite severely for ignoring you. Father once asked me whether I was jealous of your arrival. The question bemused me and he must have seen that on my face. He explained that the property, apart from this house, which thanks to Yusuf Pasha's insistence could only be inherited by the oldest son, would now have to be divided three ways. I think Father did not believe it when I said the thought had never occurred to me. I suppose when he was growing up these questions dominated discussion in their household and the arrival of every new son was greeted by the elder brother as a catastrophe."

"That may all be true, Memed," said Kemal, "but the fact remains that you and Iskander left me no other option but to amuse myself. What was really irritating was that your self-importance had infected the servants as well. Petrossian was devoted to Iskander and accompanied him everywhere. Isn't that the case, Petrossian? Well, answer me, man."

Everyone's gaze shifted to the old man with the red beard who stood near the door. He did not answer.

"Please answer him, Petrossian," my father pleaded. "Otherwise your silence will count against us in the ledger he has been preparing for twenty years."

Petrossian smiled. "I was ordered by the master to make sure that Iskander Aga did not get into trouble. They were always worried for him. He was considered very impulsive. That is why I went with him everywhere."

Kemal was not impressed. "He only replied because Iskander asked him to do so. All of you have witnessed it. Nothing changes. I have no doubt that Father gave him the instructions, but so what? It doesn't change anything as far as I'm concerned. Hasan Baba, bless him, shaved Memed and cut his hair with such delicacy that from a distance it seemed as if he were painting a portrait. With me it was always in a hurry. I was a permanent afterthought in this family."

My father burst out laughing. "I'm so glad you're here, Kemal. We hear of your amazing life from people who have run into you in the strangest parts of the world. Welcome home."

Kemal Pasha softened. "It is nice to be here, but let me get the last complaint off my chest. It has burdened me a long time. Have I your permission, sister Hatije?"

My mother smiled. "You don't need my permission, Kemal. This is your house and you must treat it as such."

Petrossian came to refill our cups and though he usually went first to Iskander Pasha, on this occasion he served Uncle Kemal before everyone else with a look of exaggerated servility. The three brothers exchanged smiles.

"I will speak my last bitterness," warned Kemal, "and then move on to more pleasant subjects. When it came to our future lives, what happened? Memed was allowed to settle in Berlin with the Baron. And I was pleased for him. Iskander went into a Sufi phase and married the lovely Zakiye. And I was pleased for him."

Everyone knew what was coming and laughter began to spread even before he had finished.

"Oh, yes, it is very funny for all of you. I was forced by Father to contract an arranged marriage. He was straightforward. The dowry was phenomenal. I was not even allowed to see the woman. I'm not surprised they didn't permit that . . ."

"Kemal," interrupted my father. "You could have spied on her in the baths."

"I tried. She never went to the cursed public baths. You think those women are unaware that we spy on them? They know. I don't think Leyla liked baths! So I was compelled to marry her, sight unseen. And as Allah is my witness I shut my eyes very tight and did my duty. Three children. All girls. Mother was delighted, till they began to develop and grow. When the youngest of my three graces turned six, our mother realised that the game was over. It was unfortunate that each of them had inherited their mother's features, but even that did not bother me. I could have ignored that if just one of them had been intelligent or, at least, not completely stupid. It is not a nice thing to say of one's own children, but it is even worse to engage in self-deception. To be bovine in appearance and half-witted at the same time is too much of a punishment for one person to bear. Did I ever tell you what our mother said to me a few months before she passed away? She had just finished her card-game with our aunt and had won some money. She was, as a result, in a generous mood that day. She kissed my cheeks and apologised to me. She's the only person who ever acknowledged the weight of my burden. She said to me: 'I'm sorry, my little sparrow. We knew your wife was no fairy, but your father and I had hoped the children would be like our side of the family. We were wrong. Terrible fate. It has dealt you such a repulsive hand.' I decided that it was pointless to bemoan my misfortune any longer. I decided to become a seafarer. Contrary to what you imagine, I have rarely been on my own. Each ship has a crew of fifty sailors and they are never of the same nationality. They speak different languages. They have different gestures to express the same thing. Some nod their heads when they mean 'no' and others will shake their heads when they mean 'yes'. Their customs are never the same. Then there is the captain. He may be the silent type who thinks only to himself and rarely speaks unless it is to issue a command or he could be loquacious to the point of irritation, talking of his adventures and presuming on the politeness of his listeners. There may be anything up to fifteen passengers. They may be adventurers in search of a fortune, traders, women escaping from misfortune, younger sons from wealthy families whose father has died and the house has gone to the oldest brother. They need anonymity in a remote corner of the world. I always have company on the boat. I have learnt a great deal in this way. Some of the conversations have been very rewarding. One does not have to cultivate insincerity as in the society we all keep in Istanbul or Berlin or London or Paris or any other big capital. My ships have made me truly cosmopolitan. I have learnt to flow like a wave and sometimes, when I am lucky, I find a wave-brother in the captain or his first mate. I am pleased to be here with all of you, but of one thing I am sure. I could never live in Istanbul again. Now if you will excuse me, I will go and shave, evacuate my bowels and take a bath. These routines are universal. Only the timing changes. Did I ever tell you that in Japan they regard you as odd unless you excrete at least three times a day? I never managed more than twice."

Later that afternoon he was in a more relaxed frame of mind. Having painted the darkest possible picture of his boyhood and youth and the bitternesses that married life had imposed on him, he decided to conclude the chapter of his miseries. He spoke now of the new worlds he had seen and how they had changed his life and his world-view. He had become adept at reading the sky and the sea. He knew why sailing ships avoided the Red Sea, why it was the prevailing winds and the currents that determined the length of each journey and not the distance. He explained why it was sometimes quicker to travel twice the distance in order to catch the right breeze rather than proceed directly to the destination. With the exception of Salman, whose face remained impassive, none of us had any knowledge of these subjects and it was like entering an enchanted world.

It was when he spoke of the night sky that his face changed, as if the memory alone was sufficient to restore some peace and harmony in his life. He had learnt to read the sky, to recognise the stars and their place in the firmament and, as the years went by, he could do so from different parts of the world.

As I listened to him speak that day, I understood why he now found it difficult to contemplate a sedentary existence. He had simply outgrown the conveniences and comforts that the ready-made world of the big city had to offer him. Each of our lives is a journey. By the time we have arrived halfway, our life, on every level, has developed its own singular routine. We do not question how we live any longer. We accept our failures and our successes. We become settled in our views. Sometimes we think if we had made a different turning in our lives so many years ago we might now be on a different road. But we accept that nothing is now likely to change. If anything, we start to look backwards. Since time and biology have circumscribed our own future, we simply stop thinking of it.

I know Selim disagrees with me very strongly on these matters. He accuses me of adopting a conservative outlook on life. He argues that just as big events can transform everything in society as a whole so they can change our lives regardless of our age. Perhaps they can and will, but is it always for the good? I know our Empire is crumbling and that is something positive, but in the end will the result be good? Unlike Selim, I am not so sure. He insists that history always moves forward. It can never regress, but he is wrong on this and Salman and I often argue with him, citing many examples from Europe and the history of our own religion. We have been regressing now for nearly two hundred and fifty years.

My Uncle Kemal may not have found real happiness in the sense that my mother meant by this phrase, but he was certainly not unhappy. He had not loved and lost someone as both Sara and Iskander Pasha had done, which meant that, for them, at least, the memories of the past never ceased molesting the present. This was not my Uncle Kemal's problem. He was escaping from the present and in his journeys had discovered his future. Salman had talked of the woman who shared Kemal's life in Tokyo and it did not seem to me that there was anything missing in his life. If anything, it was too crowded. I mentioned this last fact to the Baron, who roared with delight at this observation.

"Well judged, Nilofer. If he could push the Istanbul passengers in his life off the boat altogether, he would be even happier. How we live our lives does not, unfortunately, depend on us alone. Circumstances, good or bad, constantly intervene. A person close to us dies. A person not so close to us carries on living. All these things affect how we live. If Memed's father, for instance, had lived another twenty years would Memed have taken a decision to move to Berlin? I really do not know. Sometimes, if you are even moderately happy, it is better not to ask too many questions. That way lies unnecessary torment."

After the evening meal was over, the Baron produced a bottle of what he proclaimed to be very fine, old French cognac. On subjects such as these, I have learnt to accept his word. Kemal sniffed the glass, took a sip, and exclaimed that it was simply the best cognac he had ever tasted in his life. This pronouncement delighted the Baron, who beamed expansively at his brother-in-law.

"Tell me, Kemal," my father asked him. "how is your company doing? Will the new canal in Egypt cut down the length of your trips to the Far East?"

Kemal frowned. "I wish you hadn't mentioned that bloody canal. It is true what you say, but the canal is designed to help British trade. It is not designed for sailing ships. As I told you this morning, the Red Sea is too dangerous for us. You need fixed routes and steamships. Then the canal will be useful."

"Why not get a few steamships?" interjected Memed.

Kemal looked at his brothers and sighed. "Who would have guessed that all this time, while I've been away at sea, back at home maritime geniuses have been lying dormant in our family? Perhaps I should surprise all of you by preparing a manual on conjugal intimacy. Why on earth do you think I'm back here? I'm on my way to London to collect my first steamship. They have charged me a small fortune, but I will get my revenge sooner than they imagine. I will take it to Yokohama and we will see if the Japanese can build me ten more at half the price. If they can, I will build a steamship company that will rule all the oceans. London to New York on the Ottoman Line.

Istanbul to Tokyo via Alexandria. All becomes possible. I have raised all the money myself, some of it with the help of Nilofer's Great-uncle Sifrah. Everything is about to change and, unlike our Sultans, I am not going to wait till everyone else has overtaken me. Does that answer your questions?"

Everyone became very excited and the talk began to take on a surreal dimension, as even my mother felt obliged to intervene. The fact that nobody present except Kemal and Salman had even the vaguest idea as to what was needed made little difference. It was the sort of discussion that contributed nothing very substantial, but did have the effect of making Uncle Kemal feel that he was the only person present who was at the centre of real progress. Halil did not count since none of them realised how close the Committee was to taking power. In fact Halil and Selim had spent most of the day on horse-back and had arrived just in time for the meal. They had pretended to go hunting for quail and wild duck, and a leather bag containing many dead birds had been deposited in the kitchen, but I knew better. It was a feint. They had gone to meet the young officer from Salonika in a nearby village to hear how the eunuch-general had been despatched, the reaction in the palace to his disappearance and the latest plan for action.

"And here I was, Kemal," said Iskander Pasha, "almost convinced that you had come to visit your ailing brother. Instead it was the lure of Mammon!"

"If you have problems in Yokohama," suggested the Baron, "bring your steamship to Kiel. We might give you a better price than the English."

Kemal Pasha looked thoughtful. "Thank you, Baron. What I think I really need is for Salman to rejoin my company and start helping his old uncle again. The office in Istanbul needs a strong presence. Perhaps we can discuss this on our own a bit later. I must return to Istanbul tomorrow and sail for London."

This remark was taken as a hint that we should leave the room to the two men. We all took our leave of each other, but as I began to walk away, Salman drew me back.

"Stay with us, dear Nilofer. There are no secrets from you. Unless you are desperate to be with your husband."

I stayed.

"Well, Salman?" asked my uncle. "Are you ready to return to work?"

"I am, but one thing worries me."

"What?"

"The situation here, as Nilofer will confirm, is very unstable. The Greeks make no secret of the fact that Istanbul is their city and the Russians encourage them shamelessly. The British play both ways. The Germans are on our side. They do not want the Empire partitioned. In terms of business, Uncle, I was thinking it might be safe to move our headquarters somewhere else."

"Where?"

"I'm not sure. Liverpool? New York?"

Kemal smiled. "You must not confuse a building that serves as our headquarters with one where we bank our money. I agree it would be disastrous to keep the money in Istanbul at the moment. Sifrah advised me to move some to his branches in Paris and London some years ago and I followed his advice. If the Empire falls we will be safe."

I asked what flag flew on his ships.

"Our own, naturally. We fly the Ottoman colours. It's not a problem. I could fly the Japanese flag if I wished. When can you start work?"

"When we return to Istanbul, Uncle. I am enjoying this interlude."

Salman had dreaded any reference to Alexandria, but he knew it was unavoidable.

"I met Hamid Bey a few weeks ago. He sent you his warmest regards."

"How is he? I respect him greatly. He was very kind to me."

"He is well. His grandchildren are growing up and they make him very happy. He has something to live for. I saw them at his house. They are polite, intelligent and good-looking. What more could one ask?"

Salman gave a weak smile. He could not resist the question.

"And their mother?"

It was Uncle Kemal's turn to pale. "You don't know?"

"Don't know what?"

Our uncle was clearly shaken. He paused for a long time. "She was found dead last year, Salman. I was sure Hamid Bey had written and informed you."

Salman's face filled with pain. "What happened?"

"Nobody really knows. She went for a swim in that cove which I'm told was your discovery. She took her books with her and her towels, put them in front of that little cave and then went for a swim. When she did not return home that day, Hamid Bey sent servants to look for her. Her maid knew she often visited the cove and soon they had returned with her belongings, which included a book of poems by Verlaine.

"The next day a fisherman discovered her body. They say a current must have taken her by surprise and dragged her out to sea. She must have swum too far, got tired and was unable to return. I am really sorry, Salman. I assumed you knew but did not wish to discuss the matter."

My brother began to weep loudly, calling her name and saying he had forgiven her. My uncle and I consoled him as best we could, but the news had been completely unexpected and he was in a state of shock. He could not believe it was an accident. He kept repeating that she was a very powerful swimmer and knew the sea extremely well. He was convinced it must have been a deliberate act. She must have swum out to sea till she became tired and knew a return to the shore was impossible. That was the way she had planned her escape from the world.

As he calmed down, Salman remembered how, during the first weeks of their courtship, she had told him that if they could not be together she would commit suicide. He refused to take her seriously and had joked about it, asking which method she favoured in case the need ever arose. She replied that she did not wish to hurt herself or be discovered. She would try and swim all the way to the horizon.

"Did Hamid Bey give you any idea as to why she was so unhappy?"

Kemal took Salman's hand in his own and stroked it gently. "Hamid said she never forgave herself for the way she treated you. She told him repeatedly that the furniture man had meant nothing to her. He supplied her with seed that sprouted. As the children grew and became more attached to their grandfather, she became more and more distant from everyone. She often asked him if he knew where you were, but he would protect you by saying he had no idea at all and remind her that she had caused you enough pain to last a lifetime and if she was feeling lonely, she should look for a new victim. Hamid Bey was totally with you, Salman. He did not sympathise with her at all and their relations deteriorated over the years. She did not find another man or if she did it was a secret from her father and children."

"Poor Mariam," said Salman. "She must have been really tormented to take her own life. You look troubled, Uncle Kemal. As you can see, I've recovered well from the shock. I have a feeling you're keeping something from me? What is it?"

He sighed. "Sometimes I think how lucky I am that I have never loved like you or your father."

"Or my mother," I added. "Or me."

He smiled. "Exactly. You seem happy enough, green-eyed child, but the others have all been marked for life. I am glad that Allah has spared me this particular agony."

Salman persisted with his questioning. "Was there anything else, Uncle Kemal? I'm serious. You can tell me."

"Hamid Bey told me that she wrote you a letter each week, which she never posted. He discovered them after her death and burnt them. He did not want the children to discover them."

"What did she write?"

"He did not wish to tell me and I resisted the urge to force him. If you see him again, ask him by all means. It was not something I could do on your behalf. Who knows? Perhaps the letters were not simply the cries of a heart in pain, but were abusive, particularly in relation to her father. I must retire to bed. We shall meet when I return from London and then we shall discuss my shipping plans."

Salman and I sat alone in the library for many hours. I knew what a desolate and terrible place Alexandria had become for him. I knew how her cruelty had overwhelmed him. He would have forgiven everything else, including the carpenter, but the gratuitous pleasure she had derived from causing him pain he would never forgive. That had killed his love for her completely. All his emotion had drained away. Had anything remained?

"No, I don't think so. It was a slow process, I admit. For weeks and weeks she was in my head like a giant octopus. I would fight her with all the harsh words she had been spared when we parted. It is not easy to clear one's head of emotional waste in a few days. It takes time, but it does happen. When I was on the ship for nearly five months and then travelling through Japan, I really stopped thinking of her. Everything was over. I remember the feeling of relief that swept through my whole body. I had finally dislodged the beast that sat on my chest every day, nibbling away at my heart. I wept with joy when I realised I was free of her. It had been such a long time that I was unprepared for the surprise.

"When I heard just now that she had swum away from the cove, some old and tender memories flooded my mind, but not for long. They were replaced by other memories of what took place on that very spot. She was not an evil woman, Nilofer. I think she never recovered from her mother's decision to abandon her or her father's hostility when she abandoned me. I wonder whether the mother even wrote to condole with Hamid Bey or whether he even informed her of Mariam's death. Who knows – and who cares? It is all in the past. It is peculiar, however, to think she is no longer in this world.

For many months the only way I could recover my sanity was to think of her as dead. Now that she has really gone it feels very odd.

"Come with me, little sister Nilofer. Let sleep wait a while, tonight. Let your lover-husband read Auguste Comte while he awaits your return. I don't want to be alone as I look at the stars."

We walked out of the elegantly lit library with its six lamps, straight into the blackness of the garden. There was no moon, and it took our eyes a little while to adjust to the darkness. The sky was clear, the stars bright. In the distance the sea, like a thick, dark blanket, was calm.

Outside in the world a great deal was going on. Rebellions were being plotted. Resistance was being prepared. Sultans and Emperors were becoming uneasy. History was being made. Here in the beautiful, fragrant gardens of Yusuf Pasha's folly, all that seemed very remote. My brother Salman and I sat on a bench and began to count the stars, just as we had done when I was a child.

TWENTY

The confessions of Petrossian; the murder of Great-great-uncle Murat Pasha; the agony of Petrossian's family

'Is an old male servant permitted to address you, O Woman of Stone? I know that in years gone by it was the custom for many women in the employ of this household, after their honour had been violated by the masters, to come and weep here and tell you of their woes. Nor was this confined to the maids. In the time of Iskander Pasha's grandfather there were many young men – gardeners, watchmen, footmen and from different backgrounds, Kurds, Albanians, Armenians, Serbs, Arabs, Bosnians, Turks – who were all taken against their will. Did they come and shed tears at your feet as well, Stone Woman, or had pride forced them to erase the memory altogether?

Did the man who, sixty years ago, murdered Iskander Pasha's lecherous great-uncle, Murat Pasha, ever come to you and confess his crime? They never discovered his identity, did they?

Some of the servants must have known, but nobody betrayed the assassin. My grandfather used to say that, in secret, everyone prayed for the courageous killer never to be found. Whoever it was he must have carried on working here because, in those days, nobody left unless they were dismissed. My grandfather used to tell my father that if ever he had seen evil it was the face of Murat Pasha and not simply when he had consumed too much wine or was overpowered by lust. He was an unpleasant person in every way. His own children grew up to loathe and fear him.

It is said, Stone Woman, that he deflowered his own seventeen-year-old daughter. They say that on that occasion he was in his cups, as if that excused the crime. Did that poor child ever come and tell you her story? Did she come here and show you her blood-stained tunic, before they quickly married her off to a Bedouin from Syria? Nothing was ever heard of her again. She never returned to Istanbul. I hope she found some solace in her new life and that her children helped her to forget this world.

Stone Woman, I have something to tell you. I know who killed Murat Pasha. He told me so himself and he was always proud of what he had done. It was my friend, Hasan Baba. That is why the throat was so perfectly slit and the penis and testicles removed with expert care. Who else could accomplish this except the trained hand of a young barber? Mercifully, the finger of suspicion never pointed in his direction because he always used to help his old father shave Murat and trim his beard. The two of them were often observed in the courtyard, laughing at Murat Pasha's jokes and on the surface there was no enmity.

Hasan Baba told me that on a personal level, Murat was very nice to him, even when, in his father's absence, he had to shave him and was so nervous that he cut his cheek. Hasan feared the worst, but Murat Pasha simply laughed and muttered, "You will learn in time, young cub. Just watch your father closely."

Why, then, did he kill him? He told me that he could no longer bear the tears of the men and women whose bodies had been so brutally misused by Murat Pasha. I was never convinced that this was the whole truth. I mean, Stone Woman, Hasan Baba was a Perfect Man, but you do not take a risk such as killing Murat Pasha unless you have been personally affected by something he has done. Hasan did confess to me, after I pressed him strongly, that Murat had forced a young Kurdish washerwoman to pleasure him against her will.

Hasan had loved this girl from a distance. He would sit and watch her as she carried bundles of dirty clothes to the stream. He would notice how her body moved as she dealt with the clothes, washing them, beating them, wringing them and then standing on her toes to hang them out for drying. He had not yet summoned the courage needed to inform her of his feelings, but he was sure she knew. When unaccompanied by her mother, she would smile at him. I was not born then, but Hasan Baba at the age of eighteen must have been a very fine specimen. Before he could do anything, Murat Pasha had carried away the girl on his horse and assaulted her. When she was returned home, her mother hugged her and wept, but pleaded with the girl to remain silent or else they might both be dismissed. The daughter heard her mother's plea and wept in silence. They consoled each other. The girl promised she would not speak of the crime to anyone.

Overnight she had decided on the best way to remain silent. Early one morning, just before dawn, she made her mother's breakfast, kissed her warmly and said she was going for a walk to watch the sunrise. She jumped off the cliffs, Stone Woman. They found her broken body a few hours later. How people summon up enough courage to take their own lives is something I will never understand. Loud were the mourning wails that rent the servants' quarters that day. The young woman had been greatly loved for her defiant spirit and her beauty.

That was the day that Hasan Baba calmly decided to kill Murat Pasha. He knew he could not trust any other person. He planned everything on his own. Three weeks later Murat was found dead. His penis had been severed from the body and stuffed down his mouth.

I did not ask Hasan Baba for the details, Stone Woman. It was enough that he had done what he did. I think the whole family was relieved. Certainly no tears were shed for the monster. He was buried in the family cemetery, but very few turned up to pay their last respects. His own sons and wives stayed away.

A few months before he died, Hasan Baba was thinking of telling Selim. I am not sure whether or not he did so. I have lived with this secret long enough, Stone Woman. Over the years I often heard Iskander Pasha's father wondering who could have killed his uncle. Memed once remarked that whoever had done the deed was a modern hero to be sought out and awarded a purse posthumously. I wonder what they would have done had they known it was Hasan Baba? I think Iskander Pasha would have been proud.

I did not come here to talk of the past, Stone Woman, but your presence has the effect of dragging old secrets out of us. I came to talk of what is going on in my village. Over two hundred years ago this family gave us money to buy land in a village, close to where they themselves owned a large amount of land. As happened in those days, other Armenian families began to move in so they could be close to us and live under the protection of this family. It was Iskander Pasha's grandfather who could not bear sharing anything with his brother Murat, and therefore began to sell his land. Fifty years ago the family had sold off all its land and bought properties in Istanbul and Damascus and heaven knows where. Many Armenian merchants looking to spend their money bought some of the land, but it was the Kurds who arrived to work as seasonal labourers. Some of them settled.

Four years ago the Kurds warned my brothers and other relations that unless they moved out of their own accord, their houses would be burned and their families killed. One doesn't need more than a single warning of this nature and, as a result, many Armenians took what belongings they could and left. My sister and her husband refused to leave. She was always stubborn. She told them they could kill her, but she would never leave her home of her own accord. I informed Halil Pasha of all the happenings. He was so enraged that he did not send a subordinate to deal with the situation. He took some soldiers and went himself. He warned the Kurds that if anyone else was touched he would personally return and drive them off the property they had stolen and inflict severe punishments. He told them that if they touched my sister or her family, the punishment would come very soon. Halil was very angry, Stone Woman. The Kurds believed him. Nothing more happened.

Last week my sister's house was set on fire in the middle of the night. As her sons and their wives rushed out to escape the fire they were ambushed and killed. The same thing happened to all the other Armenians in the village. I told Halil Pasha last night. He sat at the table with his head in his hands and moaned. "The Empire is crumbling, Petrossian, and everyone is trying to get something for himself before a new order is restored. I am truly sorry, but there is nothing I can do at the moment." When Halil Pasha, who is a general, says he can do nothing to stop the killing of my people, what hope is there for us? I am an old man and will die soon, but my sons and grandsons want to make a new life.

Everyone is beginning to make stupid politics. Now my own sons want to engage in politics. They say it is the only way. What good has that ever done? My oldest boy has joined a group newly formed to fight for the creation of our own country. He says Armenians all over the world will support us. His older brother has already fled across the border to Russia.

My son-in-law says we must fight but stay within the Ottoman lands, fighting for our own *vilayets* in Anatolia to be given the status of a self-governing province with our own governor. He says a complete separation between the Ottoman lands and Armenia is impossible. Our people and lands are mixed everywhere.

He wants us to become Dashnaks. We must join the Dashnakzouthion, which is in favour of working with the Committee to defeat the Sultan. In Russia, he tells me, the Dashnaks are on the side of the Social-Democrats, whoever they may be, and against the Tsar. I have never heard talk of this sort before. If my own family is in politics something must have changed.

What is going to happen, Stone Woman? The whole world is falling apart.

All my life I have lived in this house. I have been treated well. My sons refused to stay here. They asked me many times to leave the house and come and live with them. They said that the world had changed and they had earned enough money for me to live in peace for the rest of my days. I told them I felt safe in this house. If I had been in that village with my sister I, too, would have died. Now my sons want me to leave Istanbul. One of them sells carpets in Cairo. He wants me to go and live with his family, but I don't know his family, Stone Woman. This family in this house is the only family I really know. I do not wish to leave Iskander Pasha. Am I wrong? ’

TWENTY-ONE

Selim is so impressed by the Paris journals of Iskander Pasha that he reads them twice; the Baron explains why the Parisian crowd was different from Istanbul; the troubled life of General Halil Pasha

Selim had refused to be distracted. For over an hour he had been reading and re-reading the journal that the French woman had returned to Iskander Pasha. My father had placed the journal in the library. I had lifted it up immediately and brought it to our room so we could read it together when we were in bed. Selim had betrayed me. He had started reading the entries while I was putting the children to bed and was halfway through his second reading, refusing to share it with me. When he had finished I snatched the notebook away from him, but he was in a daze.

"Don't sulk with me, princess. I was in a trance because Hasan Baba was also in Paris at the same time and talked of those months a great deal. Do you know when your father wrote these?"

I shook my head.

"In 1871. Paris was under siege by the Prussians. The self-proclaimed French Emperor, Napoleon the Third, fell and the crown slipped off his head. A republic was proclaimed and then something truly amazing happened: there was an uprising by the poor of the city, who realised that there was nothing to choose between the rich inside Paris and the Prussians at the gates. Hasan Baba always claimed that he had helped to build one of the barricades of the poor. I never really believed him. I thought it was a fantasy. He would have liked to, but could not. Your father's journal confirms the story. I'm really proud of Hasan Baba, Nilofer. Read it for yourself. Please."

To his great annoyance, I refused to read the journal that night. Instead, I fell asleep. The next morning I was woken by the noise of the birds. The sea was stormy and the seagulls were flying inland. I dressed and went down for breakfast with the journal. A strong wind was gathering pace outside and the curtains were flying everywhere. Inside, the servants were busy making sure the windows were firmly shut and the doors were bolted.

I was alone. None of the others had yet come down. I was not very hungry and poured myself a bowl of coffee and hot milk. I read the journal sitting at the table. It was a strange sensation. A storm was developing at sea and I was sitting comfortably reading about another storm of which I know nothing:

3 September 1870

I never thought the routines and the life I lead as an ambassador would permit me any space to write a diary, but these are amazing times. Today this pathetic and vainglorious figure that styled itself the "Emperor of France" was captured and his general defeated by the Prussians. Another triumph for Bismarck Pasha!

I went out for a stroll to gauge the mood of the people. Everyone looked depressed and the newspaper sellers were almost assaulted, so great was the urge to read about the day's events. I heard many people denouncing their own side much more vigorously than the Prussians. A few shopkeepers had banners outside their shops, which read "Vive Trochu". Trochu is the military governor of Paris and the man on whom a great deal now depends. In the afternoon a very large crowd marched through the streets demanding the creation of a republic. The French will never give up on their republics. We could learn something from them in this regard.

I am totally cut off from Istanbul as a result of the siege and I must admit it feels rather nice.

4 September 1870

Yesterday they demanded a republic and today it was proclaimed outside the Chamber, where a very large crowd had expectantly assembled. I was not present but Hasan, my barber, returned and gave me a complete account. This Sufi mystic is rapidly becoming a revolutionary. Since the embassy is paying his salary at the moment, I wonder whether his growing involvement might create a diplomatic scandal at a later stage. He tells me that there was applause all along the Place de la Concorde at the news. People began to tear the blue and white away from the tricolour, leaving the red intact. Hasan claims that the gilt N's on the railings of the Tuileries were being painted over and covered with crowns of flowers, supplies of which, unlike the food in this city, were never depleted. Hasan joined the mob as it invaded the palace and saw the establishment of a "Citizens' Guard". He says they were so impressed by his solidarity that they wanted to elect him to the Guard, but he declined, fearful of damaging my status here.

Excited by these reports I ventured out incognito into the streets, dressed in modest French clothes. It was a very hot and humid Paris today. Outside the Hotel de Ville there was a very large assembly. Spontaneously they began to sing the *Marseillaise*. This is how it must have been in 1789. Strange how these people feel their history instinctively; it is in their bones. The flower-sellers have joined this revolution. They are only selling red button-holes today and the Prussians are only four days' marching distance from the city. Only the French could topple their king in these circumstances. How I envy them this capacity.

Later I attended a dinner at the Montmorencys. Yvette is as well endowed as ever and the wine flowed as usual, but the mood here was very different from that on the streets. I controlled myself with some difficulty. The others were desolate. An elderly French gentleman spoke of the Germans with respect, saying that "only Bismarck can save us from this rabble". Yvette, feeling the need to speak, suggested that it might be better if the French generals dealt with the mob themselves; that if Thiers, who is an old family friend, were given his instructions there might be some blood on the streets but it would be cleansing. Then "we would all be ready to go and fight the Prussians". I suggested that the Prussian might be able to resist the French army, but Yvette might well conquer them. Apart from her nobody else smiled at my remark. My host, the Vicomte Montmorency, said that the noisy mob will only create havoc.

He declares himself for the republic, but only if it has Gambetta at its head and isolates the hotheads of the extreme left. Another guest, whose name I cannot remember, collapsed at the table, exclaiming that he had seen the most terrifying vision imaginable. Everyone stopped talking in order to listen to him. He spoke of the large amount of oil outside the gates of Paris, and his fears that the Prussians will throw it into the Seine and set it alight, burning the banks on both sides, just as the Ottoman Admiral Barbarossa threatened to do to Venice. Everyone looked at me for confirmation. I smiled.

I began to feel suffocated by the evening and took my leave. Montmorency said to me: "Don't treat us too badly in the despatches you send to Istanbul. It is all the fault of the Emperor." I smiled and said nothing.

23 September 1870
There is a terrible shortage of food in the city. As the Prussian artillery fire hits Paris, people complain of the lack of fresh vegetables and meat. Some restaurants are closing down. Others are beginning to serve horseflesh, while pretending it is beef fillet. Yesterday I was told that there were no more oysters available. There has got to be a revolution.

21 October 1870
A stranger delivered a very large parcel to the embassy. Petrossian was nervous, but brought it to my office with the attached letter. I cannot believe that he managed to do this. The letter is in the familiar hand of the Baron. He's remembered my birthday and the parcel contains the following: 2 bottles of champagne, a dozen oysters, a bottle of claret, a large piece of beef fillet, mushrooms, truffles, potatoes and, unbelievably, fresh lettuce. The cook, not knowing the Baron, was even more amazed than I am. I shared the feast with the others, though Hasan insisted that the wine he drank when he invaded the palace with the crowd was much better – as was the company. I toasted the Baron and wonder whether he is with the Prussian Army outside Paris.

31 October 1870
Everywhere I hear cries of "*Vive la Commune*". I walked with Petrossian (who has armed himself to defend us in case of attack) and Hasan Baba to the Hotel de Ville, where the embattled government realises its isolation. I fear that France is on the verge of a civil war. Paris is for the Commune, but it is isolated and will be crushed. I do not wish this to happen, but it seems inevitable.

7 November 1870

The Prussians have rejected the French call for an Armistice. Bismarck's Memorandum shows the iron will of the German leader. He has no equivalent in France. This Government, which has done so little to defend itself against a foreign enemy, is preparing seriously to take the offensive against its own citizens. A fresh egg, our cook now informs me, costs 25 *sous*.

"What are you reading, child?"

The Baron had arrived for breakfast and I put the journal away.

"Iskander Pasha's diaries of 1870 in Paris. You're mentioned."

He laughed. "The food parcel on his birthday?"

I nodded. "How did you do that? Were you actually there on the other side?"

"Yes, of course. Surely you agree that Bismarck was more progressive than that coxcomb Napoleon the 103rd or whatever he called himself. Utter scoundrel. Disgraced the name of his great forebear. Memed was very tickled that I had managed to get that parcel in on Iskander's birthday."

"Yes, I was," said Uncle Memed, yawning as he joined us at the table. He wanted to know why we were discussing the parcel. When I told him, he immediately took the journal from me.

"Hmm. I will read this later. Did you know that your Selim's grandfather played a heroic role in that ill-fated encounter?"

"Yes, but I hadn't reached that bit and . . ."

"When he first came back from Paris, Hasan was determined to organise a Commune in Istanbul. I think the Baron pointed out to him that it was foolish to mimic a defeat. Do you remember how angry he became, Baron?"

"Yes, yes. I remember. The problem was not so much copying a defeat, but the fact that the Istanbul crowd was still fiercely attached to the bloody mosques. The Parisians, thanks to 1789, had been cured of that disease. They were ferociously anti-clerical."

"You're right, Baron," said my father as he inspected the state of the table and noticed the absence of eggs, without which his day was incomplete. "Petrossian! I'm here. My eggs, please. Why are we discussing France, Baron?"

I explained for the third time that morning.

"As a matter of fact, it was the shortage of eggs during that siege, Baron, which made me pledge that once it was over I would never be without eggs ever again. It's all your fault."

Memed tittered softly. The Baron was pleased to be the centre of attention.

"Father," I asked him, "was Hasan Baba really affected by it all?"

"Yes, we all were. Petrossian became very excited as well, but the execution of the Communards by Thiers and his soldiers changed him around again. I think he saw the power of the state and it frightened him. Thiers was a bloodthirsty butcher. But Hasan was unshakeable. I agree with the Baron on Istanbul. We never had our 1789, let alone 1793. If that had happened here everything could have been different."

My father's scrambled eggs had arrived, complete with a sprinkling of fresh coriander and black pepper. As he busied himself with his breakfast, the Baron resumed the conversation.

"Yes, Iskander, but the whole point is that it could not happen here. In France there was an aristocracy that sucked the blood of its peasantry. Here, the Ottoman state was everything: Mosque, Sultan, Owner of the Land and Controller of the Army. That was its strength, as Machiavelli pointed out, but also its weakness. Your family was given fiefs by the Sultan in return for your services, but Yusuf Pasha of blessed memory had no power or land on which to raise his own army. In England and France the nobles were like miniature kings. Not here."

"Baron," pleaded Memed. "Please! Not while we're eating breakfast. You know how fragile I feel at this time of the day."

I could have kissed my uncle. I knew exactly how he felt.

"Does anyone in the house know where Halil has been for the last two days? Nilofer? You're part of the conspiracy, aren't you?"

I chose to ignore the provocation. Iskander Pasha was not convinced by the Committee and had been shaken by the affair of the eunuch-general. He had told Halil to be very careful and not to think that the eunuch was either the first or the last person to spy and report on them. It was a father's concern for his son's safety, but I felt there was something else as well. His Paris journals had revealed a side of him that had previously escaped my notice. The thought had not occurred to me before, but given the two sides of his emotional character, might there not be a similar dichotomy in the rest of his life?

There was the urbane Iskander Pasha in Istanbul who, dressed in formal clothes, called on the Vizier once a week and floated through the evening effortlessly while banalities were exchanged on the state of the Empire and the health of the Sultan. His face remained expressionless when he was entertaining visiting dignitaries at our house in Istanbul. But the charming smiles and the display of surface calm was a pure deception. This was the same man whose fists were often clenched in pain and anger. The journals were the strongest indication of this, even though he had been a young man at the time.

He was obviously worried that Halil might end up in prison or worse, but he was also irritated at being excluded from the affairs of the Committee, especially as he knew that I was involved. My interest in politics had been limited till the arrival of Selim in our house. The storms of passion he aroused had shaken the very core of my life. I had to rethink many things, both in my inner life and the world outside. These were things I had always taken for granted, such as the conviction that I and no other person would ever be in control of my emotions, and the idea of the Empire as something eternal. Iskander Pasha was looking at me impatiently.

"I'm really not sure, Father. He told Petrossian he might be away for a week or ten days in Istanbul."

"Politics or pleasure?"

"Neither," I replied. "Family."

He laughed. "Are the boys and their mother back from Damascus?"

They were and Halil, who had not seen his twins for several months, had been looking forward to seeing them again. I had always been much closer to Salman emotionally and this was still the case. On a human level and since I was a child, Salman and I had discovered we could discuss anything in the world without any sense of shyness or embarrassment. This feeling had remained, despite his long absence, and had delighted both of us this summer. Some relationships are so deep they can survive anything. I felt ours was one of these.

My relationship with Halil, while affectionate, had always been slightly formal. Ever since they were children, Zeynep and he had been close. This had nothing to do with their having a mother in common. They had always exchanged confidences and there was a temperamental affinity as well. Both of them were much more introvert than Salman and myself. Halil, in particular, could also be very secretive. Take his marriage, for example.

He met Catherine almost twenty years ago at a tea party in Istanbul. The Countess Galfalvy was an old family friend, then in her eighties. She was from an old Greek family and had run away in her youth with an impoverished Hungarian count. She spent her life on his family estate, where they had three rooms to themselves. The meals were shared with the family. Her late husband, Gyorgy, had been a painter. He must have painted over a hundred portraits of her during their life together and in every imaginable pose.

In her youth she had been renowned as one of Istanbul's great beauties and there had been rumours that the Sultan, too, had expressed an interest. Perhaps that was one reason for her unexpected flight with the Count Galfalvy. They had no children and when the count died, she found the three rooms unbearable and returned to Istanbul with all his paintings. To her amazement, a dealer, who had heard of them from a common friend asked, one day, to see the paintings. He spent several hours inspecting each one separately. He must have been honest, for he offered her a great deal of money for all of them. She kept a few she really liked and accepted his offer.

I remember going to see her with my mother on a few occasions. She lived in a large house which was fifteen minutes away from where we lived. Even in the pleasing winter sun the drapes were always drawn in her house. Perhaps she wanted to recreate the closed atmosphere of the rooms where she had spent fifty years with her count. But she was lonely. She missed the smell of oil on canvas. She began to visit the conservatory and would often invite young art students to have tea with her. If they were from poor families, she helped them financially and if they were from other parts of the Empire, she invited them to stay with her. Catherine Alhadeff was an art student from Cairo. She had been staying with some rather unpleasant friends of her father when she met the old lady at the school. Within a week, Catherine was installed in a very large room on the top floor of the house. There were no drapes and the light was perfect. The sun streamed in most of the year. Catherine was thrilled.

Halil saw her one afternoon when he and his mother went to take tea with the Countess Galfalvy. He was greatly impressed by her and probably her name was entered in his notebook later that day as one of the possible brides for him. Salman had once caught sight of the notebook and swore to me that such a list did exist, but when we teased Halil, he blushed and insisted it was a joke. I'm not so sure. I think the list, whether written or not, was always present in his mind. Catherine glided to the top of the list without even trying.

Halil was the type of person who avoided taking risks, but he was not a good judge of character. He once told me that he never trusted his own instincts because they always let him down. When I questioned him further it emerged that three young officers who he thought were loyal to him had let him down badly.

Zeynep was the first to be told about Catherine. Halil felt she would be the perfect wife for him. He did not want to live with a woman who did nothing the whole day. It would drive him mad. He told his mother, who expressed irritation that he wanted to marry a Christian. This really angered Halil. He informed his mother that if he wished, he would marry a monkey.

Then, to our great disappointment, we discovered that Catherine belonged to an orthodox Shia family. Her name was simply the result of her father's fondness for a sixteenth-century portrait of Catherine de Medici, which he had bought many years ago from a dealer in Istanbul. The painting was unsigned and Catherine's father had bought it for a very reasonable price. It was when he showed it to a visiting Venetian merchant that the trouble began. The Venetian was convinced it was a Titian and he was so sure of this that he offered to buy it for a fairly large sum of money. Catherine's father refused to part with the painting. The knowledge that it might be a Titian served only to strengthen his attachment. He grew more and more obsessed with it and when, after four sons, fortune blessed him with a daughter, he named her Catherine, despite the angry protestations of his wife.

The Countess Galfalvy favoured Halil's suit and recommended it strongly to Catherine's parents. Catherine herself appeared to be indifferent. She is supposed to have asked Halil whether he would stop her painting and after he had replied that it was one of the reasons why he wished to marry her, she accepted. She never asked him for other reasons. The owner of the Renaissance painting and his family duly arrived in Istanbul as guests of the Countess. The wedding itself was a modest affair. Only the two families and their close friends had been invited.

Catherine was a very striking woman, tall and slender with a dark complexion and shoulder-length dark brown hair. Her back arched delicately underneath her dress. She had thin lips and narrow eyes and the combination gave her a girlish quality. When I saw her for the first time I remember thinking, enviously, that this woman would never really look old.

A year and a half later, Catherine gave birth to a pair of healthy twin boys. There had never been any twins in either our family or hers, which raised a few questions, but as the boys grew all the doubts disappeared. They looked just like Halil and we grew to adore them. They were often at our house and every summer they would come here for a few weeks. Catherine loved this house and she painted it from every angle. Then she would take her canvas and paints to the cliffs and paint the sea. One such painting, in which the seagulls resemble hailstones suspended over the dark green ocean, still hangs in the library. I spoke to her often, but she was usually cold and reserved. It was the same with everyone else. Since Halil was away with the army for extended periods of time, everyone tried to be friendly with her, but, with the single exception of my mother, were politely rebuffed. For some reason Catherine liked my mother. She painted two very fine portraits of her, one of which I have in my old room in the Istanbul house.

It was a few years ago, after the twins had celebrated their fifteenth birthdays, that we realised something was seriously wrong. My source on the subject was, as usual, Zeynep.

"It's really awful, Nilo, just awful for poor Halil. Awful for poor Halil. I swore I would never tell anyone, but what she is doing is too cruel. Too cruel!"

Whenever she had important news to impart, Zeynep had developed a habit of repeating a sentence or a phrase, imagining that this would somehow double its impact. Its effect on me was the exact opposite. I would get so irritated by her manner of speaking that I could not concentrate on the content. I told her this many times, but she couldn't really help herself. The story she told me was upsetting.

Some months after the twins were born, Catherine had informed Halil that she did not want any more children. He was upset, but accepted her choice. He never pushed or pressured her in that direction. Soon afterwards she refused to share his bed and rejected his advances. She informed him that she had been very shaken by giving birth to twins and now the very thought of the reproductive process filled her with nausea. She advised him to find another wife or concubine or whatever he wished. She would accept anything provided they left each other alone. At this point I had interrupted Zeynep.

"Tell me," I asked her, "did he not open his notebook and consult the list?"

Zeynep remained serious. "No. Please. Don't try to be funny. Don't try to be funny. It's very bad."

What had made it bad was Catherine's decision to move to Cairo and take the children with her. Halil had wanted the boys to stay with him. He felt that their education at the *lycée* was being disrupted, but Catherine would not listen to reason. She disapproved of formal education and felt the twins would learn much more through travel. She had taken them back to Cairo and they had been there for a year, but the boys wanted to return to their father and their friends. She had promised they would be returned to Istanbul in the summer and could stay with their father, but their arrival was delayed, which angered Halil. He had rushed to Istanbul the minute he heard they were back. He had got his children back.

There was something else as well. Zeynep had prepared a list for him and she wanted him to view the first three names on it so that he could have a woman again.

TWENTY-TWO

What Catherine told the Stone Woman ten years ago

'It was thoughtful of Nilofer to send me to you. I've brought my easel and my oil paints. I'll paint you as I talk. I hope you don't mind. It's not going to be easy to get the colours right. You must have noticed me trying to mix them for the last hour. You look so different when the sun hits you directly. When I first heard about you from Halil, he described you as a goddess, but you're just a large rock. I'm not even sure whether you were ever carved. Perhaps you were. There are a few traces here and there. Could this have been the remnant of a woman's breast? Perhaps. That makes you more interesting. I think I'm going to paint you just as I see you. The colour is not exact, but I'm going to start.

What do you think of this family, Stone Woman? Do they ever mean what they say? I'm beginning to wonder why I ever got married. Halil is a nice man and he understands me. I have no complaints, but I can no longer bear his touch. I never enjoyed intimacy with him and I feel I've done my duty by producing two healthy boys.

It was so painful when they were born, Stone Woman. I thought my agony would never end. I lost so much blood that the midwives began to whisper to each other in worried tones. I thought I was going to die. None of my maternal emotions would come to the surface. I felt nothing. I was just a frightened girl and it didn't help when I found a child being placed on each breast. It was a strange sensation. I felt like an animal. If two women had not been found to breast-feed my boys I would have sunk slowly into oblivion, but much of the worry was, mercifully, removed from me. I don't think I was intended to me a mother, Stone Woman. I feel affection for these little boys, but I am not overwhelmed by love for them any more than I was for their father.

Did you say something, Stone Woman? I could have sworn I heard you ask why I married him. The dilemma confronting me was simple. Either I found someone of my own choice in Istanbul or returned to Cairo and faced the humiliation of having a man imposed on me by my mother, just as all my childhood friends had. I would rather have died.

My mother was completely opposed to the idea of my being an artist. It was my father who encouraged me. I learnt German so that I could go and study art history in Vienna, but my mother threatened to commit suicide and my father, foolishly, chose to believe her. She never really cared much for me. She had four sons who were all "settled in life", as she used to say. They were married. Their wives had produced children. Why couldn't she leave me alone? The agreed compromise was that I could study in Istanbul, because the Caliph of Islam resided here. One of my sisters-in-law who, like the others, is very fat, but unlike them is not so stupid, wrote and warned me that my mother was busy assembling suitors for the great day. Stone Woman, I panicked.

I discussed the problem frankly with my friend Maria, the Countess Galfalvy. She advised me to accept Halil's offer. She knew this family of old and said they were quite unconventional in their own way and would never obstruct my career. I was young and Maria had become a mother to me. So I accepted her advice. He seemed a very nice man. When I looked at him closely to see which part of him I could paint, it was his expressive and meaningful eyes that appealed to me. Unlike most men of my acquaintance, he did not like hearing the sound of his own voice. I felt he would never be unkind to me. He was not the man I had been looking for all my life, but that was because I did not think of men, only of being a painter. When I was still in Cairo, my friends would point to good-looking boys and giggle. I was unmoved by these encounters.

After I was married I found sexual intimacy very intrusive. I knew it had to be done. I had to lie down and let him put his little stick into me, but Stone Woman, I promise you: there was no enjoyment in this for me. None. When I told some women friends they thought there was something wrong with me and I grew tense and unhappy. There was no lack of passion on his part, but his touch simply left me cold. When I felt the need to be touched between my legs, I preferred to help myself. It was far less messy and much more pleasurable. I confessed this to my closest friend in Istanbul, who is also a painter, and she joked that it was like preferring the first rough sketch to the finished oil painting. I thought of this remark for a long time and it almost made me abandon oils.

I have not been intimate with Halil for three years now, ever since the children were born. I do not feel the urge to find another man. In fact I do not feel any urge that needs another person to fulfil it. I am content with my work.

One day I told some of this to Maria, imagining she would be horrified, but to my surprise, she understood perfectly. She told me some women are passionate and others are not. She herself had been very passionate in her life with Count Galfalvy, but she was lucky. She told me there was nothing to be ashamed of in this situation. Then she looked at me closely and asked me a question that, believe me, Stone Woman, shocked me deeply. Maria asked if I preferred physical contact with other women to intimacy with men. I must have gone red in the face because she burst out laughing and told me not to worry if that was the case. Istanbul was full of women who preferred each other and it was not a big problem.

I was so shaken by her question that I avoided her for a few weeks. My studio was still at the top of her house so I couldn't keep away for ever. One day when I arrived to paint I found a young woman waiting for me. She, too, was from Cairo and came with a letter from my father. She was the daughter of one of his most valued customers (my father, Stone Woman, is a merchant of antiques) and wanted to be a painter. She was spending a few months in Istanbul with her uncle prior to her departure for Florence.

Rachel, some years younger than I was, deserved to be in Florence. She had a beautiful face framed by thick, golden red ringlets, the loveliest face I had ever seen. At that moment I knew what I wanted most in this world. I wanted to paint Rachel. I wanted to paint that face in very great detail, not missing a single freckle. And, Stone Woman, I wanted to paint all of her both with and without clothes.

I showed her Istanbul. I took her to the oldest parts of the city. I sat with her on the edge of the water as the Golden Horn shimmered in the light of the full moon and we sipped the most delicious Istanbul coffee I have ever tasted.

I took her home. She saw the twins and held them in her arms. She met Halil, who liked her and was pleased I had found a friend. I asked to paint her and she was flattered and agreed. She was in Istanbul for one whole month and I painted every curve, every line of her face and body. She would not undress for me, but I imagined what was hidden underneath the folds and she was amazed at my accuracy.

Then she left for Florence. We wrote to each other regularly. She described the hills around Fiesole, the light just before sunset and just after dawn, the work she was doing and how much she missed my company. She wrote of seeing a painting, studying it for nearly an hour, trying to work out how many times the master had changed his mind, how many layers of paint had been used. She turned around to discuss it with me and became sad because I was not there looking at it with her. I was often overcome by an urge to leave everything here and join her in Florence, but Maria Galfalvy advised caution and I bowed to her experience. Instead, I would disappear with my sketchbook and draw Rachel as I pictured her in different parts of Istanbul. She lived in Florence for three years.

Now she has returned to Cairo and the leeches are gathering. Each mother wants Rachel for her son, which is not surprising. Her father is a wealthy Jew; she is very beautiful. There is an inevitability about her fate that fills me with melancholy. I am tired of living without her, Stone Woman. I will return to Cairo with my children. Rachel will have some of her own. We will console each other and paint each other and find a studio in Alexandria for the summer months when Cairo becomes unbearable.

And what of Halil? He will survive. He will find another wife, someone who will love and give him the pleasure he never had from me. I gave him two sons. I think I have done my duty.

I wish you could see this canvas. I have drawn you as a giant rock, Stone Woman, but only now do I see how much your eyes resemble those of Rachel. ’

TWENTY-THREE

A messenger arrives from New York with a letter for Sara; Memed plots to marry Jo the Ugly to one of Kemal Pasha's daughters

"Who is that noisy son of a donkey?"

Emineh thought the remark was directed at Orhan and started giggling, but it was not the children who had disturbed my uncle. It was a very hot day and Uncle Memed had decided, wisely, to take his afternoon siesta out of doors in the shaded part of the garden, where the sea breezes make the heat tolerable. I was sitting in a chair next to him trying to make sense of Auguste Comte. The children were playing some stupid game, aiming unripe walnuts at each other from a distance.

What had wakened Uncle Memed was the noise of a carriage and strange voices from the front terrace. A gardener was walking towards us followed by a strange apparition. Uncle Memed raised himself and glared at the two men.

The gardener pointed towards me and retreated. The apparition gave Memed and me a slightly awkward bow and began to speak in the worst French I have ever heard in my whole life.

"I arrived a few weeks ago in Europe from New York. I have a packet to deliver to Madame Sara, the wife of Iskander Pasha, but I am under very strict instructions to deliver it only into her hands."

Petrossian had appeared out of nowhere, annoyed that a stranger had breached our privacy. I told him to organise some refreshments for our visitor. I decided to put on my most sophisticated French accent.

"I will inform my mother of your arrival and see if she can receive you presently. What is your name, monsieur?"

"Er, Joseph Solomon, but Jo will do. Everyone calls me Jo."

"Petrossian, please show Monsieur Jo to the reception room."

As they walked away, Memed guffawed. "I'm glad you're making him sweat in the punishment room."

The name the Baron had given the ballroom after Yvette's visit had become a long-running joke in the household.

"Did you notice," my uncle continued, "how ugly he was? I mean really ugly. A perfect match for one of Kemal's daughters. Come on, Nilofer, let us matchmake a little mischief. We shall tell Kemal's wife that a new Sultan, a Sultan of money, has arrived from New York by the name of Jo the Ugly."

I laughed. Memed was cruel, but accurate. It was not simply that Jo Solomon was ill at ease with himself. The suit he wore was far too tight and the armpits of the jacket were soaked. That in itself was unforgivable. What made it worse was that he was large and fat, with a plump, placid and pock-marked face dominated by a bulbous nose, reminding me of the diseased cucumbers discharged by our vegetable gardener into the sea. Was Jo the Ugly in need of a dowry? That was the question of the moment. If the answer was an affirmative, we might send him back to New York with a bride.

At first I took him to be a jeweller bringing a gift for my mother from Uncle Kemal, who was always sending us presents. But I realised that he was too badly dressed to be a messenger. And then I knew. He must be the son of Suleman.

What did that packet contain? I threw my dignity into the sea and ran towards the house, just in time to join my mother who was sedately descending the stairway. Before I could warn her that the visitor might be my half-brother, Petrossian threw open the door of the punishment room and amazed me by announcing in a grand voice and very good French accent: "Madame Iskander Pasha et Madame Nilofer Selim Pasha."

We giggled at his audacity, but entered into the spirit of the comedy and, taking each other by the arm, swept grandly into the ballroom. Jo Solomon was impressed. Petrossian had understood his mentality very quickly. Jo the Ugly bowed to my mother.

"I am delighted you could receive me, madame. This is a very fantastical room. What a great palace you have here! I am Joseph Solomon, madame, and I have a packet which I was instructed by my late father to hand to you and you alone."

Sara paled considerably. "Your late father?"

"Yes, madame. Suleman of Damascus, as you once knew him. He never ceased to speak of your family's generosity."

My mother sat down on the sofa and demanded some water. She looked at Jo the Ugly carefully. It was obvious that his presence angered her.

"I am sorry to hear that Suleman has passed away. You look nothing like him."

Jo the Ugly handed the packet to my mother.

"He never stopped reminding me of that, madame.'

She moved to the seat near the window as I gave Jo the sickliest smile I could manage. He smiled back and at that moment I really felt ill. His mouth was maggot-infested. All his front teeth were stained a strange brownish-yellow and every single one had decayed at the edges. This was inhuman. I was relieved when Salman walked in, on Uncle Memed's recommendation, to see this person for himself, as he later told me. I excused myself and went and sat with my mother at the other end of the room.

She had her back to Jo the Ugly and Salman and was weeping in silence. I put my arms around her. Silently, she handed me the letter she had just finished reading.

My dearest Sara,

Our capacity for self-deception is infinite and I have suffered all my life as a result. This is a letter of explanation, Sara. I will write the truth. It is futile for a dying man to do otherwise.

For the last six months I have been slowly dying. The doctors have no cure because they have no idea what beast is devouring my insides. It's too late to regret that I became a painter rather than a physician. Who knows? I might have cured myself. Perhaps what is eating me is my own remorse, which has never left me since that fateful morning I boarded a ship destined for Liverpool and New York.

By the time you receive this letter I will be dead and buried. It is now over thirty years since I left Istanbul. Do you remember what you said to me that morning when I told you how desolate I felt? You gave me a cold, deadly smile and said: "You leave me with a broken heart, but a heavy purse, Suleman. I am sure one will take care of the other." I never forgot those words. How could you be so vicious, Sara? And so accurate.

Your father was generous. You were angry. I knew you wanted me to say that if there was a danger of our children being born with an ailment then we would not have any, but I was frightened that you might grow to resent me later and become bitter because I had prevented you from becoming a mother. This last sentence occurred to me only now, Sara. It's not the truth. Once you acquire the habit of speaking untruths, it is difficult to do otherwise, even for a dying man, but I am determined to break the habit here and now.

After all these years I still find it difficult to accept that I was so easily swayed by your father's generosity. You accused me of cowardice and treachery for betraying the love you had so freely given me. You were not wrong.

I do not believe your parents invented the story of the disease to stop our marriage. My own father confirmed that it was a serious problem, though my mother was equally insistent that there was nothing definite and that many marriages had resulted in children who were fine. She accepted, however, that it was a risk.

It is no consolation to either of us now, but I want you to know that all my life I have regretted leaving Istanbul. I wish I had taken the risk, Sara. I wish. I wish. Your Uncle Sifrah tells me you have a beautiful daughter. That makes me especially happy. I have not had the same luck. I know what you're thinking. Ugliness produces ugliness, in character as well as features. As you will have noticed, the bearer of this letter may have some qualities, but he is certainly not pleasing to the eye. He takes after his mother's brothers who are shysters and rogues, growing rich by robbing their own people.

In Damascus and Istanbul we tended to help each other. Not in this hell. When I first arrived here with "a broken heart, but a heavy purse", I was recommended to stay with a family of Polish Jews who had escaped here ten years ago from the pogroms against their people. I took the kindness I was shown by this family at face value. They were very nice to me as they attempted to relieve me of the heavy purse and soothe my wounded heart. They pressured me into marrying their oldest daughter, Tamara, and once I had succumbed (it was convenience, desperation and loneliness, Sara, nothing more; it never affected my love for you) I found that my purse was getting lighter by the day. I hired a studio and started painting portraits. Slowly my fame spread and when Mr Rockefeller asked me to paint him, I realised I would be comfortable for the rest of my life. But what good is material comfort, Sara, when one's emotional and spiritual cupboard is bare?

All the time I was suffering at the thought of having lost you, I wished you nothing but happiness. My own pleasures were casual, usually in my studio with some of the women who liked to pose for me. I found the lure of young flesh irresistible.

I had to find a different venue when my wife and her brothers burst in one day and surprised me with a woman. They did not harm me, but they marked the poor girl for life by carving her left cheek with a knife. I remember thinking of you after that incident and wondering what you would think if you could see how low I had sunk.

I write you all this so you know that life has punished me enough for the mistake I made thirty years ago. In this packet you will find the sketches I did of you in Istanbul and which I always treasured and used to inspect in secret to ease the misery and remember our time together. It was short, but it was the happiest period of my life. Remember that day in your father's library when you found the story of the Prophet Bilan and the Moabites and we laughed and laughed? That is another thing that disappeared from my life. Laughter.

I am also sending you a tiny oil portrait I painted of you from memory. Your child or grandchildren might like it as a memento. They are my last gifts to you, Sara. I hope you will forgive me.

Suleman

I looked at the sketches and the oil portrait of my mother. The sketches were very lively, with a lot of movement and one of them showed a bare breast. The miniature portrait was painted on a deep crimson background and my mother's eyes were very sad. It must have been the last time he saw her and the memory stayed with him.

"Leave them with me, child. You can have them after I've gone. Poor Suleman! Trapped for eternity. I do feel sorry for him and sad, but he wrecked his own life and mine."

"You had me, Mother Sara. Me! Was that nothing?"

She clung to me in an emotional embrace. "You have been everything, child. Everything. Without you I, too, might have been dead by now. We must never tell these people that you are his daughter. The thought of your being related to that fat boy makes me feel ill."

"He might still end up in our family. Memed, Salman and, I now see, the Baron are going to do their best to marry him off to one of Uncle Kemal's daughters!"

My mother's laughter was uncontrolled. She could not contain herself. I gave her some water and we joined the other group.

"Monsieur Jo, I thank you for bringing me such an important packet all the way from New York. Have you a photograph of your mother and the rest of your family?"

Jo shook his head. "I travel light, madame, especially in the summer."

Each note of the Baron's laugh was false. "Very sensible. I was saying to young Jo that, on his return from Damascus, he must stop and meet Kemal Pasha in Istanbul. Jo is a lawyer, you know, Sara, and could be very helpful if Kemal is starting up a steamship company."

Jo nodded vigorously. "I specialise in business and commerce. I can help a great deal, especially at the New York end. It will be a pleasure to meet Kemal Pasha when I return. I have no real desire to visit Damascus. They tell me it's very dusty and unpleasant in the summer, but my father's family is still there and I must pay my respects to them."

"Oh yes," said Salman. "And they'll be very happy to see you. It will come as a real surprise to them, especially since you look nothing like your father."

"Why don't you stay for dinner?" asked Memed.

This was going much too far and we all glared at him, but mercifully Jo had other plans and the coachman needed to return to the city tonight.

After he had left we all burst out laughing. My mother was a bit shaken, but not as much as I had imagined. She looked at her brother-in-law.

"Will you succeed, Memed?"

"If all of you help me, I think it can be done. The fat fool is not religious at all, which is good. He could be bribed and flattered to convert to our faith. We can pay a eunuch to dress as the Sultan and as the Caliph of our faith, and he can personally convert Jo the Ugly into Ibrahim the Worthy. Are we all agreed? Good. Iskander must be won over tonight. Kemal should be pleased with our plan. Jo the Ugly will return to Istanbul in January. Let us mark the next century with his wedding. Who knows but that the next hundred years might well be the years of people like Jo the Ugly. I'm so glad we're agreed. This has been such a productive day for me, Baron."

"I'm pleased to hear it, Memed. I do worry sometimes that your intellect is not receiving sufficient stimulation."

When I entered mother's room later that day she was sitting on the floor looking at the oil portrait.

"Would you rather be alone?"

"No, my dearest Nilofer. I would rather be with you."

She talked of the dream that had sent her running to the Stone Woman. "How can things like this happen, Nilofer? I'm not superstitious. I don't believe in the mumbo-jumbo of the astrologers, but it does make me wonder. Can we have such strong intuitions about someone we were or are still close to? I suppose that is the only explanation. The strange thing is that I had not thought of Suleman for a very long time when that dream disturbed my sleep."

I held her hands and kissed them. "Did the news of his death upset you very much?"

"No," she whispered. "I knew he was dying when I had that dream, and because I was prepared for his death I could control my emotions. It was the letter that upset me. I never thought he would admit the truth. He knew me so well, that boy. He knew I would still be wondering about the real reasons behind his decision to leave me. It was thoughtful of him to write, even though it was awful to read that my father had bought him off with money. What a fool!"

"Is the torment over now, Mother? Is it all finished?"

"Yes, my daughter. I am at peace with myself. If he had seen you and known you were his daughter I would have been even happier. Poor Suleman. He was a great lover of beautiful people and beautiful objects. It must have been a torture for him to see Jo the Ugly every day. No, Nilofer, don't frown. The problem is that the boy's character is no different from his features. All of us knew that instinctively. So did his father."

"What was that story about Bilan that made you laugh so much?"

Sara smiled and walked briskly to the small cupboard in her dressing room and returned with a copy of the Talmud.

"In our religion, Nilofer, the rabbis never gave an opponent any quarter. This was true in olden times just as it is now. And if they believed that a person had betrayed the Jews, in other words the Elders, then no mercy was to be shown. The character of the victim had to be assassinated in as many ways as possible and his name blackened in the eyes of the congregation. Bilan was one such person. They accused him of performing sorcery on his own organ. Now read the story."

I took the book from her and read the page she had marked:

Bilan's conversation with the Moabites

When they asked him why he wasn't riding a horse, he said to them:
"Usually I ride a horse. However today I am riding a donkey."
Thereupon the she-donkey said to Bilan in front of the Moabites:
"Am I not your she-donkey?"

"Merely for carrying burdens," Bilan said, trying to cut her off before she could contradict him further.

"That you could have ridden on," the donkey continued, contradicting Bilan's contention that she was merely a beast of burden.

"Only occasionally," Bilan said, implying that ordinarily he did not ride her.

"All your life until this day," the donkey went on contradicting Bilan's contention that he had never ridden her except on rare occasions.

"And not only that," she continued, "but at night I perform marital acts with you."

Thus the donkey got the best of Bilan in their verbal sparring. How, then, could Bilan claim to "know the mind of the Supreme One," that is, to know and manipulate the mind of God to allow him to curse the Jews, when it is evident that he was unable to know and manipulate even the mind of an animal?

My laughter had punctuated the reading and now it was Sara's turn, but her amusement was tempered by the memory of a wonderful day a long time ago.

"It's so childish, Mother. Don't you agree?"

"There is a childish side to every religion, Nilofer."

TWENTY-FOUR

The century prepares to enter its grave; Selim and Halil discuss the future; Dante and Verlaine; Orhan asks a question of Iskander Pasha

"The century is about to die." I heard the agitated notes of Selim's voice. "The Sultans and the Empire will go to the grave with it because their time has come. But when will our time come, Brother Halil? When will our time come? Should we die as well? I am not pleased with your news."

The two men were sitting in the library on their own when I entered. They looked up and smiled.

"Has something happened?"

Neither of them replied.

"Is it a military secret?"

Halil sighed. "No. The Committee has decided after several meetings with the palace . . ."

"And even more with the German ambassador . . .," interjected Selim.

"They have decided," Halil continued calmly, "to postpone indefinitely our plan to seize power."

"Why?"

"Because, Nilofer, we have been promised reforms of such magnitude that our action is unnecessary. It would be criminal to spill blood unnecessarily. Moreover, the Vizier accepted that next year leading members of the Committee would be appointed to the Government so that they can supervise the reforms themselves."

"Allah! That is amazing news. We have won without a single shot being fired."

"Yes," said Halil, "but they knew very well that if they did not move, shots would be fired – and not just shots. They know full well what happened to the eunuch-general. His disappearance was just accepted. No one asked us any questions. This inaction reveals a great deal about their state of mind."

Selim was looking very unhappy. "Both of you seem to have a surprising degree of confidence in the Vizier's capacity to deliver all that he has promised. He might think: appoint the ringleaders to positions of power and corrupt them in the process. Let some reforms through but resist any attempt to abolish the Sultan or diminish the powers of the clergy."

"Selim," said Halil, "if that happens, shots will be fired. Our young friends in Salonika share your doubts and your impatience. I am not as radical as you or them, but I know one thing for sure. If we fail to modernise over the next few years, we are finished. I don't mean 'we' as an Empire. I mean 'we' as a new, modern state. That is why people like me – soft, moderate, cautious – will side with the hotheads from Salonika to ensure that the reforms do not fail. We have waited two hundred years. A few more months or even a whole year will not make too much difference."

Selim relaxed a little and smiled. I asked Halil about the twins.

"Are the children back?"

"Yes, thank Allah. They are both well. I offered to bring them here, but they were desperate to see their friends in Istanbul. I left them with Zeynep."

"And will they stay with you permanently from now onwards?"

"Yes. That makes me very happy. I have told their mother she can see them whenever she likes, but I have granted her the divorce she sought. Now that the palace has given us a respite, I might do something about finding a new mother for my twins. Any ideas on this crucial question, Nilofer? Sighted any beauties of late?"

"I always thought you were the one who carried a list with the priorities clearly marked."

He began to laugh. The return of his sons had cheered him enormously and it was nice to see his forehead free of frowns once again.

"I stopped making a list a long time ago. Don't mock my lists, you wretched girl. Sometimes they can be a very useful prop for one's memory."

"No wonder women find you so romantic, Halil. You really know how to excite them!"

My brother smiled. "Once they have been selected, I release a charge of passion whose depth first surprises and later delights them."

We ended the discussion as the library was invaded from all sides. Iskander Pasha and Sara entered with my children from one side while the Baron and Memed strolled in casually from the garden. They were followed a few minutes later by Salman, whose face, darkened by the sun, was set in sharp relief to his white hair. It had become much more relaxed and he looked happy. He was carrying his old copy of Verlaine, a book I had first seen him read when I was eight years old. Its cover was now completely faded and discoloured by the Mediterranean sun and, perhaps, the tears of its owner. Everyone was pleased by the sight of him, especially Orhan and Emineh, who had become attuned to his changing moods. Children feel our problems far more acutely than we can ever imagine.

The Baron was in a mellow mood, but without permitting it to dull his competitive edge. "Why don't you recite your favourite poem from Verlaine and let me see if I can match it with one from my favourite poet?"

Salman put the book down on the table.

"This one is called 'Mon rêve familier' from his *Poèmes saturniens* and I translated it myself though, like all poetry, it is best in its own language. Here then is Verlaine's 'Well-Known Dream':

Often have I this strange and penetrating dream
Of a woman unknown, loved and loving me,
And who each time is neither quite the same
Nor yet another, and loves and understands.

For she understands me, and my heart, transparent
For her alone, alas, is a problem no more
For her alone, and the fevers of my pale brow,
She alone, weeping, knows how to cool.

Is she dark, fair or auburn? – I know not.
Her name? I remember it is soft and clear
Like those of loved ones banished by life.

Her gaze is like the gaze of statues,
And her voice, distant, and calm, and grave,
Has the inflexion of dear silenced voices.

There was a silence. Halil looked at his brother affectionately. Perhaps Verlaine had struck a few chords in the breast of my general-brother. The effect could only be positive. Salman smiled at the Baron.

"Match that if you can, Baron."

The Baron rose and walked to the shelf containing Latin and Italian poetry, one of the most under-used collections in our library. He climbed up the tiny wooden platform and, having immediately found what he was looking for, gave a little triumphant grunt to himself as he stepped down.

"It gets a bit dusty up there, especially when it isn't used much. None of you, apart from Memed and Salman, have even understood these languages. Well I, for one, will not read a translation. That would be a travesty and there is not yet a good one in German or French. It is the *terza rima* that baffles them all. It is Canto V of the *Commedia*, when our poet meets the lovers Francesca and Paolo in the Second Circle of Hell. Listen closely, Salman, and tell me honestly if the silken verses of your beloved Verlaine can match this gem from the Florentine Renaissance:

Quand' io intesi quell' anime offense,
china'il viso, e tanto il tenni basso,
fin che 'l poeta mi disse: "Che pense?"
Quando rispuosi, cominciai: "Oh lasso
Quanti dolci pensier, quanto disio
menò costoro al doloroso passo!"
Poi mi rivolsi a loro e parla' io,
E cominciai: "Francesca, i tuoi martiri
A lagrimar mi fanno tristo e pio.
Ma dimmi: al tempo d'i dolci sospiri
a che e come concedetti amore
che conosceste i dubbiosi disiri?"
E quella a me: "Nessun maggior dolore
Che ricordarsi del tempo felice
Ne la miseria; e ciò sa 'l tuo dottore.
Ma s'a conoscer la prima radice
Del nostro amor tu hai cotanto affetto,
Dirò come colui che piange e dice.
Noi leggiavamo un giorno per diletto
Di Lancialotto come amor lo strinse;
Soli eravamo e sanza alcun sospetto.

Per più fïate liocchi ci sospinse
quella lettura, e scolorocci il viso;
ma solo un punto fu quel che ci vinse.
Quando leggemmo il disïato riso
Esser basciato da cotanto amante,
Questi, che mai da me non fia diviso,
La bocca mi basciò tutto tremante.
Galeotto fu 'l libro e chi lo scrisse:
quel giorno più non vi leggemmo avante."
Mentre che l'uno spirto questo disse,
l'altro piangëa; sì che di pietade
io venni men così com' io morisse.
*E caddi come corpo morto cade.**

The Baron's histrionic performance had exhausted him and he fell back in his chair, his hand groping for the non-existent glass of champagne. Since I could not understand a word I had looked at the faces of those who could, and while Salman had remained attentive, Uncle Memed's features were filled with tenderness throughout the performance. He spoke to his friend in a soft voice.

"I first read that passage to you, Jakob. Remember? Venezia?" It was the first time anyone in our household had spoken the Baron's name.

The Baron had recovered himself. He never liked displays of public affection and ignored Uncle Memed's question.

"Well, Salman?"

My brother looked at the Prussian with a raised eyebrow.

"Dear Baron, surely you will agree that it would be impertinent for either of

*For English translation see Appendix.

us to compare these two poets. Each wrote in his own time and, as a result, each has his own special qualities. Would you compare Machiavelli to Hegel?"

"Ridiculous idea."

"Exactly. It serves no function. Likewise Dante and Verlaine."

"I disagree." The Baron was beginning to show signs of irritation. "The Florentine was a genius. The Frenchman was a poet of a high quality."

Salman was now getting annoyed. He shrugged his shoulders, but remained silent. We were beginning to wonder whether the discussion was over when Salman spoke.

"One thing puzzles me Baron. I am familiar with the extract you read from Canto V. What always puzzled me was why Dante had to spoil the effect of the passage in which the depth of emotion is truly profound by insisting that the book they were reading was the story of Lancelot, a legend which usually appeals to the soft-headed. Do you think this was deliberate on this poet's part? A way of warning the reader, perhaps, that love can make one undiscriminating?"

The Baron was livid. "The question you pose is so profound that I will think it over tonight and give you a reply tomorrow."

Salman and I began to giggle and my father intervened.

"That is enough poetry for one day. Orhan asked me a question today for which I had no answer. I told him to ask Selim and Halil to their faces. Come here, Orhan."

Orhan moved to where Iskander Pasha was seated.

"I asked Grandfather: when the Sultan is gone and my Uncle Halil and Selim and the men who visited our house take over the Empire, will the ruffians who killed my father be punished?"

Selim covered his face with his hands. Halil looked pensive and simply nodded at the question. Salman was the one who replied.

"Both of them would like to say 'yes' to you, Orhan, because they love you dearly, but because they love you they do not wish to lie. Some of the men who killed your father because he was Greek are the people who want to topple the Sultan. So the answer is 'no', Orhan. They will probably never be punished."

Orhan's eyes filled with tears and Emineh looked out of the window. My parents took them out of the room without another word. Memed, too, rose as if to depart.

"We must make sure everything we need is packed, Baron. We leave early tomorrow morning."

I had no idea their departure was so imminent. "You are deserting us in our hour of need, Baron."

"Old empires fall and new ones take their place, Nilofer. You are lucky. You will have friends in both."

Memed sat down again. "Berlin as the heart of a new Empire, Baron? I don't think the British, French and Russians are going to permit the birth of this empire."

"They are not invincible, Memed."

"We shall see."

"Let me put it to you another way, Memed. Any power which is strong enough to defeat Germany will one day rule the world."

"On that deeply mystical Wagnerian note, Baron, I think we should retire for the day."

"Good," said the Baron, "but not before inviting Salman, Nilofer and Selim to my family's New Year's Eve Ball in Berlin. It will be very grand this year. If you like, Selim, I can ask my friend Urning to get a couple of tickets for you to attend the ball being planned by the German Social Democrats. They plan everything well in advance. It is their nature."

"That would really encourage me to visit Berlin," replied Selim.

"Good. It's settled, but you will be my guests."

Selim accompanied them out of the room, leaving me alone with Salman.

"Are you looking forward to working with Uncle Kemal again?"

He looked at me and gently stroked my cheeks.

"Yes, my Nilofer. I'm ready for something new. I have tried the East and it failed me. I would like to visit America and see Chicago and New York. It is such a big country that one could lose oneself in its vastness. I'm looking forward to getting lost again. The steamship company will need to be set up on every coast."

"Father will miss you very much now. You know that, don't you? I think out of all of us he feels the closest to you. You should have seen the look on his face when you were reading Verlaine. He loves you dearly, Salman. As children we hated him for punishing you, but he loved you even then. We were too young too realise it at the time."

"It's true, and I feel very close to him as well, which I never did when I was growing up here. Don't worry. I wasn't planning on leaving just yet, Sister. I will spend a lot of time with Father."

I was in bed waiting for Selim to undress and join me. Everyone was leaving now, but he would always be with me, with his strange and obstinate gaze and his pride. He had come to me from nowhere and rescued me from loneliness at a time when I was unhappy and my life with Dmitri had come to an end. I did not wish to think about love or passion or betrayal.

Selim got into the bed and looked at me and smiled.

"I do not wish to discuss our love for each other, tonight. I do not want to know whether it has grown, deepened or which of us loves the other more. Not tonight."

I began to laugh. "Why do we always do this, Selim? Anyway, what I want to discuss is not our love, but our weaknesses. It is the knowledge of each other's weaknesses that creates what the Baron would refer to as an emotional equilibrium."

He began to rub himself against me.

"No words tonight, princess. Just passion. Passion. Passion. Passion."

TWENTY-FIVE

The full moon sets and the new sun rises

I woke up very early this morning. I wanted to be completely on my own. I dressed silently and left the house from a side entrance. Outside the lawn was still bathed in the light of the full moon.

I walked to the top of a little hill which stood just behind the Stone Woman, not far from where we had buried Hasan Baba. I had done this once before when I was sixteen years old and dreaming of the prince who would come from nowhere one day, lift me off the ground, place me firmly in front on his horse and ride away with me for ever.

Here it was, the full moon. I had not seen it so big and so close over the sea for many years. I embraced it from this hill and a mysterious strength poured into my body.

I had come to see it set in the west as the sun of the new day rose in the east. It was a very large and languid moon, to which I bade an emotional farewell from this hill behind Yusuf Pasha's summer house. How many dreams had been born here. How many others had been stored during hundreds of blissful summers, to be recovered later.

I turned eastwards. There were a few wispy clouds on the horizon. The hidden sun first lit them a glorious pink, which slowly began to turn red. It was a young beauty, visible only for a short time. I knew that any minute the sun would pierce the clouds and burn my eyes. I turned away just in time and as I walked down I saw something that had often been talked about, but never seen by any of us.

As the first rays of the sun hit the Stone Woman, they created a shadow in the shape of a giant prehistoric whale. It only lasted a minute. I had barely time to gasp in awe when it was gone. I stopped to look at the rock that was our Stone Woman and whispered my farewell, just as we used to do when we were children.

My breasts have been feeling very tender for the last few weeks and this is the second month in a row that I have not menstruated. I am pregnant once again. Selim's child will be born in seven months' time. It will be as old as the next century.

Summer is over. Tomorrow we return to Istanbul.

Appendix

When those offended souls had told their story,
I bowed my head and kept it bowed until
the poet said, "What are you thinking of?"

When finally I spoke, I sighed, "Alas,
all those sweet thoughts, and oh, how much desiring
brought these two down into this agony."

And then I turned to them and tried to speak;
I said, "Francesca, the torment that you suffer
brings painful tears of pity to my eyes.

But tell me, in that time of your sweet sighing
how, and by what signs, did love allow you
to recognise your dubious desires?"

And she to me: "There is no greater pain
than to remember, in our present grief,
past happiness (as well your teacher knows)!

But if your great desire is to learn
the very root of such a love as ours,
I shall tell you, but in words of flowing tears.

One day we read, to pass the time away,
of Lancelot, of how he fell in love;
we were alone, innocent of suspicion.

Time and again our eyes were brought together
by the book we read; our faces flushed and paled.
To the moment of one line alone we yielded:

it was when we read about those longed-for lips
now being kissed by such a famous lover,
that this one (who shall never leave my side)

then kissed my mouth, and trembled as he did.
Our Galehot was that book and he who wrote it.
That day we read no further." And all the while

the one of the two spirits spoke these words,
the other wept, in such a way that pity
blurred my senses; I swooned as though to die,

and fell to Hell's floor as a body, dead, falls.

Translation by Mark Musa from
The Divine Comedy, courtesy of Penguin Books